National Culture in Post-Apartheid Namibia

Basel Namibia Studies Series

1   Zedekia Ngavirue POLITICAL PARTIES AND INTEREST GROUPS IN SOUTH WEST AFRICA (NAMIBIA) A STUDY OF A PLURAL SOCIETY (1972) (1997)

2   Wolfgang Werner 'NO ONE WILL BECOME RICH'. ECONOMY AND SOCIETY IN THE HERERO RESERVES IN NAMIBIA, 1915–1946 (1998)

3   Lauren Dobell SWAPO'S STRUGGLE FOR NAMIBIA, 1960–1991: WAR BY OTHER MEANS. (1998) (2ND EDITION 2000)

4   Tony Emmett POPULAR RESISTANCE AND THE ROOTS OF NATIONALISM IN NAMIBIA, 1915–1966 (1999)

5   James Suzman 'THINGS FROM THE BUSH'. A CONTEMPORARY HISTORY OF THE OMAHEKE BUSHMEN (2000)

6   William Heuva MEDIA AND RESISTANCE POLITICS. THE ALTERNATIVE PRESS IN NAMIBIA, 1960–1990 (2001)

7   Marion Wallace HEALTH, POWER AND POLITICS IN WINDHOEK, NAMIBIA, 1915–1945 (2002)

8/9 Lovisa T. Nampala; Vilho Shigwedha AAWAMBO KINGDOMS, HISTORY AND CULTURAL CHANGE. PERSPECTIVES FROM NORTHERN NAMIBIA (2006)

10 Bennett Kangumu CONTESTING CAPRIVI. A HISTORY OF COLONIAL ISOLATION AND REGIONAL NATIONALISM IN NAMIBIA (2011)

11 Inge Tvedten "AS LONG AS THEY DON'T BURY ME HERE". SOCIAL RELATIONS OF POVERTY IN A NAMIBIAN SHANTYTOWN (2011)

12 Julie J. Taylor NAMING THE LAND. SAN IDENTITY AND COMMUNITY CONSERVATION IN NAMIBIA'S WEST CAPRIVI (2012)

13 Martha Akawa THE GENDER POLITICS OF THE NAMIBIAN LIBERATION STRUGGLE (2014)

14 Lorena Rizzo GENDER AND COLONIALISM. A HISTORY OF KAOKO IN NORTH-WESTERN NAMIBIA 1870s–1950s (2012)

MICHAEL AKUUPA
Introduction by M. McKittrick

National Culture in Post-Apartheid Namibia
State-sponsored Cultural Festivals and their Histories

Basel Namibia Studies Series 15

Basler Afrika Bibliographien 2015

©2015 The authors
©2015 The photographers
©2015 Basler Afrika Bibliographien

Basler Afrika Bibliographien
Namibia Resource Centre & Southern Africa Library
Klosterberg 23
PO Box 2037
CH-4051 Basel
Switzerland
www.baslerafrika.ch

The Basler Afrika Bibliographien is part of the Carl Schlettwein Foundation

All rights reserved.

Efforts were made to trace the copyright holders of illustrations and maps used in this publication. We apologise for any incomplete or incorrect acknowledgements.

Cover photograph: The cultural group Ukumwe entertains at the official opening of the Annual National Culture Festival in the Kavango region, December 2008
Photographer: Michael Uusiku Akuupa

ISBN 978-3-905758-42-9
ISSN 2234-9561

Contents

Acknowledgement	IX
Preface	X
Foreword by Meredith McKittrick	XII
1 The Festive 'Moment' of Namibia	**1**
Introduction	1
2 The 'Performance' of Culture	**14**
On 'Doing' and 'Performing' 'Culture' at State Sponsored Culture Festivals	14
Anthropology and Performance	15
Performance Theory in the Social Science Sphere	17
Theory of Performance: A Critical Analysis	19
Postcolonial Nationalism: One Namibia One Nation	24
Festival Making in Postcolonial Africa	28
Culture and Making the Nation	29
Festival with New Social Meaning and Function	32
3 Home Anthropology and Politics of Ekoro	**38**
"Whose Child are You?" The Dynamics and Politics of ekoro/likoro in Doing Ethnography at Home	38
Connectedness of Ekoro and its Workings in the Research Field	40
Analysis of Ekoro and its Working in the Research Field	45
Assumed and Imposed Fieldwork Self	49
4 Kavango the 'Domicile' in Perspective	**53**
Kavango: Whose Land is It?	53
Kavango the Place or People?	57
Kavango as Told in Legends	62
The Royal Narrative	64

	Early German Colonial and Missionary Encounters	68
	Kavango the Native Reserve	74
	Volkekunde Anthropology and Kavango	75
	Kavango After the Implementation of the Odendaal Plan	79
	Kavango in Contemporary Discourse: A Historical Sanitization Project	83
5	**Sangfees, the Antecedent of the Postcolonial Annual National Culture Festival**	**87**
	The Making of the Colonial Festival: 'sangfees'	87
	The Department of Education Administration for Kavango	89
	Division of Youth and Culture Affairs	94
	Sangfees at Ekongoro	97
	Ezuva for the 'Youth'	99
	Postcolonial Annual Culture Festivals	102
6	**Kavango Cultural Identity in Postcolonial Namibia**	**111**
	Reclaiming Colonial Ethnicity in a Postcolonial Context	111
	On the Search for 'Tradition' and 'Culture' in Namibia	113
	Kavango Museum	115
	Maria Mwengere Culture Centre: 'The Culture Booklet: An Instrument of Objectification'	121
	"Culture Booklet": A Resource of Advocacy	127
7	**Namibian Identity Through Dance**	**137**
	"Making the Nation": The Role of Local People in the Festival	137
	A Note on 'Kavango' Traditional Dances	140
	Rehearsal Performances	145
	At Mayana Primary School	145
	At Swapo Regional Office	148
	Festival Making: Exploring Local Participation and Influences in the Discourse of Nation-Building	150
	Mpungu Circuit and Kavango Regional Festivals	156
	"Daya Ngoma!", a Drumming Performance that Had Us Electrified: An Analysis of Front Stage Interactions at the Festival	164

8 **Deconstructing Postcolonial Ethnic Diversity**	**169**
Annual National Culture Festival: Discourses of *Difference* and *Belonging* in Postcolonial Namibia	169
The Annual National Culture Festival	170
The March Through Town	171
Inside the Stadium	172
'Performances' of Culture	174
Analysis of the Festival Representations in Kavango	178
Reflections on Kavango Identity	182
9 **The Postcolonial Nation as Curated by the State Through Dance**	**185**
Conclusion	185
Festivals and 'Nation Building'	190
List of Abbreviations	**197**
Bibliography	**198**

Basel Namibia Studies Series

In 1997, *P. Schlettwein Publishing* (PSP) launched the *Basel Namibia Studies Series*. Its primary aim was to lend support to a new generation of research, scholars and readers emerging with the independence of Namibia in 1990.

Initially, the book series published crucially important doctoral theses on Namibian history. It soon expanded to include more recent political, anthropological, media and cultural history studies by Namibian scholars.

P. Schlettwein Publishing, as an independent publishing house, maintained the series in collaboration with the *Basler Afrika Bibliographien* (BAB), Namibia Resource Centre and Southern Africa Library in Switzerland. All share a commitment to encourage research on Africa in general and southern Africa in particular. Through the incorporation of PSP into the *Carl Schlettwein Stiftung*, the series, by then a consolidated platform for Namibian Studies and beyond, was integrated into the publishing activities of the BAB.

Academic publishing, whether from or about Namibia, remains limited. The *Basel Namibia Studies Series* continues to provide a forum for exciting scholarly work in the human and social sciences.

The editors welcome contributions. For further information, or submission of manuscripts, please contact the *Basler Afrika Bibliographien* at www.baslerafrika.ch.

Acknowledgement

Firstly, I thank God for the strength, courage and ability to do this work. I also want to express my profound gratitude and appreciation to the following people: Diana Gibson, Olajide Oloyede, Heike Becker, Meredith McKittrick, and Sakhumzi Mfecane, for their academic support. Furthermore, I thank the entire staff at the Department of Anthropology and Sociology for being good colleagues and for their critical input during seminars when I presented my work.

I particularly want to acknowledge my academic friend and brother Kletus 'Mukashirongo' Likuwa for being very supportive and constructively critical to this scholarly work.

I am highly indebted to Dr Herbert Ndango Diaz, the director at National Heritage and Culture Programmes (NHCP), for the opportunity he gave me to work as an intern at Maria Mwengere Culture Centre in Kavango, and Simon Indongo for giving me crucial information about the national festival. At Maria Mwengere Culture Centre, I thank Thomas Shapi, *Tamwa* Joseph Mbambo, Valesca Kazanga, Donaveltha Bashir, Gelasia Shikerete, Seraphina, Theresia, Nangombe and all others for making my stay enjoyable and fulfilling at the centre.

I am equally indebted and grateful to the people of Kavango and Namibia at large who participated in this study for their time and willingness to contribute to the wealth of knowledge. Thank you so much for working with me.

I also thank my friends *Tate* Jason Ambole, John Sivute, Gerre Kakonda, Nyerere Shanghala, Mukuve Hausiku, Maggy Nepaya, Nehoa Kautondokwa, Michael Shirungu, and Shiremo Shampapi for your encouragement during this academic project. I am grateful to certain people that contributed in many ways to this study but wished to remain anonymous.

Most importantly I am also grateful to Luccio Schlettwein and the Carl Schlettwein Foundation specifically, for its generous financial support in the making of this project.

Finally, I thank my family, specifically Maria, for their outstanding support during this endeavour.

Whilst many people contributed to this study, I take credit for all shortcomings and mistakes in the book.

Preface

This study investigates colonial and postcolonial practices of cultural representations in Namibia. The state sponsored Annual National Culture Festival in Namibia was studied with a specific focus on the Kavango Region in northeastern Namibia. I was particularly interested in how cultural representations are produced by the nation-state and local people in a postcolonial African context of nation-building and national reconciliation, by bringing visions of cosmopolitanism and modernity into critical dialogue with its colonial past.

During the apartheid era, the South African administration encouraged the inhabitants of its 'Native Homelands' to engage in 'cultural' activities aimed at preserving their traditional cultures and fostering a sense of distinct cultural identity among each of Namibia's officially recognized 'ethnic groups'. This policy was in line with the logic of South African colonial apartheid rule of Namibia, which relied upon the emphasis of ethnic differences, in order to support the idea that the territory was inhabited by a collection of 'tribes' requiring a central white government to oversee their development. The colonial administration resorted to concepts of 'tradition' and 'cultural heritage' in order to construct Africans as members of distinct, bounded communities ('tribes') attached to specific localities or 'homelands'.

My central argument is that since Namibian independence in 1990, the postcolonial nation-state has placed emphasis on cultural pride in new ways, and on identifying characteristics of 'Namibian-ness'. This has led to the institution of cultural festivals, which have since 1995 been held all over the country with an expressed emphasis on the notion of 'Unity in Diversity'. These cultural festivals are largely performances and cultural competitions that range from lang-arm dance, and 'traditional' dances, displays of 'traditional' foodstuffs and dramatized representations.

This ethnographic study shows that while the performers represent diversity through dance and other forms of cultural exhibition, the importance of belonging to the nation and a larger constituency is simultaneously highlighted. However, as the study demonstrates, the festivals are also spaces where local populations engage in negotiations with the nation-state and contest regional forms of belonging. The book shows how a practice which was considered to be a 'colonial representation' of the 'other' has been reinvented with new meanings in postcolonial Namibia. The study demonstrates through an analysis of cultural representations such as song, dances and drama that the festival creates a space in which 'social interaction' takes place between participants, spectators and officials who organize the event as social capital of associational life.

NB: An earlier version of Chapter 8 was published in Anthropology Southern Africa, Vol. 33 (Nos. 3 &4), 2010. I am grateful to the editor for the permission to include the chapter in this book.

Foreword

During more than 70 years of South African colonialism, the relationship of Namibians to their state was largely defined through the lens of race and ethnicity. Terms such as "Ovambo," "Herero," and "Nama" were given ethnic content under German colonialism, but the borders of these categories were solidified under South African rule. The category "Kavango" emerged more gradually: colonial records refer to people residing along the Kavango River as Ovambo into the 1920s. Such ethnic confusion poorly served the interests of a colonial administration. And over the course of the colonial period, these categories were refined. Former political units were transformed into "tribal" entities and ethnicity came to dominate outside conceptions of Kavango's residents.

But such ethnic categories, interpreted through the lens of dominant, royalist histories, also resonated with local understandings of identity and belonging. Colonial officials administered the five former kingdoms along the Kavango River – Kwangari, Mbunza, Shambyu, Gciriku, and Mbukushu – as a single unit. It became common knowledge that these five "tribes" had more in common with each other than with others around them – despite, for example, far more 19th-century interaction between the Kwangari kingdom and eastern Ovambo societies than between the Kwangari and the Mbukushu, their fellow "Kavangos." By the early 1970s, the South African Prime Minister argued that Kavango was a "beautiful country," defined by the river that ran through it. Meanwhile, the nascent Kavango Bantustan government could state, without controversy, that "there are five tribes in Kavango" and could stipulate that those forming the Bantustan government "must have knowledge of the customs and traditions of Kavango."[1] Members of the Kavango parliament routinely spoke of "Kavangos" as a coherent category that needed no explication.[2]

This richly textured study by a talented young scholar explores what happened to this notion of "Kavango-ness" after Namibia gained independence. As Michael Uusiku Akuupa observes, what had been a "colonial identity project" aimed at separate development became "the bedrock from which contemporary identities have sprung." (156-7) By exploring the emergence of post-colonial "culture festivals," he is able to explore the nuances and contradictions of post-colonial identity construction. SWAPO's constitution commits the party to "combat retrogressive tendencies" of tribalism, ethnicity, and regionalism (among other

---

[1] *Proceedings of the Kavango Legislative Council*, Oct. 1972, p. 13.
[2] *Proceedings of the First Session of the Second Kavango Legislative Council*, Oct.-Nov. 1973, 39; for "Kavangos" see i.e. debates in the *Proceedings of the Second Session of the Second Legislative Council*, April-May 1974.

evils such as sexism and racism) – a stance based on the awareness that such categories had formed the basis of colonial divide and rule.³ As the ruling party after independence in 1990, SWAPO sought to minimize the salience of ethnicity in particular. The state's slogan, "One Namibia – One Nation," was an explicit counter-discourse to the ethnic politics of the Bantustan era. While the apartheid state had created cultural festivals, known as *sangfees*, to reinforce ethnic identities, the SWAPO government discontinued them in favor of institutions that reinforced a sense of unitary nationhood. Linguistic categories replaced ethnic ones, and the ethnically defined "homelands" were erased in favor of 13 administrative regions that, at least theoretically, cut across ethnic lines.

When the Namibian government created an annual national cultural festival, five years after independence, it marked a rather stark departure from these earlier interventions in identity construction. Other policies, too, offered state endorsement of ethnic identity: in 2000, for example, ethnic groups and traditional authorities were granted legal recognition. The result, says Akuupa, is that by 2001 the national culture policy was "the total opposite of the political ideal at the time of independence" (43). Akuupa links this shift to the state's reluctant admission that, for Namibia's citizens, these ethno-cultural categories had meaning: people themselves embraced ethnic belonging over national belonging. The state sought to co-opt this, using ethnicity as the basis for a project of constructing a national identity. On the surface, however, this privileging of ethnic identities and institutions resembled the world of the much-reviled 1962 Odendaal Commission, designed to implement apartheid in the country.

So how did something that was "conceptually colonial" (15) come to serve a postcolonial agenda? Akuupa argues that the creation of "culture" – and the ethnicized identities that are its building blocks – is more than a top-down, state-driven project. In his careful attention to local relations of power, Akuupa places himself firmly in a branch of Namibian studies that focuses on the role of local people in shaping large historical processes such as colonial rule, labor migration, and Christianization. He shows us how the content of festival performances is continually policed by spectators, participants, and judges for "external" and polluting influences. Culture thus sits in opposition to modernity. But it is also given ownership: culture, Akuupa perceptively notes, is always someone's. This fact allows local people to claim authority and authorship, and to legitimate their actions on the basis of a perceived continuity with the past. In local discourse, the performance of dances and songs is also an act of recovering something that is in danger of being lost.

---

³ http://www.swapoparty.org/swapo_constitution.pdf. Accessed 30 April 2013.

Local people thus imbue these culture festivals with larger meanings, and they give content and significance to the cultural "product" or "brand" that emerges. These culture festivals reinforce community identity and pride; they are also spaces in which young people can be socialized into a particular kind of identity, one rooted in notions of "tradition" and cultural distinctiveness. Culture festivals therefore actively construct generational relations. They also mediate fraught questions of who can or cannot claim "Kavango-ness." And they take place against a backdrop of grievances about the place of Kavango in the Namibian nation, including a pervasive sense that the region's role in the struggle to free Namibian from South African rule has been ignored. The local uses of culture festivals sit uneasily alongside the state's goals of creating a sense of "Namibian-ness" or "unity in diversity."

Michael Akuupa is in some ways uniquely placed to carry out this project. He himself has the status within Kavango of both insider and outsider: born in Tsumeb and educated in what was formerly Ovamboland, Akuupa "married into" Kavango society. He has ties to five of Namibia's regions, speaks a majority of Namibia's languages, and has spent years living as a student in South Africa; he also is one of a tiny number of Namibians who hold a Ph.D. Akuupa exemplifies how the complexities of identity cannot be reduced to colonially mediated categories. Yet when seeking to research Kavango's culture festivals, he notes that the director of the National Heritage and Culture Programmes office asked him, "Whose child are you?" and puzzled over his apparent transgression of ethnic boundaries (59). Once his ties to the community were revealed, he was deemed by the Kavango-born director to be a "son-in-law." It was this position as son-in-law – not as a Namibian – that shaped his ability to conduct his research.

Akuupa's fieldwork experience reflects a similar straddling of this insider-outsider boundary. He joined the staff of the culture center in Rundu, thereby helping to stage the very processes of culture construction he was studying. This insider/outsider distinction was crucial to the course of Akuupa's fieldwork: insider status clearly granted him access to information he would not otherwise have had. But it also limited him, sweeping him up in relations based on junior and senior status and circumscribing his ability to ask certain kinds of questions. Akuupa's own experiences remind us of the contextual nature of insider status: he is an Ovambo, not Kavango, insider when speaking to the former Namibian president in their shared mother tongue, but then comes in for presidential criticism for the (un-Namibian?) dreadlocks he sports.

Akuupa's view from the "inside" reveals the tensions and ironies inherent in this nationalist project. The staffs of the Kavango culture center are less than overjoyed when they are bequeathed the honor of hosting the national festival, because they forfeit the travel allowances and other financial rewards of traveling for work. At the same time, watching the local staff make elaborate preparations for national politicians who may or may not come and who never seem to arrive on time, Akuupa observes that this event celebrating sub-national identities does not "make any sense" without the presence of national dignitaries (260). Those same dignitaries reveal that state discourses of culture are not monolithic: they alternately reinforce the "tribal" identities that the apartheid state glorified – and the crowd cheers while Namibia's "tribes" are enumerated – and portray culture as dynamic and fluid, valorizing a secondary-school dance troupe from Kavango that contains white as well as black students.

While it is deemed proper, even exemplary, for whites to perform Kavango "culture," the role of the Nyemba is more controversial despite the fact that they are closely related to other Kavango groups. The Nyemba, who are not represented by one of the five "traditional authorities" of Kavango but who nevertheless have an extensive presence in the region dating to precolonial times, are commonly viewed as outsiders who do not "belong" in Kavango. Yet most of the songs and dances performed by Kavango troupes are, in fact, of Nyemba origin. White students are only performing Kavango culture; no one is arguing that they somehow have a hand in creating the content of that culture. They are therefore less of a threat to accepted notions of Kavango-ness than the Nyemba, who are actively constituting that identity despite the assertion of their outsider status.

But such tensions are not restricted to the local: they are written into the very structure of these festivals and, indeed, the larger units they purport to represent. While the 13 administrative regions are meant to be "non-ethnic," the culture festival is an ethnic project organized along regional lines. Thus within each region, groups perform dances, dramas and songs that represent the same ethnic identities valorized by the apartheid state. The links to "Namibian-ness" also reveal some interesting paradoxes: the group that has been most successful at the national level is a Setswana group – members of an ethnicity most Namibians would not even regard as historically Namibian, whose "true" roots are reflected in the name of the neighboring country, Botswana. This group, formed shortly after independence, predates the national culture festivals, and they take credit for motivating other Namibians to recover and re-learn their traditional dances. Thus a project of heritage recovery was originally launched not by the Namibian government, but by a group widely viewed as members of a dubiously Namibian ethnicity.[4]

Within this recuperative project, Kavango occupies a somewhat unique space. As old Bantustans were abolished and Namibia's physical space was re-imagined to fit a new, na-

---

[4] http://www.economist.com.na/2011-12-07-11-05-31/community-and-culture/2381-sing-and-dance-for-joy (accessed 8 April 2013)

tional political ideal, something called "Kavango" continued to exist – and did so within the same borders as the apartheid-era "Kavango" Bantustan. The colonial continuities do not end there. Nationally, Namibians view Kavango as an authentic repository of "culture" in Namibia, a place where tradition has somehow survived the past century and a half of European influence and colonialism more unscathed than in other areas. This is an ambivalent honor: colonial officials, too, routinely characterized the people living along the Kavango River as among the most "backward" and "primitive" of Namibia's people. Indeed, these words are used in colonial reports far more frequently for the Kavango region than for the residents of Kaokoland, who today are regarded in popular culture as exemplars of tradition and "backwardness." This shared idea of "Kavango" drives home Akuupa's point: it is simultaneously an apartheid concept, a symbol of the new national ideal of "unity-in-diversity," and a local concept through which claims to belonging are mediated. At the end of the day, however, what might seem to be a "regressive" ethnic unit can only "make sense" within the framework of the nation itself.

Meredith McKittrick
Georgetown University, DC

1 The Festive 'Moment' of Namibia

Introduction

It is early Saturday, the weather is cool but the favourable morning breeze will not last. December is a hot month in Namibia.

An event unfolds: A large number of festival goers dressed in colourful 'traditional' attire await a signal to begin the march through town to the Rundu Sports Stadium for an official opening of the Annual National Culture Festival. The dance and sing loudly, their banners display the names of Namibia's thirteen political regions. Inside the stadium the noise level rises. Opposite the stand a large canopy on the grass lawn with decorated tables and soft chairs would accommodate invited dignatories. Moments later when all protocol related to state rituals has been concluded, cultural groups were invited on 'stage' to represent their 'cultures' through dance, song and drama. The occasion was the annual state sponsored cultural festival in Kavango Region during 2008.[1]

"It is indeed a pleasure and honour as well as privilege to make use of this opportunity to sincerely inform your good office about the above-mentioned Annual National Culture Festival 2008. ... After our country attained its independence and became the Republic of Namibia, the SWAPO-Government wisely thought of reviving, preserving, researching and promoting our diversity of Cultures in our beautiful country. This process should lead towards the Namibian national reconciliation, nation building, mutual respect, acceptance and tolerance among all the communities in the Republic of Namibia. As all of us are aware, the Colonial Regime divided the Namibia people into ethnicities and language groups in order to rule and dominate the Black Communities and to cultivate destructive unnecessary hatred among the various Black Communities. This was the scenario before our beautiful country obtained its independence. Our various communities were isolated from one another. Against the above illustrated sad background, the SWAPO-Government therefore thought of an annual occasion which could attract groups from our various communities to come together and share as well as to exchange our diversities of cultures and to accept one another as people belonging only to one country and one nation. ...".[2]

After independence[3] in 1990, the postcolonial Namibian state emphasized the need for <u>national</u> cultural pride, based on the characteristics of 'Namibian-ness'. This was aimed at

---

[1] My field notes.
[2] This is a Ministerial communication about the Annual National Culture Festival (9 October 2008) to the Kavango Regional Council. On 9 October 2008, the Directorate of National Heritage and Culture Programmes (NHCP) sent the national invite of the imminent culture festival to the Kavango Regional Council and the local culture office. This would be a big event as about 2200 participants and several hundred officials from different regions were expected in town.
[3] As Namibians usually refer to the country's postcolonial period.

social reconstruction reflecting the diverse 'cultural scenes' that make up the Namibian nation. According to official sources this was the main reason that led to the institution of cultural festivals. Simultaneously, the emergence of the 'cultural tourism industry' resulted in the establishment of numerous 'cultural groups' i.e. groups of people who supposedly have an interest in preserving their customs Fairweather 2001and Mans 2002. The preservation of customs included the creation of museums, construction of cultural villages, and the initiation and identification of would-be heritage sites in an independent Namibia. Schools, community forums and regional governments are all involved in the process that has been ongoing for the past 15 years or so. Most recently, the Ministry of Information Communication Technology launched a 'nationhood and national pride campaign' with the objective of creating a sense of national belonging among its citizens, which was to embrace multiculturalism. The campaign would spread its message of unity, namely, the importance of national symbols and ideals of nationhood through the media (The Namibian and New Era Newspapers, 6 May 2011).

In 1995 the campaign was run by the ministries of Education, and Youth and Culture respectively. Their brief was to organize cultural festivals at the local, regional and national levels throughout the 13 political regions of Namibia. This was to take the form of a competition culminating at the national level, referred to as the Annual National Culture Festival (ANCF). These cultural festivals are largely performance orientated. Performances include *lang-arm* dance,[4] 'traditional' dances, displays of 'traditional' foodstuffs and storytelling. In 2008 I observed the Annual National Culture Festival in the Rundu-Kavango Region, which comprises the main subject of this study.

An excerpt from the 'letter of invitation' in reality a communication that caused little cheer to the Kavango Regional Council[5] mentions two historical moments. This letter implies that Namibia, like its neighbour and one-time colonial power South Africa, was a country that forged its culture in the 'hard mills of violent and relentless struggle, which is now changing in a rapid, uneven process of political liberalization and cultural reinvention while promoting transformations of outlook and behavior' in which ideas of economic prosperity are deeply embedded. (Barber, 2001:177) The invitation letter emphasizes the observation that ethnic diversities, previously enforced under colonialism, had led to disadvantages for an united Namibian nation and, therefore, new ways of forging a Namibian nation were

---

[4] Lit. long arm dance is 'traditional' Afrikaner music popular at farm parties.
[5] In Namibia, administrative provinces are known as regions. The regions are demarcated into constituencies. Each region has a regional government headed by the Governor with councillors. It is accountable to central government and the citizens who participate in the election in order to choose councillors. In total there are 13 regions in Namibia.

necessary. This process would have the advantage of celebrating diversity through cultural representation.

Reactions to this proposal were interesting. When the letter inviting the Namibian government's Kavango office to host the 2008 Annual Culture Festival arrived, the staff was unenthusiastic. Holding the event in a different region implied extra income for the Kavango officials who would be paid travel and subsistence allowances. By virtue of the festival being hosted in Kavango, the regional government would be held responsible for the reception of important state officials from central government. Budget constraints were a further concern to the region.

Following 1995, the competitions took place annually according to a government-issued activity calendar, at the local (constituency; i.e. district) level in primary and secondary schools for junior participants, and in other local contexts for adults known as senior participants. It is compulsory for schools to participate; for other groups the choice to participate remains voluntary. Schools and local groups compete at what is referred to as zonal (district) competition. During the preliminary round the winners qualify for the regional competition proceeding to the national festival if they did well. At the regional festival where the zones compete, government officials are responsible for the organization, including costs in all thirteen regions of the country. The regional cultural officer usually officiates at the zonal festival while the governor presides at the regional; the competition is decided by judges who may include prominent teachers, secretaries of traditional authorities and other members of the local elite who are usually state officials.

The winners compete against other regional groups at the Annual National Culture Festival, which is attended by high ranking state officers, sometimes including the head of state. The Annual National Culture Festival may be held in any of the regions.

At these events officials of the postcolonial Namibian state regularly emphasize the importance of celebrating cultural diversity.[6] Speakers seem to imply that the government regards cultural festivals as a means of politically unifying a nation previously divided along ethnic lines by the colonial rulers.[7] The professed goal is that Namibians should learn to tolerate each other in diversity. The central means to achieve this unity and ultimately lead to self-determination is the celebration of diversity through cultural festivals.

---

[6] One of the recent statements made by the Minister of Youth and Culture at the institutional cultural festival (Polytechnic of Namibia), was that "it is important to celebrate the diversity of our culture", New Era 09 August 2006.

[7] Bayart (2005) in his book on The Illusion of Cultural Identity argues that the divided ones also took part in its formations by appropriating the new political, cultural and economic resources of the then bureaucratic state.

This emphasis on tradition and culture at cultural festivals or, indeed at any other state gathering in postcolonial Namibia seems rather surprising. The format and content of these festivals appeared reminiscent of previous events where racial differences were transformed into ethnic differences through the introduction of homelands, thus realizing the colonial or apartheid central ideology that each race and nation had an unique, divinely ordained destiny and culture. Historical sources show that Namibia is a country in which the legal recognition of cultural diversity and tradition "led to the shocking injustices of colonialism". (Du Pisani, 2000:64)

At independence when SWAPO[8] took over the government of the new nation, it abolished a range of activities that ostensibly, directly or indirectly, displayed or suggested ethnicity, which was understood as an expression of the colonial apartheid era-politics of divide and rule and raised the following questions: Was the change of policy from mid 1990s necessitated by the waning threat of apartheid and the realized freedom of neighbouring South Africa as Becker 2004, 2007 tentatively suggests in her work on memory and commemoration in Namibia? Was the change due to the shifts in the sub-continental identity politics, which became rooted in cultural discourse? The official discourse of unity in diversity remains open to interpretation. How are the festivals appropriated at the local level by spectators, participants and those representing government? Do the cultural representations of the public space signify the political, ideological, social and moral imagery of the Namibian postcolonial state? When the Namibian State emphasized 'unity in diversity' was there imminent polarization among the different ethnic communities in postcolonial Namibia? How do the postcolonial cultural festivals in Namibia compare with the colonial practices from which they descended? How did different levels of the state use these? For instance, there might be contestations between the central government and the regional governments about the venue of the Annual National Cultural Festivals. If such contestations so exist, it would be useful to find out whether there are any benefits to the regional government hosting the event.

Was the postcolonial government of the Republic of Namibia employing many of the same methods and tools used by its predecessor, the apartheid government, to divide the inhabitants in order to carry out its policy of segregation? Namibia's leadership may well have realized the void left by the ending of the colonial culture and recommitted to the same format of celebration to address the issues of postcolonial nation building. As I will show, instead of simply emphasizing regional intra-ethnic cultural differences, the SWAPO gov-

---

[8] After independence SWAPO, formerly the South West Africa People's Liberation Organisation changed its name to *Swapo Party*. Hence the usage Swapo in this context refers to the postcolonial period.

ernment embarked on a national project of social and cultural "unification, which explicitly cited cultural unity in diversity" in the Presidential report of the commission on education and culture and training. (Republic of Namibia 1991:3)

The report presents the Annual National Culture Festival (ANCF) as a ritual through which Namibian citizens could visualize themselves as a new nation. The ANCF is regarded by the state as a social space in which all citizens can celebrate nationhood and belonging. It is this festive moment which is the focus of investigation in this thesis.

The study investigates the colonial and postcolonial practices of representation in cultural festivals and the meanings they derive from local people with the specific focus on the Kavango region of north-eastern Namibia. The work demonstrates the importance of belonging to the nation and a larger constituency. The focus of the study is on how the practice, which was considered to be a colonial representation of the other, has been reinvented with new meanings by analysing historical narratives and official archive documents.

I examined state-sponsored cultural festivals, with the specific focus on the Kavango region as a suitable case study in which cultural representations are produced by Africans in a postcolonial context of nation building and national reconciliation, by bringing visions of cosmopolitanism and modernity into critical dialogue with its colonial past. In the festival context, people of Kavango have been represented by both officials and participants as being distinctively different from other ethnic groups in postcolonial Namibia. Through engagement and discussion of historical narratives the study looks at the notion of Kavangoness as a colonial construct and the way this is reconstructed and appropriated through the medium of the state organized culture festivals.

The study presents several interrelated arguments. Firstly, I argue that the culture festival event should be viewed as a social practice which produces ideas of being and meaning within a particular context. I will show that, although the festival was used under colonialism, it has been reinvented with new meaning and purpose, namely that of forging the Namibian nation. The festival creates a social space in which social interaction takes place and it is viewed by participants, spectators and officials as the social capital of an associational life. Festival rituals are seen to develop community stability and pride. The festival evokes understanding among people seeking "to give birth to new and viable nations" as argued by July 1983:124. Most importantly, the festival is seen and presented by its organizers and participants as a social space where the younger generation can learn the history and culture of the Kavango people.

Furthermore, the study aims to show that the state sponsored culture festival is a space of intensive social interaction. The interaction includes expressions of belonging, the emphasis of difference and the right to be heard and an acknowledgement of what is believed could enhance the social and economic life of citizens, praise of leadership and the making of the nation through presentation of cultural dances.

The second key argument in my research relates to anthropological studies, which deal with the question of nationalism through investigation of fairs, festivals and carnivals in the analytical context of ritual performance. In this context it relates to the work of Kelly Askew 2002, which focused on Swahili music and cultural politics in postcolonial Tanzania; and Paulla Ebron's 2002 study of praise singers locally known as *jaliya* in transnational encounters in The Gambia. Theoretically, my own research speaks to their complex usage of performance[9] in Anthropology, relating to the contemporary theoretical and methodological concern of looking at performance as processes of practice in analyzing nationalism. Ebron's study is of particular importance to my work here. Ebron uses performance as a mode of enquiry on three levels: in the analysis of formal events in which artists perform for audiences; in informal contexts in which one can observe the enactment of social categories and, finally, as a way in which to analyze scholarly modes of enquiry.

Askew's work is of importance to my study, specifically in the sense that it provides an alternative way of looking at nationalism so that it can be investigated and understood in social practices and not necessarily in publicized political rituals.

While contemporary scholarship of performance in rituals has moved away from studying these as systems of representations to regarding them as processes, (Schieffelin, 1998) my study specifically stresses the importance of analyzing festival performances not only as processes, because of their public enactment, symbolism and aesthetic activities, but rather as social practices. I do not view the festivals, or any celebratory ritual, as mere celebrations without clearly showing the performative aspect within their context and meaning. Due to the ambiguity and complexity of performance as a concept, festivals should be studied as a practice of making meaning. I propose the use of the phrase *showcase* as conceived and used by festival producers and participants when referring to the various presentations and representations in the festival space.

Significantly, I look at the way in which local people and performers see themselves in the context of festival performance and how the state views the spectacle it has organized, hosted and mediated. While the festival organizers (the state) perceive and present the festival as a performance, which can be objectified and in which various groups can be distinguished, participants and spectators consciously saw themselves as showcasing reality.

Thirdly, I present 'culture' as a central resource and analytical tool in this study. As a result of hosting cultural festivals in various social contexts of postcolonial Namibia, 'culture'

---

[9] I will discuss the anthropological genealogy of performance in chapter 2 in detail.

has become a vehicle through which political and social agenda are driven. In Kavango, people refer to culture, which is performed in the festival space, as *mpo zetu*. (Akuupa, 2006) *Mpo* is generally used by older people to refer to something that is old and different from the modern – in other words, synonymous with tradition. (See Spiegel and Boonzaier, 1988) It is generally linked to *zetu*, meaning <u>our</u>, indicative of ownership. The phrase 'our tradition' thus clearly signifies something that carries the authority of the past. It is commonly used to refer to practices that are assumed to have "been handed down for generations and that need careful protection against foreign influence". (Sahlins, 1993:4) Although my engagement with the vernacular understandings of 'culture' is rather tangential to this dissertation, the study shows how culture as a resource is variably appropriated by people and state representatives alike in the festival context and its usefulness in understanding social life.

Finally, the study contributes to the anthropological methods of doing research and methodology through addressing matters about access and negotiation of the field from the perspective of an insider. Methodologically, my study contributes a new insight from that of doing anthropology at home with a specific focus on forms of kinship insertions and their workings during fieldwork. In that context the study shows how local social and kinship relations in the field create conditions of possibility for research in the field.

My research was set in Kavango[10] with frequent travels to Windhoek the capital city of Namibia. My fieldwork was characterized by an extended period of creating relations, as I will show later in the study. During my fieldwork which was largely observational, I was stationed at Maria Mwengere Culture Centre in Kavango region. The Maria Mwengere Culture Centre serves as a regional culture office of the directorate of National Heritage and Culture Programmes for the Ministry of Youth, National Service, Sport & Culture where I worked as an intern for a period of seven months during 2008. As an intern I participated in all office activities such as meetings and preparation for culture festivals. I travelled with the state officials to various constituencies to host culture festivals. I worked closely with the official responsible for the museum at the centre. At the centre I occasionally went to visit and chat with labourers at various sections such as the botanical gardens, the dining hall and dormitories, especially during tea and lunch breaks.

My role in the festival context was that of an assistant. As an intern I acted in an official capacity[11] in the festival space and was privileged to access all aspects of the festival such as

---

[10] My family lives in Rundu the administrative capital of Kavango region.
[11] I discuss the process of gaining access to informants and information during my research in chapter 3 where I reflect on my fieldwork. Although I was seen by festival participants as an official of some sort, the senior culture officer explained my role in the festival as that of a 'student of culture' when he introduced his team to the audience before the events began.

talking to group leaders and taking pictures. Although I did not participate in the festivals dances – not being much of a dancer – I joined in certain aspects of the ceremony. During the festival I made video recordings or took pictures and spoke to both participants or spectators. I observed all the circuit festivals, including the regional, which were organized by officials at Maria Mwengere Culture Centre. I observed the Annual National Culture Festival and served on the local preparatory committee as an ordinary member.

I conducted over 25 interviews with various people in Windhoek and outlying villages in the traditional authorities[12] of Shambyu, Mbunza, Gciriku, Mbunza and Mbukushu including Rundu[13] town. My interviewees ranged from officials in the education sector and at the culture office to youth[14] and older people. Officials conversed about their experiences of the culture festivals, while the youth narrated their life stories, experiences and perceptions of the postcolonial festivals. I asked the elders about their life stories including narratives on their memories of the colonial culture festivals. I held interviews with cultural group members. Interviews were useful for the insights they produced about many of my observations in the field. Only interviews which were made in the official contexts were formal and duly recorded. I could not record some of the interviews due to what I refer as cultural barriers locally known as *yidira* pl. I summarized these later in my field notes when I was home.

My research extended to everyday life outside the sphere of the organized festivals and their preparations. I frequented various social spaces in Rundu such as bars, cuca shops[15], and churches, the latter especially when there were weddings or funerals. As a member of the local community in Rundu and *ekoro*[16], I attended community meetings, traditional courts and government offices. My participation in either family or social activities led to

---

[12] What was known as 'tribal' lands during colonial time are now referred to as traditional authorities after the acts for traditional leader and traditional authorities were gazetted in 1997 and 2000 respectively.

[13] Rundu is an administrative town of Kavango region.

[14] Youth and elder are "elastic concepts" in Namibia. For example young people are described variously as young adults, teenagers, adolescents or juveniles and "they all qualify under the rubric youth". (Mufune 2002:179) This youth age group has been selected, because of the legislative impression and definition of a youth. The Namibian legislation has opted for an age-based definition of youth for the effective implementation of its programmes and development initiatives. Due to the complexities of determining exactly a youth or an elder, it is fair to regard these as part of the negotiations and contestations of the cultural process.

[15] A cuca shop is a small business holding which usually sells small merchandise such as traditional alcoholic beverages, sugar, salt, bottled beer and many other household needs. It also serves as a social space where villagers come to relax after their long day at work. The name cuca is derived from the beer that was sold by the Portuguese merchants in most northern areas in the early 1970s.

[16] Ekoro is a very important communal relationship tightened in clan affinity. I will discuss the workings of ekoro in detail in chapter 3.

the creation of casual and adopted kin relations, an aspect that would become a crucial determinant of access to my fieldwork.

I spent about two months at the National Archive of Namibia in Windhoek. Newspapers of the time such as *Kavangudi* and *Muruli* served as important sources of information about the people and social life of Kavango including the colonial culture festival which was previously known as *sangfees*. Archive resources complemented by oral sources from interviews were helpful in constructing perspectives on colonial festivals and the history of Kavango specifically and Namibia in general.

The main limitation of this ethnographic study was the 'field' of research. Generally, observation as a very important aspect of ethnographic studies in my research context was fairly even. My study was largely observational and took place mainly in public places especially where culture festivals are held. When I observed the circuit and regional festivals respectively I travelled with the officials and spaces were not secured by police[17] unlike at the Annual National Culture Festival. The former events are relaxed unlike the latter.

During preparations of the Annual National Culture Festival those of us who wanted to record the proceedings had to apply for clearance. On one occasion, I witnessed how the deputy director[18] reprimanded and warned some European[19] and Chinese tourists taking pictures at the proceedings not to make video recordings as they did not hold rights to do it; they could, however, take pictures.

The situation could get difficult when local organizers were joined by others from head office whom I did not know or had not met before. I had to begin to make new relationships with these 'strangers' from head office in Windhoek. In the event that there was an impromptu meeting for the organizers, the deputy director was not always willing to share information. During the last meeting held at Maria Mwengere Culture Centre to review the whole festival, the deputy director asked me to leave the room. In order to get information from those meetings I relied on certain officials who attended and briefed me later when I invited them for a drink at a local bar. Why there was so much secrecy around certain aspects of the festival is a question worth reflection, but one which I cannot answer in this study.

---

[17] Security at the Annual National Culture Festival is always tight as the presence of senior state officials is anticipated.

[18] The deputy director is second in charge after the director of National Heritage and Culture Programmes. He also removed all the culture booklets which the various cultural groups submitted to the judges; as a result I could not get hold of those from other regions except from Kavango which I had witnessed being made.

[19] One woman who said that she was a PhD researcher from Europe, had to produce her student card and letter before she was allowed to sit in the space which was designated for the media.

The other serious limitation was in doing interviews. I realized that conducting interviews in Kavango and also in Windhoek has become difficult. I came across instances when research informants[20] insisted on payment before an interview. They mentioned names of certain researchers and radio broadcasters[21] who had paid for doing interviews with them. It is not important now as to which party paid for interviews first, but the consequence is detrimental to future research data produced from such an environment. I had to abandon many of the interviews due to this.

I entered the field as a black Namibian and as a result I was somehow expected by my research participants to have some knowledge of the subject. For example, when I asked questions about usage of certain local implements and assured them I had no prior knowledge of this, they answered with reservations. Specific subjects asked about from certain individuals were regarded as being taboo, because of our relationship. As I later realized it was important to bring certain knowledge to the field. There seemed to be some idea among local people that if someone is black one somehow needs to know local basic practices. In my research context, which was rather complex in terms of relations, people often treated me as an insider at certain times, especially when I spoke local languages and, as such, expected me to know various things. They would, however, feel compelled to answer certain questions without hesitation and reserve when a person who asked them was 'obviously' foreign, such as whites. This supports what Mfecane 2010:33 says about the importance of not entering the field on a 'blank slate' as this will limit one's ability to question various aspects of the ethnography.

Culture discourses and related issues are sensitive especially if they involve the state and, therefore, require cautious handling. During my stay at the state institution, the culture office in Rundu, I was entrusted with certain confidential information, which I have not used in my study as it may create problems for those who have given me access to such data. Before interacting with the research participants, I informed them about the nature of the study and those who needed anonymity for fear of reprimand (officials) were guaranteed confidentiality. However, certain subjects were more than willing to have their names publicized in the outcome of the study.

Regarding interviews I sought informed consent from the participants on an ongoing basis as I had more than one interview with some. There were certain issues we spoke about which they did not want to be on record and in such instances I duly complied and switched

---

[20] This has become an issue especially with people who are regarded as knowledgeable about certain subjects.
[21] One could understand the context of state radio broadcasters especially in Namibia as they have an obligation to reward people for their intellectual property, when they make recordings which will be stored and aired occasionally.

off my voice recorder. Due to the nature of the study which required people's names to be revealed especially when I sought to reconstruct the history of my research area, participants were encouraged to withdraw from the study at anytime they wished to do so, or when they were not comfortable with the subject.

Public spaces may not require any form of permission but, as we have seen in the context of the ANCF, I was required to seek clearance in order to record the event and all proceedings. I duly complied with that process. There is an ongoing ethical debate on the usage of visuals. It appears to be very complex because there is no standard procedure that can be adhered to when producing such data. This study has made extensive usage of visual materials and, as a result, I have obtained permission from participants who are depicted in the pictures to use them for analysis and publication. However, pictures that I took from a distance are displayed without permission.

The book has two parts which locates the material studied both historically and at the present time. The first part outlines the local history of Kavango as a research scene in three contexts namely pre-colonial, colonial and postcolonial times. This historical discussion presents evidence on the migratory and settlement patterns of the people in Kavango and the way they have changed over time. The focus is on pre-colonial identity construction and the influence on this by colonialism and its eventual appropriation in the postcolonial time. The second part deals with 'making the nation' in a postcolonial context through participation in state sponsored culture festivals.

In chapter two I locate culture festivals within the wider theoretical discourse of representation and performance. I show that festivals are about the practice of identity "pride" by those involved. (Meyer, 1999:103) Representations of culture performances in the festival produce meaning. I show that festivals are not just celebratory in the postcolonial discourse of nation building in independent Namibia but serve also as a social practice and resource for social cohesion.

In the third chapter I reflect and discuss my fieldwork experiences with specific focus on the workings of kinship relations and its influence on my access to the field. I interrogate the workings of *ekoro*[22] as a very important social relation and the practice of *kukutongonona*[23] and how these determined my access to various aspects of social life in Kavango specifically and Namibia generally.

---

[22] Ekoro is a very important communal relationship rooted and reinforced by clan affinity.
[23] Kukutongonona is a practice of introduction. It is an extensive introduction which does not just end with the name, but with presentation of your extended relatives including your parents, grandparents and previous domiciles.

Chapter four sketches the historical background of inhabitants in Kavango through oral legends, which speak about issues of early migrations and colonial representation over the years. The idea of Kavango-ness inherent in these legends is subsequently reconstructed, appropriated and asserted in various historical periods. I show that, historically, Kavango has played a special part in Namibia culture politics by presenting evidence of contemporary academic discourse, which is an attempt by local scholars to re-locate and sanitize the history of the region.

Chapter five deals with the inception of culture festivals, which was officially known as the *sangfees*[24] in colonial South West Africa/Namibia with a specific focus on Kavango as a homeland. Using the reminiscences of my research participants and archival materials, I reconstruct the story of the colonial festival in order to understand the intentions of its making and relevance in what was then the Kavango homeland. The focus in this context is the former Department of Education in the Administration for Kavango and culture activities at *Ekongoro*[25] or Maria Mwengere Culture Center as local contexts where colonial identity was asserted.

In chapter six I present an ethnography of the Maria Mwengere Culture Center as a space in which the state produced and articulated identities of the local people through the compilation and promotion of the 'culture booklet', a collection of oral stories, songs and research on various musical instruments and the Kavango museum. I discuss the booklet (then known as a *Sangbundel*) originating from the colonial South West Africa period, when it was commonly held that the 'culture of the native' should be captured and stored in museums for ethnographic presentations and the tourists and, finally, the way the project of colonial cohesion is reinvented with new meanings in the postcolonial period.

In chapter seven I deal with the theme of making the nation with specific focus on the role of local people, participants in the cultural performances and audiences and state officials in the festival space. Following Goffmans 1959 conceptualization of backstage and front stage, I detail rehearsals and regional festival sessions in order to explore social interactions of the people in the festive context with the specific focus on *maliyombiliso*[26] and *kulinyanyukisa*[27]. I show that the contribution and participation of lay and local people to the activities of the various culture groups in the state sponsored festival context makes

---

[24] Sangfees literary translates as Song festival in English
[25] The phrase Ekongoro is used in situational contexts to refer to a very important water serpent believed to be living in the Kavango River, or the rainbow. In this case it can be understood to refer to the rainbow which is also locally believed to symbolize the various population groups in Kavango which have been celebrated during colonial culture festivals hosted by the Maria Mwengere Culture Centre.
[26] Lit. rehearsal
[27] Lit. to make ourselves happy or to entertain ourselves.

them active role players in the processes of a nation-making project, as mediated and prescribed by the state.

In chapter eight my analysis shifts to the postcolonial state sponsored culture festival. In particular, this chapter draws on the events of the festival's 2008 programme, which took place in December of that year in Rundu, the capital of the Kavango region in northeastern Namibia. I present a detailed ethnography of the processes of the 'making' of Kavango identity which unfolded during the festival as distinctively 'different' from that of other ethnic groups in postcolonial Namibia. The ethnographic description and analysis focuses on the cultural performances of two groups, namely the Ntunguru Cultural Group and the group from the Noordgrens Secondary School.

Chapter nine draws major arguments from other parts of the thesis as a conclusion. I conclude that, although the state sponsored culture festival has undergone various stages of transformation in which it has acquired new meanings, it is an important social investment for associational life. The event is important for post colonial states and its citizens as it enhances social cohesion, an aspect of life with which many states have struggled since independence. The chapter shows other possible avenues, beyond the scope of this study, for further academic research such as how the festival is conceived and politicized in other political regions of Namibia.

2 The 'Performance' of Culture

On 'Doing' and 'Performing' 'Culture' at State Sponsored Culture Festivals

In this chapter I discuss performance as a social practice. Performance has recently been used as a key concept in several widely read studies on culture, nationalism, and the making of national and Pan-African identity (e.g., Askew 2002, Ebron 2002). Specifically, my study draws on Askew 2002 key argument, namely the connection between performance and power and the imagining of the nation state as it contributes to understanding the emergence of momentous realities in the world. By situating postcolonial identities within their broader political and economic context, Askew demonstrates how performance has been fundamental to both the active and reactive processes of transformation. In order to locate and make sense of how performance is conceived in my research and anthropological and academic discourse respectively I explore how the term is used and perceived by those (state officials, cultural groups and audiences) who participated in the making of the state sponsored culture festival in Kavango north-eastern Namibia. I argue that in this context performance is used to refer to the practice of particular symbolic or aesthetic activities such as ritual, or theatrical and folk artistic activities that are enacted as intentional and unintentional expressive productions in established local genres. I set out to show how academics analyze ritual processes as performance framed as they are with their symbolically rich enactments.

Social rituals such as culture festivals are employed as a means to achieve national goals, and are important in understanding the processes of nationalism. I engage what I believe to be challenges posed by our usage of performance in anthropological theory in order to understand social life in its *realness* or as a social practice. The tendency to refer any aspect of social action as performance (Schieffelin, 1998), I believe presents the danger of misreading and reducing the significance of what we as social scientists observe as performance. With reference to the festival under investigation those involved in its making see themselves as "doing or practicing culture"[1]. Thus, as students of performance it is important for us to distinguish and contextualize performance as process from practice as a single act in the process.

Secondly, I turn my focus on the links of the cultural festival in Namibia to related politics in order to understand the state's nationalist policy. In order to make sense of the

---

[1] I will discuss this aspect later in the chapter.

festival's complexity and its place in the social space, I draw on insights from my research to show how the state sponsored culture festivals assert identity, and contest citizenship and belonging through representation of ethnic and traditional dances and drama in order to signify a unique ethnic existence within the national context. (Akuupa, 2010) My preliminary archival research shows that while colonial power linked the concept of nationality to ethnicity, the postcolonial government linked nationality to the state. In Namibia both the concepts "nationality and ethnicity are in use and in discursive negotiation with one another" as KJÆret & Stokke 2003:580 have argued in their analysis of national discourses in postcolonial Namibia. In the following section, I discuss Anthropology and Performance in order to lay down the foundation on which I locate the theoretical discussion of performance.

Anthropology and Performance

Postcolonial nationalism takes a significant interest in the study of performance in Performance Studies and Anthropology. Recent studies show how festival fairs and other political rituals have become spaces and resources through which ideas of nationhood are constructed, making them well suited to understanding the processes of nationalism. In Africa, explicit anthropological studies of performance and politics of nationalism were undertaken by Kelly Askew in Tanzania and Paulla Ebron in the Gambia (2002). In the restorative context of the Truth and Reconciliation Commission (TRC) in South Africa, Catherine Cole 2010 researched the stages of transition as performance in the process of national reconciliation from a performance studies perspective.

Kelly Askew observed Swahili music and cultural politics in Tanzania. She focused on the imbrications of power and performance and their application to multiple levels of social life, from the individual to party politics at the national level. She constructed her theory of performance from events she encountered upon her arrival in Tanzania such as customs checkpoints, state holiday celebrations, *ad hoc* funerals and weddings, concluding that performance constitutes a means of countering and destabilizing established power. She has suggested that in the context of the above, performance is best viewed as an active dialogic interaction between and among performers and audience, rather than the traditional emphasis on the product (the text, the message communicated), and argues that the recent emphasis on the process and concern for the form and the politics of context can be united and integrated into a single model. This interaction, she argues, is not proved to be dialogic and the distinction between the communicators can become highly fluid. She emphasizes that the seeds of an integrated theory on politics of performance lie within the many theoretical contributions of performance theory. Askew argued, in the context of her study, that elements of performance that directly relate to politics are the processes of its production, its communicative function, the messages it communicates, its reflexivity, its capacity for an enhancement of experience and the capacity for active power negotiation and contestation in local and national, private and governmental performances. It is this aspect which forms part of the focus of my study.

Ebron's work in The Gambia is equally important. She calls our attention to the importance of reading literature on performance and representation with and against each other in order to understand contemporary politics of nationalism in Africa. She explored the implications of performance as both social encounter and practice, as well as its significance as an ideological construct through a discussion of Mandinka praise singers. Her study on praise singers, locally known as *jaliya*, produced evidence that suggests that performance as an act or practice creates a perception of Africa for the tourist sector on that part of the continent.

Catherine Cole's Performing South Africa's Truth Commission (TRC) explores the question of a larger cultural memory in its many guises of performance. She focuses on the commission's public enactments of what was said, scripted, produced, rehearsed and represented by witnesses, commissioners, perpetrators and victims. She examined the layers of performance from witness to interpreter to journalist to audience. Because of the TRC's presentation as a public enactment, Cole analyzed it as performance. Based on a closer reading of sources, raw video footage of the TRC hearings and interviews she has come to the conclusion that the ritual (TRC) as a performative act had multiple and ambiguous meanings.

Studies elsewhere in the world and on the continent implicitly employ performance as an analytical concept. Examples of this are the examination of *lafête* in Quebec by Richard Handler 1988, Guss 2002 on transformed cultural landscapes in Venezuela, Van Binsbergen's 1994 Kazanga festival in Zambia and Lentz 2001 Kobine and Kakube festivals in Ghana.

Guss has dealt with the contestations of nativeness and the notion of *mestizaje* in the celebration of the monkey dance on the Day of the Monkey. At the centre of these contestations is the myth of *mestizaje*, which carries a discourse of all- inclusiveness among the blacks, whites and those of mixed race in this part of South America. However, as he has argued, the *mestizaje* was employed for the precise purpose of excluding those who are seen not to conform to national ideas of progress and a market economy. Similarly, although in a different context, in Handler's study (1988) we see how French speaking Canadians negotiate belonging to the nation of Quebec (a province on mainland Canada) and claim allegiance to the province and mainland, whilst others felt the province should not be attached to Canada.

This was based on evidence gathered during the celebration of *la fête* when Parti Québécois won the provincial elections in 1976. He observed elements of differentiation and belonging in other social spheres such as sport and argues that the processes of cultural production are political insofar as they involve controversy over identity formation.

Van Binsbergen 1994 focused on the Kazanga Festival in Zambia through which he explored the cultural dynamics of ethnicity in the context of a postcolonial African state. With particular attention to the participation of the Nkoya ethnic group in the Kazanga festival, his analysis brings out an instance of ethnic self representation *vis-á-vis* the national state and argues that in the festival space ethnicity transforms local historical cultural forms into a global idiom of performance, inequality along class and gender lines and commodification of culture.

In West Africa, Carola Lentz 2001 has shown why it is important for provinces to hold cultural festivals. In her extensive research in Ghana over the years Lentz has demonstrated and argued, through what she calls politics of invitation and participation, the importance for local chiefs to host Kobine and Kakube cultural festivals in their areas. Unlike the festivals held by the state, local chiefs hold festivals to show the political influence they can generate at the level of their administration in addition to deriving benefit from business and community contributions. Attention is also drawn to the area of the chief at the level of the state, which, in turn, has used the gatherings to disseminate information about its political agenda. The above studies speak about performance explicitly or implicitly and deal with processes of representation, which mark belonging, ethnicity, exclusivity and the development of social relations.

Performance Theory in the Social Science Sphere

The most influential students of performance theory such as Erving Goffman, Victor Turner, Clifford Geertz, Richard Bauman and Robert Schechner have largely concentrated on how performance is used to address human social interaction. In his representation of everyday life Goffman 1959 in a dramaturgical context suggested that when an individual plays a part he or she implicitly requests his observers to take seriously the impression that is presented to them. They are asked to believe that the character they see actually possesses the displayed attributes and that the tasks performed will have the consequences that are implicitly claimed for it and that, in general, matters are as they appear. He argued that there is a popular view that the individual offers their performance and puts on his show for the benefit of other people. What interested me in Goffman's view of performance is the idea of turning the consideration from what is on show towards the individual's own belief in the impression of reality that is presented. In this regard, Goffman 1959 argued that the notion of performance has two extremes. One of which is when "the performer can be fully taken in by his own act and be sincerely convinced that the impression of reality which he stages is real". (Goffman, 1959:28) If his "audience is also convinced in this way about the show he/she has just put on and this seems to be the typical case then for the moment at least, only the socially disgruntled will have any doubts about the realness of what is presented"[2]. (Goffman, 1959:28) It is within this extreme that I locate my usage of the term 'performance'.

For Turner 1979 performance is an interaction between social actors and their environment, understood to be 'social drama', a model of life performance. Social dramas may occur at all levels of social organization ranging from state to family. The dramas are never amorphous or open-ended, they have diachronic structure, a beginning, a sequence of overlapping, but distinct, phases and an end. However, these dramas seem conflict driven and require interventions at most times. Man can be regarded as a performing animal not in the sense of an animal in a circus, rather that of man as self performing animal, his performances are *reflexive*; in performing he reveals himself to himself. These performances (drama) are enacted in the social context, which Turner termed communitas.

Turner and Goffman differ in their conception of ritual as performance. Turner views rituals as dramatic events in which participants not only do things, these actions are performed for an audience. Goffman, using a scenographic approach, views the world as a stage on which performances are staged. Both critics stress the importance of processes and processual qualities. Turner's approach poses certain problems in that he reduces every human act, which he refers to as social drama, to a mere process. We need to distinguish process from practice. Goffman's presentation of the world as a stage too gives a reductionist impression of actors on that stage as mere performers. However, his analysis of the stage according to what happens in the hidden and exposed realm and the belief in it by actors is of particular importance in understanding the festival under investigation.

In the essays published posthumously on Turner, Richard Schechner 1993:16-18 presented a useful idea on understanding the interrelationship between social drama and stage drama or cultural performance, namely that the manifest social drama feeds into the latent

---

[2] The other extreme alluded to in the work of Schechner and Appel (1990, reprinted in 1993) is when the performer is not taken in at all by his routine. This possibility may be understood especially when there is no one with skills to read through the act. When the individual has no belief in his own act and no ultimate concern with the beliefs of his audience, he may be called 'cynical' while reserving the term 'sincere' for individuals who believe in the impression fostered by their own performance. (Goffman,1959:28)

realm of stage drama. Its characteristic form in a given culture at a given time and place unconsciously, or perhaps precociously, influences not only the form but also the content of the stage drama of which it is the active mirror. (Turner, 1993:16) Although the "stage drama is always meant to entertain, it becomes a meta-commentary, explicit or implicit, witting or unwittingly on the major social dramas of its social context in *which it happens*" (my italics). (Turner, 1993:16) In turn, the stage drama feeds back into the social drama and life itself now becomes a mirror held up to art and the living now perform their lives; for the protagonists of social drama a drama of living have been equipped by the "aesthetic drama with some of their most salient opinions, imageries, tropes, and ideological perspectives". (Turner, 1993: 17) Therefore, performance in the culture festival in question is conceived as a "completion of a more or less involved process of various acts; which are done by those involved". (Turner, 1979:82) A process, which according to the ritual stages Turner invented, is that of redressive action in a conflict perspective. However, conceptual complexities emerge when some of the acts represented in these processes also happen in daily life and not only when the festival is enacted.

Bauman 1986 has argued that "display events such as rituals, festivals, fairs, ceremonies and spectacles can be viewed and analyzed as cultural performances". (Bauman, 1986:133-134) It is important to treat cultural performances seriously as these are meta-cultural enactments, occasions when members of the society put their culture on display for themselves and others through performance. The nature of such display, he argued, includes "cultural forms about culture and social forms about society in which central meanings and values of a group are embodied, acted out and laid open to examination and interpretation in symbolic form, both by members of that group". (Bauman, 1986: 133) Festival participants represent cultural forms including artifacts, rehearsed traditional dances and drama about the ways of life.

Theory of Performance: A Critical Analysis

In a critical review of performance theory, William Beeman 1993 argues that anthropologists have studied performance largely for what it is able to show about human institutions such as religion, political life, gender relations and ethnic identity in a *functionalist* perspective. (my italics) He claimed that less study has been devoted to performance, its structure and cultural meaning apart from other institutions, the conditions under which it occurs and its place within broad patterns of community life. As a student of theatre he noted the particular neglect of "performance activities which are designed specifically to entertain:

theatre and spectacle even though both were universal human institutions to which societies devoted much time and energy". (Beeman, 1988:370-371)

It appears from a critique of performance as a theory of social interaction that it is only useful when applied to processes and not to practices. For the purposes of analysis, we need to clarify and distinguish *processes* from *practices*. When Turner spoke of performance he had in mind a "processual sense of bringing to completion or accomplishing. To perform is thus to complete a more or less involved *process* rather than to do a single act". (Turner, 1979:82) In my understanding, a process happens over an unspecified period of time and depends on what it entails and how it is sanctioned. Practice broadly refers to anything people do in the Bourdieuan sense of practice. Practice can, therefore, be understood to be a customary action, habit, behaviour, a manner or routine. I argue that process constitutes practice. Although process constitutes practice, it does not happen at just any time. A process is sanctioned. On the contrary, practice happens on a daily basis. In the context of my study, certain elements of representation, which are showcased in the festival, are practiced on a daily basis and not necessarily only during processes which are sanctioned in order to mark a particular occasion in the ritual sense.

There seems to be a neglect of agency and what I call the psychosocial element in performance theory. Although the psychosocial element present in human practice, commonly referred to as reflex or meta-cultural enactment in the theory of performance is difficult to analyze, it still remains important. "Individual agency in performance also presents a problematic role" (Walker 2003:149 cited in Cole 2010:10), which cannot be ignored. Walker (cited in Cole 2010) has argued that performance resonates simultaneously in several different registers including reason, emotion, and experience. The early authors on performance mentioned above have one aspect in common, namely the element of meta- commentary or meta- cultural enactment in their writing, which is largely ignored or overlooked by contemporary authors on performance theory in anthropology. Even though Turner 1979 thought that cognitive reductionism was misleading of social life, matters of the brain, body and culture seem to have dominated his later work.

This oversight in contemporary performance theory has been noted by Edward Schieffelin (1998), who argues that it has resulted in performance being conceived as a particularly symbolic or aesthetic activity such as rituals, or theatrical and folk artistic activities, which are enacted as intentional expressive productions in established local genres. Although the contemporary scholarship of performance in anthropology has moved away from studying these as systems of representations (symbolic transformations, cultural texts) to looking at them as processes, they have time and again used performance to refer to bounded, intentionally produced enactments, which are usually marked and set off from ordinary activities, and which call attention to themselves as particular productions with special purposes or qualities for people who observe or *practice* them. (Schieffelin, 1998, see also St John, 2008) Hughes Freeland 1998 in the introduction to the collection of essays on recasting ritual performance argued that there is a danger of misreading performances and allowing the symbolic to dominate the functional if we in the social sciences do not appreciate performances as constituents of social practice and start to look at them as such. If we do not see social practices as constituents of performance, Schieffelin 1998 maintains 1998, performances seem to be inquisitively robbed of life and power, especially when distanced within discussions concerned largely with meaning. Thus, I suggest, it is important that we not only acknowledge the psychosocial elements and agency in rituals, which conceptualize processes, but that we illuminate them as practices and determinants of power, which influence the lived experience we in turn claim and analyze as performances.

The omission of psychosocial elements and agency in practices, which make up processes, has resulted in most contemporary authors on ritual presenting them as staged acts, especially in the festive context. The work of Boonzaier and Sharp[3] 1994 is a useful point of departure in dealing with the issue of performance in the southern African context. They argue in their essay on Namaqualand that ethnic identity is a carefully controlled performance. The essay was written on the occasion of celebrating the signing ceremony in a reserve park where the Nama choir presented the singing of Nama songs and the construction of a traditional matjieshuis. Through investigation of the events surrounding the signing ceremony, which marked the park establishment in Namaqualand, they concluded that the acts were role-play, a highly self conscious statement which was formulated collectively through dialogue and modified according to context; they did not, however, problematize the perfomative aspect of role-play in relation to what people said they were doing. (Boonzaier & Sharp, 1994:405-406)

In Namibia, Ian Fairweather's (2003) work on heritage is of particular importance. In his attempt to elucidate meanings in the series of dichotomies presented by his research subjects, he focused on local distinctions between pagan and Christian, traditional and modern and, finally, rural and urban, which he analyzed in the light of Fergusson's work on the adoption of local and cosmopolitan styles by mineworkers in Zambia. His case study described a

---

[3] In my personal communication with Boonzaier, he has indicated that the context in which the essay was written was a complex one, especially when some of their informants indicated to them that they were in the true sense of the word 'just' role playing; and that what they presented was not 'really' their daily culture. That sentiment itself begs careful attention. It seems that they (people in Namaqualand) were weary of the new developments in the politics of 'belonging' and 'differentiation' especially among the 'coloureds', which were emerging at the time. He expressed similar sentiments in his talk during the launch of a journal special issue on: Engaging difference: Perspectives on belonging and exclusion in contemporary southern and East Africa.

wedding ceremony held at Olukonda in northern Namibia in a refurbished early Lutheran church situated next to an old mission house serving as a museum. He analyzed the wedding as a staged nostalgic construction of tradition, which was implicit in the proceedings, and allowed for a multi layered performance. Although Fairweather's ethnography demonstrates his subject's lived experience since the arrival of missionaries, his argument seems to suggest that the practice has become static and, thus, can only be staged.

Askew in her study set in Tanzania acknowledges the influential insights on reflexivity derived from Schieffelin. She demonstrates through her presentation of musical ethnography that performance of *ngoma* and *taarab* musical dances has the capacity to constitute, negotiate and transform social relations. However, she does not clearly bring out her research subjects' view of their performance making it difficult to clearly locate her usage of performance as process or practice. Implicitly she refers to a process, as her work is largely influenced by Turner's perspective of performed social drama as a process of social interaction.

Boonzaier & Sharp 1994 and Fairweather 2003, make sensible assertions with regard to the cultural situations they have investigated, however, they tend to reduce the "practical relationship between agents [*actors, observers, organizers*] and fields to a utilitarianist vision" as argued by Bordieu in his theory of action. (1998:79) As a result their theory reduces every action to having been motivated by "economic interest and monetary profit" which, in this case, was access to the reserved land and the material display in the wedding. (Bourdieu, 1998:79) Fairweather located the staged wedding within the realm of performance ignoring the aspect of nostalgia and its challenges as an important psychosocial variable. Turner 1988:84-85 calls our attention to the "observance of static models for thought and action such as cosmology, theology, philosophical systems and ideologies in the epistemological tradition of lived experiences".

Although these three authors acknowledge the importance of psychosocial elements, especially for the performers in the performances they discuss, it is an aspect they have not fully exhausted analytically. Their focus falls more on the symbolic representations they observed. The question of people's belief in what they do within the context of the symbolic representations is omitted. It is this aspect of reflexivity that stands at the centre of my research and theoretical understanding. In order to clarify my position, I employ Goffman's belief in the part one is performing, and Bourdieu's notion of habitus as it manifests itself in the interested and disinterested acts of human beings.

Bourdieu refers to cultural capital as that which is implicitly believed by actors in the social field and which is somehow stored in the habitus. In his theory of practice he argues that actors have embodied a host of practical schemes and appreciations, which function as instruments of reality construction as a principle of vision and division of the universe in which they act. He implies that actors are not just subjects faced with an object that will be constituted as such by a process of thought; they are absorbed in the affair. It is in this context that I locate my study of state sponsored culture festivals. Although, as Ebron 2002 has suggested, we read performance and representation with and against each other, in my research context I use performance as a term to refer to the process, and not the practice which makes the process.

In my research, local people refer to the cultural festival as *sipito soudano wompo,* which translates as the feast of traditional/cultural dances/play/ literary. Herein the *sipito* (feast) is composed of *udano* (dances/play) and are believed to be traditional/cultural by those who participate in the feast. These dances or plays are <u>done</u> thus the saying *kwa ku rugana yompo* (we are doing things of culture) during the culture festival gathering. By implication it means that because dances are done, they are practised and not performed only during festivals, but in other instances of social life as well. State officials who produce the festival, however, refer to the act of symbolic representations as performance. In this context they use the concept performance as a noun to refer to what transpires in the festival. Interestingly as I have observed, state officials use the same idea as ordinary locals in reference to the practice of dances/play. In the English language, which is also the official language in Namibia, they say "people are doing the performances"[4]. This usage of performance as a noun creates some ambiguity especially when contexts of conventions are not clearly explained. Respectively, the cultural/traditional is said to be <u>done</u> in order to be showcased to the public or to those in attendance. Showcase in this context is locally conceived to be an act of public display. Hence I argue that what is <u>done</u> in the festival context is believed and seen by all actors as facts of the "habitus", which are embodied in an "incorporated state" from the local perspective and "objectified" segments practised in real life by state representatives and participants alike. (Bourdieu, 1998:80-81; Handler, 1988:1-3) In other words, I view the state sponsored cultural festival as a social space, which contains practices through which perceived social reality is showcased by actors. Following Bourdieu's idea of disinterested acts suggesting the difficulty of measuring these and not assume that people do not act randomly; that they are not foolish and that they do not act without a reason, I acknowledge the challenge we face in dealing with performance theory. Thus, in the context of my research I present subjects in the festival as actors who are present in the event unfolding and that there is an immediate correlation of practice, which is not posed as an object of thought, but which is inscribed in the presence of the event. The above discussion

---

[4] My field work notes.

on performance as a process and analytical tool is necessary in order to locate and make sense of how the phrase is conceived in my research and in relation to the anthropological academic discourse respectively.

An important issue is the way we deal with the question of performance as a process, when those who participate consciously see themselves as doing or practising acts of reality, and not performing during that process. My research of the state sponsored cultural festival data shows that the state representatives regard the event as framed, heightened and public with symbolically rich enactments; they refer to this as performance. The state representatives view and present the festival representations as acts that can be objectified in order to distinguish the participating groups ethnically. In this context, performance is used to refer to the particular symbolic or aesthetic activities, such as ritual, or theatrical and folk artistic activities, which are enacted as intentional and [unintentional] expressive productions in established local genres. (Schieffelin, 1998)

Postcolonial Nationalism: One Namibia One Nation

In a rather surprising move, five years after Namibia gained independence, the postcolonial state created the Annual National Culture Festival in order to enhance a "polyethnic participation and heterogeneous cultural expression" (Cohen, 1993:8) which, it was argued, would enhance social cohesion. This was contrary to their earlier condemnation of the practice at the time of independence. The desire to replace different ethnic identities with a Namibian national identity is expressed in the constitution adopted in February 1990, in the Swapo Party[5] slogan which is synonymous with that of the state of "One Namibia- One Nation", in the use of linguistics rather than ethnic categories and in the replacement of the ethnic homelands with the new administrative regions. (KJÆret & Stokke, 2003, Swapo Party) Nationalist politics are normally dated from the launch of South West Africa National Union (SWANU) and the Ovambo People's Organization (OPO) which dealt with contract labour issues from the late 1950s before being transformed into a broad based movement, SWAPO, on 19 April 1960 with a different mandate that mobilized all people in the country. It became a liberation movement recognized by the United Nations. The slogan 'One Namibia, One Nation' was born out of the Swapo Party's realization that "divided the nation shall fall"[6] hence the call for a united nation. Ethnicity, tribalism, and regionalism are listed as the main enemies in the ruling party's constitution.[7] At the adoption of the constitution,

---

[5] Swapo Party is the current ruling political party.
[6] See Swapo Party website: www.swapoparty.org/history.html accessed 31 August 2011.
[7] See Swapo Party website: www.swapoparty.org/history.html accessed 31 August 2011.

Geingob[8] 2004 identifies ethnicity as one of the building blocks of the Namibian nation: "once the house has been painted no one would see the bricks or different ethnicities" (Geingob, 2004:144). The Swapo Party constitution and political agenda informs government policies; in fact in Namibia the formally liberal democratic state often appears to be an extension of the ruling party.

The Swapo Party government discontinued the cultural festivals previously created by the colonial state, only to resurrect them five years after independence. It appears the idea of discarding thoughts of ethnicity presented the ruling party with a conundrum: how was it going to define its citizens? Becker 2003 has indicated the same idea particularly with reference to ownership and remembering public heroes and national monuments. In Namibian postcolonial nationalism, Becker 2011 demonstrates how ethnic affiliation played a role in defining and determining a sense of belonging to national ideals of nationhood and ethnicity. She describes a picture with images of a greater desire for ethnic association than national belonging, which she conceptualized as the "culturalization of Namibian nationalism". (Becker, 2011:21)

Similarly, in a South African context Brown 2001 and the Comaroffs 2001 argued that postcolonial states found themselves faced with enormous diversity and few unifying elements. African leaders developed different approaches to the problem of internal unification and almost all placed great importance on the production of national culture. The postcolonial period has been marked by a great deal more than just a move to democracy. At independence, the idea of belonging was about nationhood based on "One Namibia, One Nation". Those in power spent much energy emphasizing the importance of belonging to the nation. At the independence of Namibia, their South African neighbours were striving towards the abolishment of apartheid. In this context the idea of the *Rainbow Nation* championed by Desmond Tutu and Nelson Mandela as the first black president became the bedrock of South African nationalism. "Unity in Diversity" subsequently replaced the slogan "One Namibia, One Nation", as citizens began to emphasize ethnic belonging in preference to national belonging. These changes are at the core of this study. This is an epoch in which most countries experienced unprecedented waves of demand for democracy, including the lessening on power of state institutions, which was passed to transnational corporations, associations, nongovernmental organizations and, at times, crime syndicates.

The challenge for the state was to define *Namibianess* in the light of the waning of apartheid and continental shifts in identity politics. Responding to these shifts, the Swapo

---

[8] Hage Geingob was the chairman of the Constituent Assembly which drafted the Namibian constitution. At independence he became the first Prime Minister of the republic.

led government devised the policy: *Unity, Identity and Creativity for Prosperity*. This was accepted in principle by the Namibian cabinet in 2001. Contrary to the Swapo Party constitution, which shunned ethnicity and tribalism, the new policy, built on a constitutional guarantee, presented a new political vision:

- We envisage ourselves as a united and flourishing nation, celebrating the diversity of our artistic and cultural expressions, and globally admired as is the skin of an African leopard.

- We envisage ourselves as a united and flourishing nation, achieving sincere reconciliation through mutual respect and understanding, solidarity, peace, equality, tolerance and inclusion.

- We envisage ourselves as a united and flourishing nation, treasuring and protecting our material and spiritual heritage and customs, developing creative talents throughout our lifetimes, and employing our skills and knowledge for economic development and common good[9].

This vision was totally opposed to the political ideal at the time of independence. It presents a new idea of enhanced diversity as expressed in the metaphor of an African leopard skin. It focused on the notion of tolerance among different cultures. The underlying goal of the policy was to promote widespread cultural and artistic expression through representations in cultural festival and the arts. (Culture Policy, 2001) As a result, officially recognized ethnic groups gather in order to present and perform what is believed to be their "exclusive culture" (Cohen, 1993:6) under the banner of Namibian Culture.

Article 19 of the constitution of the Republic of Namibia guarantees that:

> Every person shall be entitled to enjoy, practice, profess, maintain and promote any culture, language, tradition or religion subject to the terms of this constitution and further subject to the condition that the rights protected by this article do not impinge upon the rights of others or the national interest.

Implicitly the constitutional guarantee supports and encourages diversity. Although diversity is strongly encouraged in the festival context, festival organizers and the state have a "conscious concern about and preoccupation with the possible development of exclusivity". (Cohen's (1993:6) Exclusivity is of utmost importance where ethnicity is viewed by those in positions of social influence as a tool to be used for accessing various social fields. (Bourdieu, 1998) In postcolonial times I argue that exclusivity has become synonymous with ethnic-

---

[9] Culture Policy, Government of the Republic of Namibia 2001.

ity especially due to the negative social consequences they have produced elsewhere on the continent.

As Dickson Eyoh 1998 explains with reference to social realist cinema and representation of power, the justly celebrated resurgence of popular movements for democracy in Africa retreated into ethnic and kinship networks as a sanctuary from the violence and intensity of competition over dwindling resources; this presented a major pattern of response to the erosion of the utopian dreams of independence. The above perspective gives an impression that Africanist discourse on postcolonial nationalism had previously been dominated by the management of social tensions, generated by ethnic interaction with modern and traditional forms of production, institutions of political power and cultural systems. I acknowledge Magubane's (1969) caution of understanding postcolonial social tensions labelled as ethnic or tribal in isolation from the colonial context that created them.

In the South African context, the Comaroffs 2001 argue that global neoliberal capitalism constructed the modernist subject- citizen characterized by the explosion of identity politics during the late 1990s. This led to shifting relations between the concepts of citizenship, community and national sovereignty under neo liberal conditions in South Africa. In fact, xenophobic attacks on foreign immigrants in the later years of 2000 could be understood in terms of the politics of identity, belonging and access to resources.

In the context of Botswana during the 1970s, The Comaroffs point to the tension between the model of a one party state and multiparty democracy. The one party state model was seen by the majority of Botswana citizens as an African alternative especially by looking at the "comparative ethnic homogeneity of the time, different from the deeply taken-for-granted European political practices and institutions". (Comaroff and Comaroff 1997:20) However, the antagonism against the postcolonial Botswana state was in turn seen to be opposed to the Setswana tradition by those that represented the state. With reference to the South African apartheid period lasting forty years and the bloody war in Rwanda, Duncan Brown has attributed such painful historical moments to increased sensitivity of "inclusive and exclusive conceptions of identity". (Brown, 2001:758)

The recent publication by Peter Geschiere 2009 presents interesting changes in the discourse of belonging in Cameroon since that country's independence in the 1960s, and points to inherent ambiguities within the concept. He describes various forms of political rituals signifying local ideas of belonging in the context of nationhood, and has demonstrated how these changed over time. He focuses on the particular expression of the local namely the idea of autochthony and allognes in Cameroon and in his native Netherland in the 1990s. In question is the history of violence against allogènes in both countries in order to inform the making of contemporary ambiguities in Cameroon and Netherland. Of course this process is influenced by different factors such as immigration and access to postcolonial resources. The idea of autochthony and its working is similar to the workings of ethnicity; more specifically when local rituals are essentialized by leaders and believed to display allegiance to a particular cultural group. Geschiere discusses the manner in which autochthony operates to mediate exclusion and inclusion of citizens in democratic processes and resultant hostilities in Neoliberal Africa.

Significant research in the field of nationalism studies indicates that festivals may be instrumental in the way national identity is constructed and presented. (Handler, 1988) In his seminal study on political ritual Handler argues that processes of cultural production are political insofar as they involve contestation over identity formation. In such processes[10] identity formations are manifested and enforced, contested and manipulated in order to emphasize the required display. In the context of constructing nationhood, he sees nationalism as an "ideology about individuated being", because it is concerned with boundedness, continuity and homogeneity encompassing diversity. (Handler 1988:6) In his exploration of nationalist discourse in Canada, Handler frequented fairs, festivals and folklore exhibits. He found "that celebration of *la fete* expressed more than partisan joy – it marked their belief in the coming of age of a collectivity and their pride in belonging in that collectivity". (Handler, 1988:4) In the next section I focus the discussion of the notion of culture as an important political resource for enhancing sovereignty and belonging in wider postcolonial Africa.

Festival Making in Postcolonial Africa

In this book I attempt to show how during the state sponsored cultural festivals, ethnic identity is expressed through cultural representations. Furthermore, favoured cultural representations are those deemed 'traditional' and include characteristics that signify a unique ethnic existence within the national context. Schieffelin 1998 argues that African states make use of cultural representations to refer to bounded, intentionally produced enactments, usually marked and set off from ordinary activities, which call attention to themselves as particular productions with special purposes or qualities for people who observe or perform them. It is these particular productions, I argue, which mark the postcolonial ethnic and inner-ethnic differentiations in my research context.

In my ethnography of the state sponsored cultural festival it is evident that the state representatives regard the event as framed, heightened, public and symbolically rich enactments. I argue that through festival participation and interactions individuals create their

---

[10] Recently the Namibian government embarked on a National Pride campaign in order to create awareness of national identity.

self-identity, which is appropriated collectively. My research showed people to be more concerned with who they are, their descendants (clan), ethnic orientation and, finally, their national identity. Like others in the field of the social sciences, I acknowledge that identity as a concept is rather complex to unravel. However, in this context for participants and spectators, the state sponsored culture festival provides an opportunity not only to practice what is referred to as their culture and tradition, but also to express their identity in essentialist terms, as argued by Hall and Du Gay 1996. In that sense, identity is presented "on the back of recognition of some common origin or shared characteristics with another person or group and with the natural closure of solidarity and allegiances established on this foundation". (Hall & Du Gay, 1996:2-4) The importance is the emphasis on the participants and spectators who harness the social space in order to present their identity to the audience through the culture performances, which are acted out in the festival context.

For those who organize culture festivals, including politicians who officiate at the gatherings, the social space presents itself differently and is differently regarded by the spectators and participants in the festival. In contrast to participants and spectators, culture festival organizers assume a perceived identity of those who will participate and those who are represented respectively. This conception and simultaneous presentation of these perceived identities "is not *necessarily* an essential one, but a strategic and positional one". (My italics) (Hall & Du Gay, 1996:3) What is significant here is the point that identity as a construct becomes subject to manipulation during the presentation of cultural performances and, as with all signifying practices, it is subject to the play of difference. At the same time it is "reconstructed, given new meanings and used as a means to forge solidarity". (Hall & Du Gay, 1996:2)

I use identity in this study as a category of practice as suggested by Brubaker and Cooper (borrowed from Bourdieu) in their essay on *"Beyond Identity"*. I use the notion in the context in which it is practiced by lay people in some of their daily settings in order to make sense of themselves, their activities, what they share and how they differ from others. From the perspective of politicians, I employ the notion as used to persuade people to understand themselves, "their interests, and their predicaments in a certain way, to persuade people that they are identical with one another and at the same time different from others, and to organise and justify collective action along certain lines". (Brubaker & Cooper 2000:6-8)

Culture and Making the Nation

With reference to postapartheid culture politics in southern Africa, Richard Wilson 2001 examined practices, methods and discourses of culture and race. Focusing on two main human rights institutions in South Africa, namely the constitutional court and the TRC (Truth and Reconciliation Commission), he studied how local people's notions about reconciliation differed from those of these central institutions of the post-apartheid South African state. He explained that post-apartheid nation building appealed to civic nationalism as a new basis for national integration. The key term here is *Ubuntu*. Wilson 2001 contends that *Ubuntu* was an African concept used by leaders to address and justify amnesty during the truth and reconciliation commission. The usage of *Ubuntu*, he argues, created an artificial polarity between Africanist and Western perspectives of reconciliation. He took the historical trajectories of race, culture and group rights in South Africa into consideration in his attempt to deconstruct the post- apartheid politics of culture. He argued that, even if human rights became the paradigmatic discourse of compromise and constitutionalism, these rights had been subordinated due to the priority of nation-building. An example in that respect was the abolition of the death penalty in South Africa when an appeal was made to African ideas of unity and community through the new "culture of rights". (Wilson 2001:210)

In order to realize state programmes in different ways human rights may be combined with symbolic markers of cultural difference as a strategy of nation building. Conversely, the state may assign them to categories of culture and race in a literal, legalistic and procedural liberalism. (Wilson, 2001) The vocabulary of human rights has become the central language of nation-building in democratizing countries such as South Africa. In South Africa, Wilson 2001 observed that state officials tend to combine elements of both liberalism and communitarianism in their interpretation of nationhood and rights. In the context of nation-building, the language of human rights is deployed with significant culturalist and Africanist referents in order to legitimate the project of post-apartheid nation-building. Wilson's work is important, because of its implications for the anthropological conception of culture as an analytical tool and its usage by the elite in the process of legitimizing their projects of bureaucratization and nation building.

Oomen 2005:8 argues that culture, which had been considered in the early phases of the postcolonial state as backward, tribalist and an obstacle to modernization, now led the way in engaging a fast changing world. Its revival was not only about the wider economic processes, it was essentially political. This South African observation relates to global developments where ethnic and indigenous groups all over the world in recent years have revived their cultures in order to attract tourists and to assert authenticity for a range of reasons. Governments, on the other hand, have sponsored what Chanock 2000:17 refers to as cultures which "brand best" in order to strengthen their identities.

A recent study emerging from Zimbabwe by Ndlovu-Gatsheni and Willems 2009 shows how music festivals have shifted from the celebration of the imagined united African nation to attribute new meanings to concepts such as independence, heroes and unity in the changed political context of the 2000s. In their essay on making sense of cultural nationalism and the politics of commemoration under the third chimurenga in Zimbabwe, Ndlovu-Gatsheni and Willems show how the gala event of music performance effectively syncretized the elite memorialism of the 1980s and 1990s with the cultural practices of the 1970s liberation war. In the process, the ruling party delegitimized the MDC (through musical performances)[11] as a political party without liberation credentials and as a threat to the country's independence and unity.

While little directly relevant literature has been written about Namibia, a body of literature on the politics of identity and cultural performances is steadily developing. Becker 2004 and 2007 expresses views about the reclamation of traditions, developments of *efundula* (women initiation in northern Namibia, Ovambo) and other practices such as the commemoration of heroes in Namibia in the mid 1990s. Fairweather 2001 focuses on identity politics and the heritage industry in the northern regions of postcolonial Namibia. He argues (2006) that cultural performances in any form have a more complex role in the production of postcolonial subjects than simply reproducing colonial ways of organizing experience. He foregrounds the role of the rapidly developing heritage sector in enabling postcolonial Namibian citizens to negotiate the local, national and global contexts in which their identities are asserted. A fairly recent work on performances from Namibia is by Wendi Haugh 2009, who analyzed song performances in order to understand the construction of Christian and national identities in postcolonial Namibia.

In his reflection on opportunities for "rebuilding societies from below", Reinhart Kossler 2003 used the Witbooi festival among the Nama of Gibeon in Southern Namibia to demonstrate society building amid forces of globalization. The festival commemorates the death of Kaptein Hendrik Witbooi during the historic defeat of the Nama by the German troops in 1905. Kossler argues that the festival narrative changed from being an inward looking ceremony centered on church and cemetery to a political manifestation of the struggle for liberation and Witbooi's aspiration to regain what the Nama considered their legitimate heritage. In postcolonial Namibia he demonstrates how the festival incorporated characteristics of traditionalism, syncretism and inclusiveness showing that while the festival's character of traditionalism and syncretism was not surprising, its inclusiveness presented a reflection of a conscious political effort of symbolic inclusion on the narrative of "One Namibia, One Nation".

---

[11] MDC stands for Movement for Democratic Change. It is an opposition party in Zimbabwe led by Morgan Tsvangirai.

Literature from elsewhere on the African continent and beyond demonstrates a similar emphasis on the sentiments of ethnicity predominantly during festival fairs and carnivals and, more especially, on issues such as access to resources, and the articulation and mobilization of rights.

Festival with New Social Meaning and Function

With respect to Ghana, Birgit Meyer argues that festivals are about performance and presentation of "identity pride" by those involved. (Meyer, 1999:103) The representation of 'culture' in the festival produces meaning. In this section I show that festivals in the postcolonial discourse of nation building are processes of creating social meanings. As an associational practice and a resource for social cohesion they provide a space in which people can 'renew' their being. (Owusu-Frempong, 2005:735) Thus, I argue that their meanings should be read not only through representations enacted during such gatherings, but in the context in which they take place. In the context of Ghana and in relation to the African American festivals, Owusu-Frempong 2005 has argued that festivals are a medium of cultural education and intergenerational communication in the community. It is, however, important to note that these festivals are produced and held for different reasons, and since postcolonial times have transformed and acquired new meanings and functions. The organization and representation of genres of music, dance and drama are altered in order to meet the demands of the festival agenda, which is set by the state.

In Ghana, Meyer 1999 speaks of an interesting heritage initiative by the state at independence. Kwame Nkrumah launched a project on Sankofaism referring to the Akan symbol of a bird looking back over its tail, which means: go back and take it. This idea and cultural revival project "...posits that the indigenous culture and religion from which Ghanaians have been alienated through colonization and missionization, yielding a brainwashed, colonial mind-set, needs to be retrieved. The African personality which Nkrumah had in mind is to reincorporate his/her roots that got severed in the past and forgotten". (Meyer, 1999:3)

The body of literature on festival emanating from Ghana presents two perspectives. One representing festivals as an invaluable source of knowledge about folklore, history, philosophy, aesthetics, music dance, art and myth all of which form part of the African collective existence as argued by Owusu-Frempong 2005. In contrast to this rather essentialist expression of African cultural nationalism, another more instrumentalist perspective suggests that festivals create an opportunity to those involved not only to salvage traditional heritage[12] but also use it in order to sustain their existence.

Ghanaian research further suggests that festivals provide an interface between local communities and the state, as well as providing a space for interaction. (Lentz, 2001) Despite the interface between those in attendance and the state, Carola Lentz 2001 observed that in northern Ghana festivals seem mainly to be regarded as a space were local people address the state and where state representatives could lobby for political support. The situation is significantly different in the south of Africa, as I will show shortly. Following her research of the festival, Lentz 2001 has argued that research into festivals can advance anthropological and historical analysis of cultural innovation and the creation of new ethnic and local identities as well as political dimensions of culture.

Further south on the continent, history and culture represented during culture festivals seem to be regarded as a "precondition for development and progress" by those who organize and participate in them. (Meyer, 1999:103) There seems to be a difference in the way people of the continent in the south and those in the west of the continent relate to the culture festivals. While festival politics in West Africa are about lobbying for political support, in southern Africa the emphasis seems to have shifted more towards assertions of belonging and differentiation. (Van Binsbergen, 1994; Van Heerden, 2009; Akuupa, 2010) The situation could be attributed to the different colonial histories creating different encounters and experiences. What interested me most were the different reactions to the making of festivals by those who organized, participated in and witnessed them. Specifically, in southern Africa culture festivals did not only feature ethnic self representations, they brought out the extent to which cultural representations of ethnicity transformed local historical cultural forms towards a global idiom of performance, inequality and commoditization of culture. This argument has been used in slightly different terms by both Van Binsbergen 1994 in his work on the Kazanga festival in Zambia and the Comaroffs 2009 in Ethnicity INC.

Van Heerden's (2009) research on post-1994 Afrikaner identities is of particular importance in understanding festivals in the Turnerian sense of social communitas. Van Heerden 2009 presents an interesting insight on how ethnic Afrikaner identity is presented, contested and reconfigured among Afrikaans speakers through their participation and attendance at the Klein Karoo Nasionale Kunstefees en Aardklop (KKNK) festivals. The festival

---

[12] Of late, festivals in the postcolonial context play a very important role in what is believed to be the "preservation of cultural heritage" for economic purposes and interactions with Diaspora blacks. (Pierre, 2009:60) The importance of the above theme is confirmed by the emphasis that numerous influential bodies place on heritage as a component of sustainable development and poverty alleviation, as documented by Flint (2006) in his essay on the Kuomboka festival in Western Zambia.

emerged during a time of perceived crisis among the Afrikaans speakers. The Afrikaans language and its artistic expressions were in need of change, especially in a post apartheid context. Van Heerden compares and contrasts the Afrikaans oriented art festival to the former Afrikaner *volkfeeste*. She argues that whereas the *volkfeeste* were designed to advance the apartheid ideology of Afrikaner nationalism, the newly established Afrikaans oriented festivals were envisioned as inclusive celebrations. Similarly, my research in Kavango shows that there is a significant ethnicization taking place in the colonial and postcolonial culture festival. (See chapters 6 and 8 below)

The literature indicates that the postcolonial African festival has a social function. I argue that one of those functions is to provide space and opportunity of expression to those who participate. In a more far reaching statement it has been argued that the festival has a political function, that of decolonizing the mind. (Wa Thiongo, 1986) From this perspective festivals involve the crafting and shaping of the postcolonial national identity by carefully selecting, locating and legitimizing certain historical memories and literary works that reflect indigenous ways of life. (Opoku, 1970; Wa Thiongo, 1986) Furthermore, it has been argued that the festival provides not only a medium through which certain histories and ways of life are "legitimized", but also relates to "state authority". (Arnoldi, 2006:56; Ndlovu-Gatsheni & Willems, 2009:946)

The festival provides an opportunity to the organizers and participants to present and create their perceptions of identity. The festival has enormous popular appeal, therefore, it should not be viewed as a mere venue for celebration and entertainment. Arnoldi, 2006 whose research on the Malian youth festival and the National Museum which focuses on their role as official sites where nationhood is imagined, has argued that the festival seizes the opportunity to indoctrinate the citizens in socialist principles and decolonize the national culture while exciting outpourings of nationalist sentiment in the process. She suggests that festivals serve to transform local genres into modern national forms. Many local performances, which are either ethnically or regionally based, are inserted into a national cultural discourse in order to allow citizens at large, regardless of their specific affiliations, to identify with and embrace these arts as a wholly national identity. (Arnoldi, 2006)

Postcolonial rulers saw cultural festivals (and similar events) as opportunities through which to strengthen their hegemony. In the context of this study, I shall demonstrate later how Sam Nujoma, the first postcolonial president of Namibia, decided to introduce cultural festivals, which were abolished during the early stage of independence when the nationalist narrative was "One Namibia, One Nation" a narrative discouraging all sentiment suggesting separateness or uniqueness at the time of independence in the country. When citizens began to emphasize their ethnic uniqueness coupled with issues of access to resources and ethnic recognition in the time of freedom, the state adopted the "unity in diversity" narrative that encouraged tolerance of difference. During my research interview Sam Nujoma expressed the view that:

> "Otwa ukeni miita iidhigu yo ku kwatela po eemithigululwakalo dhetu. Opo kadhi tewe po".[13]
>
> (Our heritage is facing a difficult war and we have to preserve our heritage so that it is not broken.)

The expression of the importance of cultural preservation should not be read in isolation from other state activities of that time. During Nujoma's tenure he not only introduced the festival, he worked towards creating a law that recognizes ethnic groups in traditional authorities. This state initiative does not differ greatly from the colonial Odendaal Plan[14] of 1960s, nor is the narrative of 'unity in diversity' significantly different in principle from that of the 'Rainbow Nation' and 'Ubuntu'advocated by Desmond Tutu and Nelson Mandela in neighbouring South Africa.

In West Africa the popular African Second World Black and African Festival of Arts and Culture (FESTAC 77) in Nigeria (initially held in Senegal) is dealt with by Apter 2005. The organizers used this festival to introduce new ideas about African identity and the perception of culture. The idea of this festival was conceived and supported by African leaders who had recently succeeded the colonial administrators. The study did not aim to extract an authentic tradition from its fictive colonial and postcolonial forms choosing instead to focus on the transformations culture undergoes when it is produced and consumed in festive mood. Apter describes the production of national culture and tradition, a process that converts cultural objects and materials into icons of a higher symbolic order, during the boom of the Nigerian oil economy. (Apter, 2005:7) Festivals and fairs in the western part of the continent were inspired and influenced by the makings of FESTAC. Apter's investigation into FESTAC shows how heroic narratives of progress and modernity were explicitly presented in the architecture of cultural representation. In this sense he argues FESTAC's path from tradition to modernity was one of progressive abstractions and singularity, building upon a culturally differentiated past to unite the black and the African worlds.

Elsewhere, off the continent, David Guss 2000 argued that forms of behaviour, previously condemned are now being granted new meanings and even more complex lives. His study is embedded in the discursive constructions in which the traditional and the modern are seen as interpenetrating rather than opposing each other. These forms not only dis-

---

[13] Interview with Sam Nujoma, Office of the Founding President, Windhoek 25 November 2008
[14] I will discuss the Odendaal Plan extensively in chapters 4 and 5.

solve into the market-driven global cultural landscape, but enlarge the semantic fields where meanings are multiplied rather than reduced. (Guss 2000:4) Those involved consciously engage in the act of inclusion and exclude elements, which do not conform to the new meanings. David Guss's (2000) study of transformed cultural landscapes in Venezuela (South America) focuses on the reappearance of contaminated visions of a primitive paradise as the alternative to modernity. Guss observed the celebration of San Juan (one of the oldest church festivals). The context involves a conscious creation of a tie with the past where the history is "exploited and reworked within indigenous rituals and social life".

The above literature review shows that instead of treating festivals as occasions where people come together and enact nostalgic traditional representations or carefully controlled performances, they should be treated as complex social practices in processes with intended and unintended ends. (Fairweather, 2001; Boonzaier & Sharp, 1994) I suggest that we view and treat them as social practices because we need to separate them from the processes in which they take place. I argue that festivals are processes in which practices are manifest. Although there are contradictory usages and conceptions of the notion of culture among local people, state officials and academics, it is believed and felt by those who participate in festivals that what they do is reality and hence a practice of society. (Akuupa, 2007; Bourdieu, 1998)

The literature on performance shows festivals not only as celebratory but also as events through which we can read meaning about society and its roles. Witz 2003 suggests that, although festivals are depicted as boisterous and carefree occasions during which festival goers feel and act in unison, it is important that we read the "intentions of the festival organizers and the (usually diverse) reactions by the event critically". (Van Heerden, 2009: 49) It is only once we have grasped the various contradictions that we will be able to conclude that, indeed, festivals lead to the formation of social communitas, in which people are united and renewed. (Turner, 1979; Van Heerden, 2009)

This study shows how the conception and meaning of the festival in question varies and that it is context driven. It examines the assertions and contestations of different identities and social issues as presented through a variety of cultural representations. In the context of the state-sponsored cultural festivals in Namibia, which take place over three phases, namely the circuit, regional and national, the festival is conceived diversely. The showcased content is very much influenced by social issues such as access to resources. At the circuit and regional levels, issues range from the assertion and contestation of intra-ethnic identities, the state of local governance, and praise of local leaders. At the national level, the festival is conceived of as an important medium through which development[15] and belonging can be enhanced. In the context of belonging to the nation, Lindholm 2008 has argued that active participation in collective rituals allows individuals to become greater than themselves. Many different kinds of collectives such as "religious, ethnic, political and aesthetic provide the said experience, but the nation state is one of the most potent existing today". (Lindholm, 2008:98) He argues that the state, in order to accomplish its mission of establishing a sacralized connection with its citizens, not only selects, codifies and publicizes indigenous aesthetic productions as concrete expressions of the national soul, it also writes its own history books recalling its mythical origins, designs a distinct flag-totem, composes an anthem praising itself, celebrates its glorious past, and constructs all the other standard symbols. Through collectives such as rituals people not only celebrate the being of their citizenry in culture festivals, but also legitimate its being and belonging to the nation. (Handler, 1988)

The study shows that the festival has a function, which is to provide space and opportunity to those involved to express themselves politically and economically. Political and economic independence is seen as incomplete unless the citizen's mind, which is the *sine qua* of any genuine independence is also independent and decolonized. (Wa Thiongo, 1986) The festival, therefore, performs the function of enhancing associational life. As a ritual, the festival serves as a medium through which dances, drama and song are presented and given meaning. In relation to the above, I argue that such political rituals are social capital for associational life.

---

[15] Development in local terms is 'ekuliko' or 'ezokomeho'. The two words both refer to the advancement and betterment of social life as a result of state intervention through projects such as the building of roads and clinics. I use the phrase development in the same context.

3 Home Anthropology and Politics of Ekoro

"Whose Child are You?[1]" The Dynamics and Politics of *ekoro/likoro*[2] in Doing Ethnography at Home

During 2006 I visited the directorate of National Heritage and Culture Programs (NHCP) informally in order to find out more about the Annual National Culture Festival (ANCF). I did not get any information.

Some months later, I wrote a letter to the Permanent Secretary at the Ministry of Youth, National Service, Sport and Culture (MYNSSC) in Windhoek to ask for an internship position within the directorate of National Heritage and Culture Programmes (NHCP). As my research was to observe culture festivals in Kavango region, I wanted to do an internship at their office at Rundu. I never received any response from the Office of the Permanent Secretary or any letter from the department back at university.

I went on to make an appointment at the office of the director of NHCP. This time his secretary obliged me by scheduling an appointment. I was preoccupied with how I would explain to him what I was planning to do during my research. As it turned out, other aspects were much more important.

On arrival the secretary directed me to knock at the director's door and after his acknowledgement, I entered and greeted in *Rushambyu*[3]. Morokenu! (Good day!)

I introduced myself by name and surname only and mentioned the institution to which I was affiliated. He then asked me the following:

Director: Mona re ve?
(Whose child are you?)

After telling him that I was the son of Lukas and Dorkas Akuupa more questions came.

Director: Kuni va tunga kwinya kwetu?
(Where is their settlement in our land?)

Michael: Vavo ne kuVambo va tunga.
(They stay in Ovamboland)

Director: KuVambo nka! Oro Rumanyo una kughamba ne weni?
(In Ovamboland! How come you are speaking Rumanyo?)

---

[1] Conversation with Herbert Ndango Diaz the director of NHCP in Windhoek, 2008.
[2] Ekoro or Likoro is a very important local relationship closely linked to clan affinity.
[3] Rushambyu and Rugciriku languages are collectively referred to as Rumanyo.

> Ame ne muRundu na tunga. Mukamali wande mona Nanguroni wa Tandavara na Fau yaHaididira
> (I have settled in Rundu. My wife is the child of Nanguroni the daughter of Tandavara and Fau the son of Haididira).
>
> (The Director still asked with air of disbelief.) Mona re wa kwara ve?
> (Whose child have you married you say?)
>
> Michael: Mona Nanguroni and Fau.
> (She is the child of Nanguroni and Fau.)
>
> Director: Nanguroni wa Tandavara yaHaimbili?
> (You meant Nanguroni the daughter of Tandavara born of Haimbili?)
>
> Michael: Yii. Ndjewo monaTandavara.
> (She is the one, the child of Tandavara.)
>
> Director: Kaa! Kenga shi,va liro lyetu vanya. Liro lyetu lyene lyene. Vantu ne mwa hepa ku kutongonona ndi ku kombana Tamweyi[4] yande.
> (My goodness, look at you! Those people are my relatives, real relatives. People should always introduce themselves properly otherwise one can get lost, my son in law.)

After the above introduction we did not enter into details of what I wanted to do in the directorate. All he asked was how his relatives were, because he had not seen them for a very long time. He instructed me to go to Rundu, inform the senior culture officer, Thomas Shapi, about our meeting and request an office. "Tell him the letter will follow shortly".

> Director: Wa ru yiva shiri Rumanyo! Paku ku teerera na ku vhura ashi uyayhare shi ove mona vaWambo.
> (You know Rumanyo very well! One could not tell that you are a child of the Vambo people when listening to you.)

We stood in the front of his office door and with his very loud voice he laughed as I made a joke of myself :

> Mulyo unene nange shi kughamba liraka lyamukwarero, ndi kapi u vi yuvha omu vakughambera mumudona.
> (It is very important that one speaks the language of your in laws, lest they gossip you in peace.)

---

[4] Tamweyi a Rukwangali and Rumanyo a word which is used interchangeably in Kavango to refer to son/father or brother in law. One's maternal uncle is also referred to as Tamweyi.

The conversation above shows that after I did proper *kukutongonona*[5], I established a new position, that of a son-in-law with the Director at headquarters. The practice of *kukutongonona* informed the director who I was and whom I was related to. As it turned out it was my newly established position as a son-in-law that mattered.

Connectedness of Ekoro and its Workings in the Research Field

As I learned, although it initially appeared easy to access the field and gather data, my non-adherence and observance of my in-laws' local relations and connectedness of *ekoro* made it complex and difficult. *Ekoro* in Rukwangali and */Likoro* in Rumanyo refer to a very important communal relationship strengthened by clan affinity. Rarely, in an average family life in Kavango does something happen without the involvement of *ekoro*.

Ekoro may be roughly referred to as an extended family, but it is more than that. It is a relationship rooted in clan affinity and is not necessarily determined by blood connections. The clans are ranked according to seniority and whoever belongs to a junior clan, irrespective of age, is deemed young by those in the senior clan. There is an expectation of a command of respect and a high level of obedience from the senior clans. Others can also become clan members by seeking allegiance due to various circumstances, such as hunger[6]. Thus the local idiom "Muntu gekoro kuparukira mo wakuauo" (One who has relatives lives through them) or "gekoro kapi azi mu li nzara" (One who has relatives does not die of hunger) as explained by Kampungu in his thesis, which investigated the concept and aim of Kavango marriages. (1966: 28) Those who seek allegiance to a particular clan do so through a process known as *"kupirura makankara"* whereby those who wish to be adopted enter the homestead and turn the three stones which makes the fireplace where cooking take place. That kind of relation or "connectedness" (Carstens, 2000:1) is maintained as if it is constituted through blood. It depended on the circumstances in which this adoption happened and, historically, its constitution remained a secret among the clan elders especially if the adopted persons became slaves in the process.

On many occasions people look to their *ekoro/likoro* in the event of the death of a relative or when a marriage is to be consummated or when there are family disputes. Reference is made further to *ekoro/likoro* if there is a need to access a particular resource, which may

---

[5] Kukutongonona is a practice of introduction. It is an extensive introduction, which does not just end with the name but with the presentation of your extended relatives including your parents, grandparents and previous domiciles. I will explain its workings clearly in the chapter.
[6] The word hunger in this context should not be understood in its literal sense, because the same term can also be used to refer to poverty, war and any other circumstances, which may disrupt societal functioning.

be unobtainable under certain circumstances. In the context of marriage the importance of *ekoro/likoro* is high, "because marriage creates new relations and modifies old ones". (Kampungu, 1966:35)

In contemporary Kavango, the ideal conception of *ekoro* has not changed although the practice of it may have changed. People support the idea of *ekoro* through rendering assistance to their relatives in many ways such as contributions to funeral costs, the negotiation of marriage and weddings, education and child support. Many people who have settled in Rundu, the capital of the Kavango region, still maintain their *ekoro* relations with those in their village of origin which is locally referred to as *kembo* or home. In this case, Rundu is regarded as a temporary settlement for work purposes only and it is expected by those in the village for town people to come home occasionally for holidays, funerals, and weddings and also help with village work. If one does not go *kembo* or assist people at home you risk losing very important relations.

In Kavango, the notion of going home is of utmost importance. For example, I have observed during my stay in the region that whenever someone in Rundu died, it was very rare for them to be buried in the cemetery in Rundu. Memorial services, and in many cases church services, are held in Rundu, but the actual burial takes place in the village where the deceased originated. The death of a person who had lived in Rundu is announced on a local radio program *Madiviso gonomfa* (lit. death announcements):

> Apa nyame Elisabeth Haididira, na ku gava madiviso kekoro nalinye gonomfa damugara gwange Faustinus Haididira ogo ka dogorokere mosipangero saRundu. Elikwamo yimo nye li na kara ngesi, ukeleli tau ka kara poMillenium moutano kositenguko moRundu, momapeu ngurangura kokira zaRundu, povili zohambombali tatu katundilira pembo tu zekongereka Kokayengona. Konyima zoukeleli pongereka tat u kasindikila nye nakufa kembo lyendi lyokuhulilira komayendo.[7]

> (I am Elisabeth Haididira announcing to the whole '*ekoro*'the death of my husband Faustinus Haididira, who passed on in Rundu hospital. The following is the arrangement regarding his funeral, the memorial service will be held at Millenium Park in Rundu on Friday afternoon. On Saturday morning we will meet at the mortuary. At seven we will leave the house to go to church at *Kayengona*[8]. After the church service we will escort the late to his final home at the graveyard.)

---

[7] This extract is taken from the death announcement script of my father- in- law, which was broadcast on 29 July 2010. At the time of his death, I was in Windhoek and had to quickly rush home as a son- in- law and member of *ekoro* so that I could participate in various activities pertaining to the funeral preparation.

[8] The palace of Vashambyu is at Kayengona village.

The excerpt above shows that, although it is known that the deceased lived at Millennium Park,[9] it was not considered his home, because *home* is where he originated; in this case this was Kayengona. In that context Kayengona, i.e. the place from whence he came before staying in Rundu, was considered his home and, therefore, is where he was to be buried. Home in this context is not only an important reference in life, but in death as well. It is evident in the excerpt that no one other than *ekoro* is specifically informed in the event of death. *Ekoro* in this context would make the funeral event possible especially the ritual aspect of it. As a result, many people who work and have settled in Rundu occasionally visit the village in order to maintain ties. The working of relations in *ekoro*, especially between those who are in town and those who remain in the village, is not limited to monetary assistance from Rundu. Those in the village also visit their kin in town and when they come to town they bring goods such as millet flour, meat, fish and any seasonal delicacy available from *home*.

In the context of my research one's position is not really clear whether you are an outsider or insider. I suggest that it is the relations such as the above, which an ethnographer creates in the field irrespective of whether they are insiders or outsiders, which influence our understanding of local ways of life and eventually access to local knowledge. Insider-ness or outsider-ness can be relative and should be understood contextually. One interesting observation that emerged during my fieldwork was that one's connectedness to *ekoro* and its (ekoro) relations/operations to other people in the field determined access to many aspects of social life in the field and outcome irrespective of one's knowledge of the local language and conduct of other social practices such as funerals and wedding rituals[10].

One's self presentation in the field is of particular importance. The self in this context refers to the social self and is a medium in which one appears and how one is subsequently labelled or constructed by people in the field. In this regard Anthony Cohen 2007:114 has asked whether our "self" in the field matters more than the peoples' "self knowledge" we study. Such questions have brought issues like "reflexivity and subjectivity of the ethnographer into serious critique, raising concerns as to whether ethnographies will not end up being about the authors while omitting the subject" [the people studied]. (Cohen, 2007: 114) However, I think it is important to reflect on our relations and activity in the field in order to make sense of what we abstractly construct of the *other*.

---

[9] Millennium Park is one of the new housing developments in Rundu which is the residence of civil servants mainly. It was developed at the dawn of the new millennium.

[10] Practices which make rituals such as weddings and funerals including any other rite are locally believed to be conducted according to 'culture' and are thus referred to as practices of 'culture'. I am aware of all the problems associated with the term "culture" and have elaborated on this issue in the Kavango context elsewhere. (Akuupa, 2006)

The distinction between insider and outsider is widespread in the field. Through power relations of *ekoro/likoro* and the practice of *kukutongonona*, the distinction between the two concepts is harmonized. In this context factors such as education, gender, class and sexual orientation were secondary and the basic distinguishing feature of my fieldwork was how well I was connected to *ekoro* and its relations.

Generally, the success of ethnographic fieldwork is largely measured by the ability to establish a good understanding and develop meaningful relations with research participants. (Sluka, 2007) These relations range from friendship to hostility and may be influenced by ethnicity, religion, class, gender and age. (Sluka, 2007:123) In her essay on How Native Is a "Native" Anthropologist? Narayan 1993:671 has argued against the fixity of the distinction between "native" and "non-native" anthropologists and suggests that anthropology as a discipline or academic enterprise will flourish if all view each anthropologist in terms of shifting identities amid a field of interpenetrating communities and power relations. In my view such an argument may be of value within disciplinary circles where there seems to be a virtual wall between readers of stories (thus theory driven professionals) and between narrative and analysis, but not in the field from which such stories or data are produced. In the field context where such data originates, the distinction of insider/outsider is significant in terms of access to data and field. Whether people and/or researchers are always clearly distinguished into insider/outsider categories remains a complex discussion. However, the people we study use social means to either include or exclude us as researchers. These are the perceptions which people have about us and the way we portray ourselves. Nationality, race, gender and age are but some of the aspects which are used in order to distinguish whether a person is an insider or outsider.

I was aware of this process from my early days as a student researcher. From 2005 until the time of my research I have always had dreadlocks as a hairstyle. When I attended festivals I always carried a bag with cameras and a tripod, though not when visiting other social venues. I have always socialized at the local bars and other public space in town. However, as I will show below, these physical attributes and my linguistic abilities were always a distinguishing factor whether or not I was an outsider or insider in various contexts. There were various times when I was treated differently or with suspicion when I arrived at a venue or requested an interview. For example when I went to visit Kayengona village that is home to my wife and also where I run a small *cuca* shop[11], I am not regarded as an

---

[11] A cuca shop is a small business holding which usually sells small merchandise such as traditional alcoholic beverages, sugar, salt, bottled beer and many other household needs. It also serves as social space where villagers come to relax after their long day of work. The name cuca is derived from the beer that was sold by the Portuguese merchants in most northern areas in the early 1970s. All the little businesses which then sold beer and small household needs became known

outsider. There are two main reasons for this, firstly because of my relationship to them as a son in-law, and as a result of my clan's relationship to that ascribed by many as the royal clan of the *Vakankora*[12]. My clan name is *Omukwanambwa* (singular), literally translated as the clan of those who hunt with dogs. It is also the royal clan of the *Aakwaluudhi* people in western Ovambo in the present-day Omusati region from which my parents originate. Kings of the Aakwaluudhi people are selected from the *Aakwanambwa* (plural) clan. This implies that I have adopted the *Vakankora* clan, because its conception is similar to that of my *Omukwanambwa* clan. However, I was also always an outsider, because of being a *Muvambo*[13]. Sometimes local people would jokingly refer to me as:

"Ame si ogo ne Muvambo[14]"
(That one is a Muvambo)

This happened, for instance, when I made a linguistic error but also when I carried out a social deed of which they approved, for example when I was the director of ceremony at a wedding in Rundu during the December holidays. When I introduced myself I said the following:

"Ogu ana kuhuyunga ige Michael Akuupa. Ame sitenya!"
(The one speaking is Michael Akuupa. I am a son in-law!)

In acknowledging what I have just said the wedding attendees exclaimed:

"Wee sitenya wee! Wee Muvambo Gwetu wee!"
(Wee our son in law wee! Wee our Muvambo wee!)

This anecdote shows how complex it is to establish relationships. It shows that one needs not only to focus on what I call research relations, but on other social relationships such as kinship in order to understand and gain access to other unsaid aspects of life. For example, studies[15] in North America have showed that kinship relations are universally believed to be constituted by blood, thus leading to assumptions that biology is the foundation of the social. (Carstens, 2000) However, it is important to note that the boundaries between biology and the social are blurred leading to the destabilization of such relations as it could not be applied elsewhere than in societies of America and Europe. Stone 1997 has argued against the idea of universalizing patterns of kinship as this might lead to possible distor-

---

as cuca shops.
[12] Refer to the myth of origin narrated in chapter 4 which deals with the historiography of Kavango.
[13] Muvambo is used to refer to anyone who is believed to have come from the former Ovamboland.
[14] My fieldwork notes.
[15] The work of Schneider on American kinship systems is widely cited in studies of Kinship.

tion and encourage us to consider the diverse culture contexts in which these relations are constituted. My argument is that if anthropology as a discipline is to advance to the next level in its unending evolution, it needs to consider the workings and belonging of kinship as an important resource of establishing research relations. In certain aspects of my research I had to seek[16] belonging to the clan and *ekoro* in order to make my fieldwork a success.

Of course not everyone knows their *ekoro* and its networks do not always yield the expected or positive results. Sometimes one has to look for one's *ekoro/likoro* as it can also get lost due to geographical distance or a lack of contact. In the event when it is believed that *ekoro* is lost, those who seek for it have to go through a process of *kukutongonona* in order to make known who they are and how they are related. If you do not *tongonona* yourself clearly it is likely that you may not be known and this may adversely affect your intention of seeking your lost *ekoro* and obtain any help. *Kukutongonona* can resurrect old grudges. Observance and understanding of such relations complemented by the practice of *kukutongonona* in every social context increases or diminishes chances of the ethnographer's entrance to and explanations of various taken for granted local cultural aspects.

Analysis of Ekoro and its Working in the Research Field

Doing ethnography at home has its challenges. There are two sets of commonly held assumptions that ethnographers or anthropologists on familiar terrain will gain a greater understanding than elsewhere as they are not impeded by linguistic and cultural barriers. Sichone 2001 has argued in his review of Ferguson's *Expectation of Modernity* (1999) that only when one is doing anthropology at home can one understand that there is noise everywhere. He used the concept of noise to illustrate the benefit of knowing language in order to minimize the risk of doing pure anthropology[17]. A further claim is that a local ethnographer gets entrée easily to privileged information unlike the outsider. (Strathern, 1987)

There have been some critical reflections on doing anthropology at home, mostly relating to the difficulty that a researcher may take phenomena and relationships for granted and, therefore, may overlook significant aspects. (Mascarenhas-Keyes, 1987; Narayan, 1993; Tsuda, 1998). In my fieldwork experience I found, however, that the reality is more complex. It is worth mentioning that I am not a native of Kavango having worked there as bank clerk

---

[16] I do not imply that all researchers need to marry into the field where they will do fieldwork. In this context I was married long before I started graduate studies and it is just one of the relations which made things work for me. However, seeking allegiance and ways of belonging to clan and ekoro to create "research relations" may work in this context.

[17] Sichone (2001) in the same review criticized pure anthropology for its lack of practical value.

before I married a woman from that area. In this case, my position as an insider is a complex one even if I know the local languages of the region. On the other hand, I am a citizen of Namibia, of which Kavango forms a part. Like Vale de Almeida 2002 I regard citizenship as a process and not a status, a set of rights and obligations in a formally democratic social contract practiced by an anthropologist and those who are studied. When I did fieldwork in Kavango, I had knowledge of local ways of life and language but, and because of this, my access to field (interviews), observations and information was strongly influenced by relationships[18] with my in-laws (mother and father), their extended family and clan, which in turn provided a large base of connectedness locally. They were, for example, connected to the local elite as well as to many others having relations with the Shambyu royal family as my father-in-law was an advisor in the traditional authority council at some point in his life. Above all, my wife is named after the one-time queen of the Vashambyu, Maria Shingoma Mwengere wa Mbava na Mukosho.

A letter of introduction is regarded to be one of the very important components to access the field. In his essay on "Ethnicity and the Anthropologist: negotiating Identities in the Field" Takeyuki Tsuda 1998 has demonstrated how important letters of introduction were during his fieldwork in Japan. However, my experience demonstrates that while Tsuda 1998 might be right for the Japanese context, elsewhere documentation with regard to research matters only to a certain extent. The secretary to the director asked whether I had any documentation, which would outline what my discussion with the director entails. She thus followed the set bureaucratic procedures. However, for the director, it was the relation I had or shared with his ekoro that was important.

My access to the director's office presented interesting dynamics. When I spoke to him in his vernacular the moment created a sense of familiarity. As it is customary in the exchange of greetings in Kavango, the older person asks whose child you are and what your visit entails. 'You' as a being in an individual capacity at that moment did not matter as much as who your parents were. In this context the director assumed the role of *mukondi* (an 'elder') and asked me who my parents are and whether their health was fine. My responce to his question did not immediately create a sense of connection as my parents lived in another region and he had not heard about and did not know them. Despite my ability to converse fluently in his vernacular and observe the Vakavango manners, my background and origin created a sense of momentary outsider-ness. I refer to this as an uncertainty

---

[18] I use relationship in this context as a component of being 'known'. In Kavango being known is not an instance in which people are only aware of your name and presence. In this case one can only be known through your relation to somebody else related to you through family, marriage or clan and who is preferably older than yourself.

rooted in the disruption of the expectation by the director that I could have been from the same ethnic group.

However, my added extended introduction which included information about my affinal ties and relations to Kavango was what created a sense of re-connection between us, which resulted in my redefinition as an insider. My relation to Kavango through marriage created a kinship affinity to the director opening the field in the space of the national government.

The situation was not very different when I sought out interviews with people in Rundu town and the nearby villages. Every time I introduced myself as a student from the University of the Western Cape doing research on *yompo* (things of culture), I did not need to produce a letter from the university in order to prove that indeed I was doing research sanctioned by a legitimate institution. This was due to my connection and associational links with local people in the Kavango, specifically in the town of Rundu. As a result my access to that social space was fairly easy. However, when I visited the villages in the Kavango region (except for Kayengona) I had to do extended introductions with reference to my connections with my-in-laws. Even if it was in areas very far from my-in-laws 'traditional' village domicile, I was likely to meet a person who was related to them through clan links. Clans transcend ethnic boundaries and the same clans are found in all tribal[19] areas of Kavango. In cases where I went with Kletus Likuwa, a postgraduate student in History, who was born in the Kavango region, he would introduce me not just as his friend, but as one of his in laws married to their relative, indicating that I indeed belonged. He would always refer to me as '*wetu*'[20] in the practice of *kukutongonona*, whenever he introduced me to people we wanted to interview. The above juggling of positions as an insider or outsider including extended introduction leads me agree with Michael Agar 1980:52 that it is not easy at all to work in one's own society, because "you cross the line between the field and home often and very rapidly".

The situation was different when I attended festivals in various constituencies. At the festivals in the constituencies, I was introduced as '*munasure gompo*' (a student of culture) temporarily based at the culture office in Kavango. The senior culture officer, Thomas Shapi, would extend my introduction and even tell the audience that I am studying to be a "doctor of culture[21]". His introduction separated me from the official status which made me an outsider thus mediating my access to the audiences who came to watch the performances.

---

[19] Local people refer to areas, which are believed to be the domicile of the five ethnic groups in Kavango, as tribal areas. This tendency can be attributed to the earlier colonial construction of its citizens into tribes which has since been internalized by people and hence used as somewhat 'normal' 'category' of reference.
[20] Gwetu' or wetu means 'ours' in local Rukwangali and Rumanyo respectively.
[21] My field notes.

Although I had access to the field through the connection of ekoro, various encounters did not yield the expected results. My interview with the director showed the extent of power and authority he had in terms of content and direction of the conversation. This authority is highly significant and it is not really influenced by the person's professional title or the office he holds, but through his social status of being *mukondi* which literally means elder. The level of *mukondi* is reached when one has fulfilled certain social expectations such as having a family and the ability to act on its behalf and ekoro.

In Kavango the notion of *mukondi* refers to anyone who is older than you. As a sign of respect one is required to submit to any person who is older in order to show *nonkedi* (good manners). At times I could not ask or speak about certain things, because I had to *dira* which literally means to refrain from asking or speaking about them. *Dira* is a stem of the word *kudira* or *sidira*. *Kudira* is an act of restraint while *sidira* is a taboo. *Sidira* in Kavango refers to the unwritten social rules observed in order to maintain harmony.

Due to these proscriptions, my relation to the director as an adopted son in law prevented me from speaking about certain topics, which he deemed inappropriate, because of the relationship of respect between us. It influences the format of the conversations open to a researcher. For example, tape-recorded interviews were refused as unnecessary as I could always return if I needed further input. Although the director had undergone the same academic ritual and initiation I was going through, (he holds a PhD in Religious Studies from University of Cape Town since 1992) that did not change his conduct towards me in terms of the etiquette of communication as that would have caused him to break the *sidira* or observe *nonkedi doVakavango*, (manners or ways of life of the Kavango people). So, as much as I was an insider through my relations of ekoro, there were some limitations to certain aspects of the field because of y*idira*[22].

In his thesis on Kavango elites, Fumanti[23] 2003 demonstrated how he was treated as a child or a 'student' among the senior elites of the region. It is evident that his status as a student and observance of local *nonkedi* influenced his access to his subjects.

The ekoro relation is very important and powerful but is only invoked when a need arises. The professional status of the director did not play a major role our relationship after our ekoro status had been established. However, his professional role was of particular importance when he gave instructions to Shapi at the regional office in Kavango. For the staff in the Kavango office, his communication was a directive from the director. Those concerned would only act on official instruction. It was not necessary and perhaps not even desirable to inform the officials at Kavango office that I had a relationship of ekoro with the

---

[22] Yidira is a plural form of sidira.
[23] Fumanti was an Italian and doctoral fellow at Manchester University.

director. However, such a relationship could be discovered by those who may be interested about who you are and your local relations when you *tongonona* yourself to them. I have heard of debates in the local radio programs and elsewhere in private social settings where practices of nepotism were discussed. For example, it said that people were given jobs, because of the relations they shared with those in positions of power, but no information surfaced which was directed to any particular person in the region. It is easy to conclude that such a relationship may lead to accusations of nepotism and favouritism in the context where access to resources is competitive, especially among those who may not understand the workings of ekoro. However, it is essential to understand the functioning of ekoro as expressed in local proverbs such as "he who has relatives lives through them" or "he who has relatives does not die of hunger". It means that the working of ekoro can be situational and the primary intention is that of assistance if one is in need. It is important to note that it does not invoke any debt to the ekoro of someone who has rendered this assistance, which can be in any form.

Assumed and Imposed Fieldwork Self

Josef Mbambo, the assistant culture officer, received me at the Maria Mwengere Culture Centre in Kavango, My relation to Mbambo was an important one as we refer to each other as *Tamweyi*. Although our spouses are from the same village and related through ekoro, he preferred to relate to me as a brother-in-law because I had married someone from Kavango. The other reason was that I was not a Mukavango as a result I become a *sitenya*[24]. In this context Tamweyi means brother-in-law. My relationships with the other staff members at the Maria Mwengere Culture Centre were guided by bureaucratic procedures only and not by ekoro. The senior culture officer, Thomas Shapi, allocated me an office and requested other officials to assist me with any questions I might have. This was an official request which was made during the meeting where I was officially introduced to all the officials at the centre. I was not introduced to the institutional workers[25] officially; I had to do that myself by meeting them on an individual basis especially when they came to sign the register at the beginning and end of their working day.

Another interesting aspect of my fieldwork was my access to official documents and archives at the centre. I learned that the majority of the office workers, including the senior culture officer, were all fairly new in their jobs whereas some of the institutional workers had been working there since the establishment of the centre in the early 1970s, thus pos-

---

[24] See my earlier discussion when I directed a wedding ceremony.
[25] Institutional workers are cleaners, gardeners and drivers.

sessing substantial institutional memory. It was my association with them, which led me to information about which the officials knew nothing. None of the officials had ever heard of the Kavango anthem, which had been in use during the apartheid era, however, one of the older male labourers directed me to where copies of the anthem had been stored. I received much valuable information from both male and female institutional workers when I chatted with them during their tea and lunch breaks.

Many of the people I was studying were interested in what I would be doing at the centre. Seraphina was one of the female employees. She came across as a friendly person, talkative and inquisitive. She features in many pictures I took during the events at the centre, because she wanted to be seen by people in the other world, as she referred to South Africa. During my entire stay at the centre she cleaned my office and wanted to know how my family was doing.

> Seraphina: "So Meneere to mu ya tujoina nye? To mu ya kara siruho so ku hura kupi?"
> (So sir, have you come to join us? How long will you be with us?)
>
> Michael: "Ah, na tu tara tupu. Ngano dogoro Desemba apa ngasi pwa sipito sokulcha."
> (Ah! Well we will see. I am supposed to be here until December just after the culture festival.)
>
> Seraphina: "Makura oyina ko mu fanekere to mu yi randesa ndi? Nose mwa kona ku tu faneka tu yali mone morwa TV nazo pozili."
> (What will you do with the films you captured? Will you sell them or what? You should also record us so that we can see ourselves on TV, we have one here at the office.)
>
> Michael: "Ooh, oyina yange tupu yo ku ruganesa eyi naku tjangatjanga. Nyee ngani mu faneka tupu."
> (Oh, those ones are just for personal use when I am writing something about them. Don't worry I will record you as well.)

Eventually I became known especially among the institutional workers as "*ogo gokufaneka kulcha*" meaning "he who photographs culture".

The ways in which you present yourself in the field is always important. This I learned also in a different context when I had an interview appointment with Sam Nujoma, the first president of independent Namibia. After I had interviewed Nujoma for over 45 minutes in Otshingandjera, his mother tongue, he asked me to switch off my tape recorder so that we could have a conversation off record. He then went on:

> "Otshinima nee tshimwe ngele oto longo nomithigululwakalo omafufu goye na ga kale geli onatural ashike. Iilonga yoye iiwanawa lela."

(One important thing is that when you work with things related to heritage your hair needs to look and appear natural. You are doing a good job.)

What I deduce from the above conversation with Seraphina the institutional worker and the statement by Sam Nujoma, as well as my observation during my visit to the office of the Founding President, is that my appearance determined how I was perceived during those moments. To Seraphina and her other colleagues I was a photographer of culture, because of the camera equipment I always carried during the festivals and at the office. For Sam Nujoma, I appeared like some Rasta individual because of my hairstyle. Rastafarians have never had a good standing in Namibia because of their reputation for smoking marijuana. In his eyes people who smoke and abuse alcohol are a danger to society, which is why he saw it proper to advise me against keeping such very long hair as it would blur the very important work about heritage I was doing. Perhaps, one could also view it in terms of traditional age relations of young and old where an elder is likely to give advice to the younger person at any convenient time, hence the observation that those we studied would "listen to you, watch your behavior and they will draw from their own repertoire of social categories to find one that fits you". (Agar, 1980: 54)

Another interesting dimension during the interview with Nujoma was the language in which we communicated, we conversed in Otshingandjera and not in English the official language. This is how it occurred: While I was waiting for him to emerge from one of the doors, I sat there with one of his personal assistants whom I have met and conversed with several times in the past. While Ndoze and I conversed in Otshikwambi in the lounge, Nujoma appeared unexpectedly from one of the doors and found us speaking. And the first thing he said was:

"Moro comrade!"
(Good day, comrade!)

He went on to greet me in Otshingandjera. It appears in that context, I was an insider of some sort, because we spoke in the same language and I was looking for information about 'culture' a subject he claimed to be important. However, my insiders-ness was limited, because of my appearance, especially my dreadlocks, despite the formal suit I had put on for the occasion. As a result he criticized my hairstyle. In this context, <u>appearance</u> was a determining factor. In fact, Goffman 1959 has argued that each performer (here the fieldworker) is presented with the problem of communicating to his audience a particular image of himself and for that purpose may make use of much kind of dramaturgical devices and materials which may include clothing, appearance, décor as well as behaviour which may promote dramatic realization. Goffman's view is presented in a theatrical context, which is a significant component of how I understand the festivals. I can guess that a person like Sam Nujoma might not have agreed to meet me had he known of my appearance and dreadlocks before the interview. However, one can also argue that a great deal of what you are "depends, at the beginning on how you offer an explanation of what your interests are and what you intend to do". (Agar, 1980:55)

The discussion above shows that self-reflexivity in anthropology is critical, because our position in the field directly constitutes the acquisition of anthropological knowledge. Knowledge is never found in the abstract, but is always situated in a certain context, which is obtained from a particular perspective. This is the case when the researchers' access to knowledge depends heavily on his or her social position in the field. (Tsuda, 1998) I have observed that the course taken to get access to the field is in itself a moment of knowledge acquisition. The manner in which we present ourselves to those we study determines and/or leads us to various levels of knowledge. It is those presentations which lead to various relations that in turn create platforms for us as researchers to work from as adopted sons and daughters or members of clan or ekoro.

Recent reflections on doing ethnography emphasize that it is at the core a collaborative effort, involving the researcher and his or her subjects in knowledge production. Our self-growth in that perspective is not about other people's culture only, but relates to them as they define us. I have come to learn the importance of observing local social relations in the field for they create conditions of possibility. We should not only undertake to explore the lived experiences of the knowing, but the "social condition of possibility and therefore the effects and limits of that experience" which in my opinion includes the social relations we come across in the field. (Bourdieu, 2003:282)

In this chapter I have tried to demonstrate that "anthropology carried out in the social setting which produced it has its limits". (Strathern, 1987:16) I have shown that the two generalized assumptions about doing ethnography at home need to be viewed and situated contextually. It is through the relations that one has to observe and also create that which determines the success of fieldwork. Although distinctions between insider and outsider existed in the field, the challenge still lies ahead when the fieldworker returns to the institution in order to write up the research. The challenge is similar to the one that Narayan 1993 argues against: that of the fixity of a distinction between native and non-native anthropologists. I follow her suggestion that it is crucial for anthropologists to focus their attention on the quality of their relationship with those they seek to represent and these relationships need not necessarily determine research relations; any social relation (be it kin or clan) has the potential to increase the depth of an ethnography.

4 Kavango the 'Domicile' in Perspective

Kavango: Whose Land is It?

This study investigates the re-appropriation of a colonial practice and the politics of culture in Namibia in the postcolonial era; specifically, I am interested in how these play out in the Kavango region of north-eastern Namibia in order to understand the wider national politics. My ethnographic research is centered on the making of Kavango-ness and its subsequent belonging to the larger nation through the expression of culture performances during state sponsored cultural festivals in Kavango. I look at these during different specific historical moments. Today Kavango participates, as do all of Namibia's thirteen regions, in the nation-wide festivals. However, historically Kavango played a special part in Namibian culture politics, which shapes the contemporary discourse of unity in diversity as advocated by the postcolonial state.

This discussion is guided by the position of the Kavango region in Namibia's history and politics; specifically, the omission of Kavango heroes from the national narrative of the liberation struggle, which more than one local historian and member of the region's elites have intimated in conversation with me. The feeling of exclusion is not only common among the elite, it is expressed by ordinary people on the street through music[1]. The case in point is how the region participated and contributed to the struggle of liberation from the time of German to South African colonization and its role in the very shaping of colonial rule. Kavango is one of Namibia's ethnic and political regions. Like all of the country's regions, it has been part of Namibia's historical and political metamorphosis.

Situated in north-eastern Namibia, the area's most prominent physical feature is the Kavango River, which runs from central southern Angola to the Okavango Delta in Botswana. The river forms the border between present day Namibia and Angola and ends in the lower flood plains in Botswana known as the Kavango Delta. The rains in central and southern Angola begin in September or October, increasing in frequency reaching a peak in January and then decreasing until March or April, these they are followed by the dry season. The level of water flowing into the Kavango River consequently rises and falls annually. Next to the river the area has fairly virgin vegetation and large numbers of game such as kudu, giraffe and elephant. Wild animals and birds such as hyena, buffalo, and eagle are significant for the determination of clan names as do many trees and foods found in the area. Unlike

---

[1] A local musical group by the name B-square recently released a controversial music album, which criticizes government and its programmes in their songs.

the densely populated former Ovambo areas to the west, the Kavango region still has large tracks of unutilized land suitable for agriculture and cattle grazing.

The Kavango region is one of Namibia's thirteen administrative regions. Its neighbours are the Ohangwena, Oshikoto, Otjozondjupa and Caprivi regions. The administrative capital, the town of Rundu has approximately 72000 residents. Established in 1936, Rundu has transformed from being an office of the native affairs commissioner into a vibrant economic centre, which also caters for neighbouring Angola across its northern border. It has an ever growing hospitality industry serving continental and international travelers with lodges and tourist camps on the banks of the river. Most lodge owners originate from outside the region but have entered into partnerships with local people in the vicinity who may supply firewood or perform *traditional* dances for the visitors in the evenings.

Many South African retail brand stores are housed in the new shopping malls, which have been built in Rundu since the past three to five years. Chinese retailers are significantly evident. This economic sector is, therefore, dominated by foreign expatriates employing a large number of local people.

The main aim of this chapter is to show how different factors have influenced the narratives of Kavango as a space and the idea Kavango-ness throughout history. I argue that the current central issues of Kavango-ness and belonging seem to have roots in both historical legends as well as being the outcome of colonial politics such as the official recognition of the five tribes[2]. Colonial recognition seems to continue through the contemporary postcolonial invention of identity politics as expressed in the culture festival. The chapter looks at how the notion of Kavango as a space came into being and how the idea of Kavango-ness was imagined during colonialism and how it is reconstructed and asserted in the postcolonial time. Drawing from oral historical accounts and archive documents I reconstruct various pre- colonial and colonial eras in order to make sense of the contemporary politics of culture starting with the German colonial era followed by the period of South African rule.

During the time of colonial South West Africa the area of Kavango, according to the administrators of the time, was said to be inhabited by five ethnic groups, namely Vambukushu, Vagciriku, and Vashambyu from the far eastern part of the region and Vambunza and Vakwangali from the west; since then these five groups have been collectively identified as Vakavango. These groups are believed to have migrated either from the Mashi[3] plains or

---

[2] My usage of the word tribe or tribal does not in any way connote or imply that my research participants are such but rather is the terminology as recorded from official research data and several interviews.

[3] The Mashi plains are situated in what is presently known as south-western Zambia. Early inhabitants of Kavango are believed to have migrated from that area before they settled in their current place.

Makuzu[4] gaMuntenda and settled on either side of the river, depending on the climatic and political context at the time.

Professor Josef Diescho, a Kavango born academic, suggests that it was only after the 1970s with the colonial independence of Kavango that people of the region became united and identified[5] as such. This came about as the result of the colonial Odendaal Plan which was synonymous with the Group Areas Act and separate development policy of apartheid South Africa. The Odendaal Plan was established by a commission set up in 1962. The commission contained several recommendations based on the concept of dividing the country into 12 ethnic homeland settlements. Ideally, those identified as Vakavango were to live in the region in areas believed by the commission to be of tribal ancestry. Such an arrangement would place the Vashambyu in Shambyu, Vagciriku in Gciriku, Vambukushu in Mbukushu, Vambunza in Mbunza and, finally, Vakwangali in Ukwangali. Collectively the area was proclaimed as Kavango and became an independent homeland in 1970. I discuss the making and workings of the commission below.

The issue of the excluded groups or those not uniquely recognized by the colonial administration has serious ramifications for the notion of Kavango-ness and a sense of belonging in the postcolonial moment. Especially during the creation of tribal trust funds in the early 1930s and after the implementation of the Odendaal recommendations, these were regarded as 'others' or recent arrivals from Portuguese West Africa (PWA[6]). Discussion about these non-recognized groups is significant for understanding various themes addressed in this study.

The ethnic group concerned is locally known as the Vanyemba and refer to themselves as such. The Vanyemba are the most significant among the groups in the contestations in contemporary Kavango. They are concentrated in areas of the region initially recognized by the colonial administration as containing the *real* residents, namely the Vakwangali and Vambunza in the west, the Vashambyu and Vagciriku including the Vambukushu in the east of the area. The Vanyemba have lived along the river with the *locals* since time immemorial. Although there is no literature on the early settlement of the Vanyemba in the region, historian Inge Brinkman 1999 and 2005 has dealt with the question of Vanyemba refugees who fled from Cuando Cubango[7] in southern Angola during the Unita[8] wars and settled in

---

[4] Makuzu gaMuntenda is a place in what is today south-western Angola.
[5] Some of the interviews I conducted with Kletus Likuwa seem to suggest that earlier people imagined themselves as either Vagciriku or Vakwangali etc. from Kavango, especially at the time when they were recruited for contract labour i.e. not as Vakavango.
[6] NAT1/1/54 File 25 Official Communication dated 1937/2/21 Tribal Trust Fund: Okavango Native Territory.
[7] Cuando Cubangu refers to provinces in southern Angola.
[8] UNITA stands for National Union for the Total Liberation of Angola. It was a guerrilla movement

Kavango. She has argued that the refugee Vanyemba used the lack of a fixed identity as a means to become inconspicuous members of the cosmopolitan culture among other Kavango residents and so avoid expulsion and exclusion. Her study dealt with the Vanyemba who fleeing the war settled in the area of Kaisosi on the outskirts of Rundu town. This particular group of Vanyemba should be clearly distinguished from Vanyemba who had been in Kavango long before and who did not settle in areas of Kaisosi or Sauyemwa. Brinkman's findings should be viewed in the context of the period of her study, conducted in the mid-1990s. The situation has changed significantly since then. My research findings suggest two sets of the Vanyemba in Kavango: those who are said to have arrived along with the five groups to Kavango in historical legend, and those who came during the wars in southern Angola, which lasted until after the independence of Namibia in 1990. It was this latter group on whom Brinkman focused. There is today a high level of Nyemba awareness among those who claim to belong to the Vanyemba. I argue that the situation can be understood in terms of the peaceful conditions that prevail in Namibia generally and in Kavango specifically, allowing people to claim belonging and association freely. Although the position of the Vanyemba in the social space of postcolonial Kavango is highly contested, especially in the festival context, significant oral historical accounts indicate the longevity of their presence.

Within this group there are various other sub groups such as Vachokwe, Vangangela, Valutyazi and many others. Oral accounts of migration routes and settlements refer to some Vanyemba travelling along with the five groups mentioned above, namely those who are locally believed to be the original discoverers and inhabitants of Kavango. Some of these accounts, however, are contested by various clans who believe they have been excluded from the mainstream history of origin. During my research I witnessed a high level of Vanyemba awareness in the Kavango. Beliefs of those autochthonous to the Kavango region have come about during the region's complex history specifically that of South African occupation. The making of Kavango-ness is a significant theme in this study.

A third sub-section of the population covers those who claim to have been the earliest inhabitants in Kavango, namely the San[9] locally known as *Vaduni* or *Vagcu*[10] whose

---

in Angola which, since the death of it leader Jonas Savimbi, has been transformed into a political party after the civil war in Angola.

[9] The term San is commonly used by academics to refer to a diverse group of people who live in(and are believed to be the first inhabitants) of southern Africa. They were generally defined as hunters and gatherers and colloquially known as Bushmen. At the independence of Namibia usage of the name Bushmen was discouraged as it was believed to be negatively loaded and 'othering'. (See Legal Assistance Centre report of the regional assessment of the San in Southern Africa published in 2001 and authored by James Suzman). Today, the term San in Namibia is widely used to refer to those population groups for purposes of being politically correct.

[10] The two words Vaduni and Vagcu are used by other local population groups to refer to the San

presence has been acknowledged in various oral accounts. However, they are presented as people who did not like to settle along the river banks. The San lived in areas far from the river, their dietary needs did not necessarily include fish and they did not cultivate the land as did the other groups. There are other social and political issues dictating their way of life in terms of the old anthropological notion of culture.

Generally, relatively little is known about Kavango and its inhabitants. Eckl 2007 investigated the accumulation of knowledge about Kavango and its people by the German colonial administration during the period 1891-1911. He has argued that under German colonial rule the region was not fully brought under colonial control due to its remoteness. Information was mostly limited to matters of economic value while interest in the people of Kavango remained weak. According to his perspective such limited knowledge of the region led to its conspicuous absence from Namibia's contemporary public history. However, Eckl continues to essentialize Kavango as a space presenting it as an area inhibited by the five groups, which were recognized by the colonial administration and ignores other groups such as the San and the Vanyemba who have been inhabitants of the region for the same duration, or even longer as in the case of the San.

The chapter is also informed by an essay by the Namibian-born anthropologist Robert Gordon, 'The making of modern Namibia: an anthropological ineptitude'. Published in 2005, Gordon's paper documents the role of the South African anthropologist Johannes Petrus van Schalkwyk Bruwer in the creation of the then apartheid South West Africa. Gordon emphasizes the usage of anthropological expertise to the world court in order to support the creation of apartheid in the then South West Africa.

Kavango the Place or People?

Early missionary and colonial encounters with inhabitants of the region largely influenced the contemporary conception of the Kavango in postcolonial Namibia. Historically, people in Kavango have been conflated with their western neighbours in the former Ovamboland. Kavango people were regarded as "simply offshoots" of the people of Ovambo. (Grotpeter, 1994 cited in Eckl 2007:8) This is also evident in the colonial administrative practices of the time, especially as the two regions were jointly administered by one native commissioner under the banner "Ovambokavango[11]". Missionaries are no exception to the practice

---

people. Even the local San in the region refer to themselves as such, although the terms may be negatively loaded according to context especially when used by other groups. In the study I will use the terms interchangeably.

[11] NAT1/1/54 File 25 Official Communication dated 1937/2/21 Tribal Trust Fund: Okavango Native Territory.

of confusing the 'uniqueness' of the two groups. Kampungu (1966: 78) bemoans in his work "Unfortunately, there is a tendency among the Missionaries particularly those who are sent from Ondangwa, of adapting the Kwangali peoples and their language and customs to those of the Ovambos". The case of the Vakwangali, the residents of the westernmost part of Kavango, is interesting especially in the context of the relations with their western counterparts. There is a history of Vakwangali *Hompas* (kings, queens) seeking asylum in Uukwanyama in Ovamboland and also further to the west in Uukwambi district of Ovamboland when they had disagreements at home. Some of the hompas were born in exile and only returned to Ukwangali after those who made their parents flee had died. During the time of the South African colonial administration, the Uukwambi king, Iipumbu yaTshilongo, who was regarded as dangerous and uncooperative by the authorities, was exiled to the Ukwangali area of Kavango. The uncertainty about the boundaries between the two groups could, therefore, be understood in terms of the relationship of the hompas who moved to and fro between the two areas. While practices by the colonial administration were largely informed by the observable physical attributes and closeness in language people in Kavango, as elsewhere in the territory, believed that they were different as emphasized by one of my research participants below:

> Actually people should just accept certain things how they are. Certain people started to say that the (boere) whites came to divide us so that a Vambo stays in Ovamboland; a Kavango stays in Kavangoland or a Damara to stay in Damaraland. But, if one critically looks into that statement does it contain some truths? Where did they find us, the people of Kavango together with the Herero, Vambo or Damara? Where was it? At which place did they find us? We know ourselves how we came along! It is true that the Vakwangali and the Vambo came together until [they separated] at Makuzu. As the words clearly say the part of the Vambo known as Vakwanyama went on to hunt game because they like to eat meat, while the Vakwangali remained behind lying on their back as their name implies. During that time, the whites had not yet arrived! Neither the Germans nor the English! Those who went to hunt went and stayed there while the Vakwangali remained and instead followed the river along[12].

As oral research about legends of a Kavango origin shows, the Vakavango as a generic ethnic group have always imagined themselves to be different[13] from other ethnic groups of the territory. Their migration tale presents a picture of a group of people who initiated a journey and settled in an area, which they believed catered for their needs exclusively and, as such, they believed they were a distinct group.

---

[12] Interview with Rudolf Ngondo at Katjinakatji, 15 January 2010.
[13] The notion of difference in this chapter should be understood according to various specific historical contexts.

Most importantly for my research is that people who reside in this area and participate in the postcolonial culture festivals identify themselves as *Vakavango*. There are various stories of how the name Kavango for the space, the river and inhabitants came into being. Actually, there is currently a local debate going on whether the name Kavango referred to the river (space) or its inhabitants among authors[14] who have written about the region. There is a series of extensive communication between Maria Fisch, a retired medical doctor and amateur anthropologist and Kavango-born historians, Shampapi Shiremo, Kletus Likuwa and Kavango Elders.[15] One of the contested matters is the origin of the name Kavango. Fisch asserted that the name Kavango was given by the Herero to the river at the time of the Swedish explorer Anderson's travels in the region in the 1850s. Likuwa and his colleagues argue that the name was given to the place by its inhabitants who had settled in the area in the early 1700s. As I will show below, one needs to understand the name according to two contexts, namely, that of local historical narratives and alternatively, after the creation of Kavango as a colonial homeland. During the latter process the inhabitants of the region were collectively identified as Kavango, with emphasis given to the name's origin in space rather than on the people.

According to Likuwa 2005:50, "Kavango means a small place". The name he argues was given by early *Vakankora* (clan of the toad) clan hunters who were on trail of an injured elephant that crossed the river to the other side. When they returned to the rest of the clan, they reported that they had found *"kavango ko kawa*[16]*"* and urged further movement to the new found area. Likuwa's inferences suggest that those who called the space Kavango came from elsewhere and found this place referring to it as their small place perhaps due to its unbelievable natural endowment with resources. (Likuwa, 2005)

Those who came to make Kavango *shirongo* (a country[17]) found the river, which had an abundance of resources as Djani Kashera narrates below:

There was a man from the Mbukushu people who also lived among the Vakandjadi clan (clan of the eagle) by the name of Kangumbe[18] who also met with the Jao and

---

[14] See one of the communication letters from Likuwa to Dr. Fisch dated 31 July 2006, a copy of which is available in the National Archive.

[15] Kavango Elders is a group of local elders who are believed to have knowledge about matters of the region. Kavango Elders constitute about six men, who have worked or served as teachers in their life. Specifically, two of them headed the Education department in the region while three others are Education officers and one is retired.

[16] "Kavango ko kawa" literary translates as "a small beautiful place".

[17] The research participants during my interviews referred to their area as shirongo or sirongo which literally translates as the country or land. They intimated that those who came at the time of migration made the environment habitable and created a political system to regulate its affairs.

[18] Kangumbe is the Mbukushu man who is believed among the Vambukushu to have discovered theKavango River. Thus they refer to it as ruwhare ruaKangumbe (the river of Kangumbe)

Canikwe[19] people and asked them where they were coming from. They told him that they were coming from Mashi area in search of land to settle but he told them that this country belongs to Mankoto[20]. We, of the eagle clan moved onward until we reached Ncushe area. Nobody should ever lie to you my child that this is their country, this land belongs only to the Vakandjadi (eagle clan) who found it first. The Vakandjadi clan settled all over the land and later on the chiefs of the Vashambyu arrived too and needed the same land.[21]

The notion of *shirongo* or land was presented as follows by David Hausiku a local headman in Sauyemwa area in western Rundu during an interview in which Kletus Likuwa[22] participated to suggest that the term *sirongo* referred to settled land as opposed to wild *wiza* which means bush:

> Q: When people were just moving around and fishing was that considered as living in the bush or as living in the country?
>
> Hausiku: It was in the country. When people moved along the river in canoes they hunted, moved further and slept at Guma. It did not really matter a lot because they lived in a country. It was the Bushmen only that were living in the bush.[23]

People used the terms *sirongo* interchangeably to refer to their domicile as country or land. It appears that places only became countries when the royal clans arrived with their skills in cultivation and cattle herding as Hausiku further narrates below:

> They started to cultivate their fields. Those that did not cultivate or have the strength to do so move in with those that had lots of food and those that had lot of foods and strength to work hard were in high regard and sometimes were made chief.[24]

Historically, the Mashi people (as they were previously known) settled and lived along the banks of the Kavango after their arrival from the Mashi plains (in what is today Western Zambia) around 1650. They were a riparian people. The Kavango River is a most crucial aspect in the life of contemporary Vakavango especially when it comes to the assertion and determination of local identity (Kavango-ness), hence its space in the historical legends about the origin and being of the Vakavango. The river space as a domicile bestowed the

---

[19] The Jao and Canikwe are sub groups of the San who are believed to have been moving around the area near the Kavango River.
[20] Mankoto was a leader of the household of the Vakandjadi clan, which claimed to have arrived first in the area. He was not a chief.
[21] Take note of the usage of the word country or land in the interview excerpt.
[22] Most of my oral interviews were conducted by myself and Kletus Likuwa whilst researching together.
[23] Interview with David Hausiku on 20 July 2007 at Sauyemwa in Rundu.
[24] Interview with David Hausiku on 11 April 2007 at Sauyemwa in Rundu.

identity of being a riparian people as Likuwa 2005 argues: "The people in turn came to identify themselves not with the land within which the river was found, but with the river itself. They became known as Vakavango, meaning those who belong to Kavango, the river, as they refer to their early migration in the mid 1750s. It is that process of living along the riverside and identifying yourself with it by taking part in all river activities which identified you as a Mukavango[25]" (Likuwa, 2005:50). It is important to note that certain people from the area saw themselves as either Vakwangali or Vashambyu from Kavango and not just as Vakavango, especially in the situation of recruiting and identifying contract workers. This contradiction of a Kavango identity seems to suggest that there was no sense of Kavangoness until the time of the Odendaal Plan as Diescho intimated in his speech during a public lecture. What is of importance here is the period in which people began to go on work contracts to the south. This was the time when the tribal trust funds were created and the situation forced young men to work on contract in order to afford the taxes. The tax issue appears in the narration of Mbambangandu who had also gone on contract at various times:

> When that tax story started they said we should all assemble to be recorded and we were given papers. They said we should keep those papers as a sign of the number of people who live in the land while it was in fact a trap. Some people started whispering to one another that they saw the same thing in Botswana and that this was the beginning of tax payment. Commissioner Nakare Harold Eedes, Native Commissioner for Kavango in the 1930s, heard about this talking that was doing rounds around the Kavango and he threatened that if he will hear of any one saying that this was the beginning of tax payment, such a person will be beaten with branches or will be jailed. Well, in the end of everything, people were called again to bring along those papers they were given. They wrote on each one's paper and asked each to pay fifty cents. Tax started at the amount of fifty cents.[26]

Migrant labourers had to give clear information about their origin to the contract official and were told that this was necessary for tax purposes. When tax was deducted from the employees' earnings it was remitted to the correct tribal authority[27], thus the importance of correct information about the worker's origin.

With the advent of colonialism, especially during the South African administration, those who had settled along the banks of the river especially in the area of Rundu from the villages of Nkunki, Ncwa, Nkondo, were forcibly moved to higher ground away from the river during the 1950s. (Likuwa, 2005) There were other reasons for the removal such

---

[25] Likuwa used oral and archival sources in order to present a perspective of identity which is derived from the river. He has also relied on the minutes of the debates on the question of Kavangoness taking place in the Kavango Legislative Council during the 1970s.
[26] Interview with Mbambangandu waShivako on 20 January 2007 at Kambowo.
[27] NAT 1/1/54 S/U-20 File -25

as the administration's attempt to curb influential political activities[28] from both sides of the river, especially during the 1950s and the early 1960s. Likuwa 2005 refers to this in his study as having influenced the authorities of the time to police the border extensively. People continued to live along the river banks in other areas of the region despite fluctuating climatic conditions, which over the last decade have culminated in terrible floods during the rainy seasons.

This brief historical account will enable us to understand the historical construction of present day Kavango ethnic identity from the foundation legends, which I present below. The legends show that the earlier foundations of inhabitants were predominantly clan-based and that Kavango-ness is a new colonial construction and is context specific. It becomes evident that legends told in Kavango are about royal clans and families and not necessarily about others living in the region.

Kavango as Told in Legends

Legends about Kavango show that the majority of its inhabitants, or their ancestors, have migrated to the region from elsewhere. Even the San who are generally believed to be the earliest residents of the area seem not to have settled permanently in the area, as they have not set up permanent structures that symbolize the *sirongo*. Instead, their settlement in the area was temporal, determined by seasonal food resources and the migrations of game, which they hunted. Although the San moved about the region they did have relations with the visitors. Oral sources show the San participating in the activities of the time such as trade exchange, medicine and food. There are indications and evidence suggesting that they intermarried. Below I present accounts that confirm that all the groups living in the area today are immigrants to Kavango as a space; the only exception are the San[29] whose legends are virtually non-existent in local discourse. Thus, they were regarded as first visitors by the group known as the *Matjaube*[30] or the *Vakandjadi* (eagle clan) under the leadership of Mankoto, which claims to have found the Kavango land first before any other groups arrived.

---

[28] There isvarious official correspondenceduring 1969 referring to the above activities that resulted from the inability of the Portuguese to control their people. See archive documents: NAR/11/55, File 9 and Vol.3 and NAR/11/55, File 20, "unregistered confidential correspondence, 1962-1967".

[29] In his paper on the possibility of universal suffrage in Kavango in 1967, Kampungu addressed the question of who is a Kavango. In later years the Kavango Legislative Assembly debated on whether the San could participate in the elections, which were to be held in South West Africa territory, as Vakavango or as something else. (BAC-1/1/55.NAR10 File 7)

[30] The chronicles of the Matjaube is dealt with extensively in the work of Fleisch and Mohlig (2002); The Kavango Peoples in the Past: local historiographies from Northern Namibia.

This narrative was told to me by Djani Kashera who is regarded as authoritative on the subject of the *Vakandjadi* clan in Kavango. Djani is a male elder of the Vakandjadi clan who lives at Kambowo in Shambyu. He is one of the living Mukandjadi who is believed to still have knowledge about the Vakandjadi clan and its dealings with the royals in Shambyu:

> It was at this place where he was met by the first visitors in his land. There were no *Vaduni* or any other chief around. All other groups were by then still in Mashi land. The first visitors which Mankoto received were the *Vaduni* who were running away from the wars in the south of Africa. When he asked them where they were coming from, he was told they were running away from people who shot at them. So, Mankoto stayed there and then moved along the valley of *Ndongalinena*[31] up to the area of *Ncushe* where he parted with his *Vaduni* visitors. After all that has happened he also received groups of *Canikwe*[32] and the *Jao* people[33].

While everywhere else they are presented as early settlers of the southern African region, the above account gives the San[34] only the status of visitors. However, what is interesting is that most names in the area of Kavango such as *Ncushe, Ncaute* are derived from San languages, an issue deserving further research. Another question arises as to whether or not the *Matjaube* are actually one of the San groups. Kashera actually denied this:

> Q: What language did Mankoto speak? I am asking you this question, because some people told me that the Matjaube were actually a group of *Vaduni*.
>
> Djani: They call us *Vaduni* just because they found us living together with them. We did not live along the river, but in the bush.
>
> Q: So then, when the other chiefs came from Mashi they found your clan and concluded that you were all *Vaduni*?
>
> Djani: Yes! But we were not *Vaduni*; we were rather as human as them. When they came they found that we have mixed. They thought that we were *Vaduni* and they thought that this land belonged to them (*Vaduni*). But then, we are a different group, the *Vaduni* were our first visitors[35].

It seems the group claiming to have arrived first in the area did not establish structures that could be recognized as those of a 'country' as in the case of the San. Instead, the *Matjaube*

---

[31] *Ndongalinena* and *Ncushe* are valleys situated not far from the Kavango River in the present day Gciriku area in eastern Kavango.
[32] The *Canikwe* and the *Jao* people are believed to be subgroups of the San population.
[33] Interview with Djani Kashera on 20 January 2007 at Kambowo village.
[34] I have not interviewed people who claim to be San in Kavango, but it is one area I will look at as a matter of concern arising from my wider research.
[35] Interview with Djani Kashera on 20 January 2007 at Kambowo village.

roamed freely and lived on hunting game like the San. However, they seem to have lost their ability to protect their land from the other groups, namely the royal clans of the Vashambyu who killed them during a fight after a meeting that went wrong. They occasionally joined the San in the bushes and intermarried with them. Relations with the San were not limited to the Matjaube; other groups such as the Vambunza claimed to have had relations with them as asserted by the following response:

> "Yes, they (Mbunza) were co-living with the *Vaduni*. The *Vaduni* could come to the river and find them or the Mbunza could also go to the field[36]."

The intention of the above narrative is to locate the presence of the San within the wider discourse of the origins of the inhabitants of Kavango. However, it begs further attention. Too many questions about the origins of Kavango-ness remain unanswered. It is evident that the San had been present in the region and various forms of interaction had existed. Why they are left out of most historical accounts lies beyond the scope of the present study.

The Royal Narrative

There are general legends which depict the mainstream officially recognized groups in Kavango to have come from Mashi. Below are the legends as told by *Hompa*[37] Maria Kandambo from the *Vakankora* clan in Gciriku[38] area, and by *Hompa* Alfons Kaundu Mattias from the *Vakwasipika* clan in Mbunza[39] area respectively:

> When they came to Kavango, they only came in one group as *Vakankora* clan. When they reached in the valley of *Kalikenuke* on their way towards Kavango River, one wife of the elder family member was about to give birth. They sat down and broke down their own bow to use it to get some wild fruits called *Ntja* for the women in labour. The younger family of the clan decided to live behind the elder family and reached Kavango and found a pond full of toads and killed them and said that they have now become the chief of the land. When the older family of their clan arrived they found the young family saying that they were the chiefs of the land and not their older family members. They said they were now the *Vakwafuma* (famous clan)

---

[36] Interview with Samuel Hausiku, headman of Sauyemwa, on 11 April 2007.
[37] The phrase Hompa locally used to refer to a king or queen.
[38] Gciriku is the area in southern Kavango between Mbukushu and Shambyu. The royal palace of the Vagciriku is situated at Kadedere in Gciriku. In post independence Namibia it has come to be known as Gciriku Traditional Authority after the Traditional Authorities Act was gazetted in 2000.
[39] Mbunza is the area in western Kavango between Ukwangali and Shambyu. The royal palace of the Vambunza is situated at Sigone in Mbunza now known as Mbunza Traditional Authority after the Traditional Authorities Act was gazetted in 2000.

and not the *Vakankora*. But when we came from Mashi, we were all the *Vakankora* clan[40].

Well we are from the chiefs' clan of Mbunza but our clans are the same as those of Ukwangali chieftainship because of our elders Kapango and Mate za Mukuve. Kapango is of the Sitentu or Kwangali family and Mate is of the Mbunza family. Most of what you are asking is inside that copy of the history, however following what I read is that when they were staying at Makuzu ga Muntenda there deep in Angola they were just one family. So Mate's family found a pond full of fish and they started catching fish there, but they refused to give some of the fish to her sister's children Kapango. Later in time the Kapango family found some animals that could be tamed easily, in fact they did not know that they have picked cattle and apparently this animals came from Cuito[41]. They domesticated these animals and started to milk them. Mate's family wanted to be given some milk by the Kapango family, but they refused totally. That's where the division of the family started and Kapango and her children went further west while Mate and her children moved to the east. The cattle were animals that could be tamed easily and people just picked them. The place Makuzu was on the other side of Ukwangali area across the river. The Mbunza came here and the area was named Mbunza of fish, derived from a lot of fish known as the "*nza*" that was found here. In fact Mbunza means a lot of "*nza*" fish[42].

These narratives show how the royal clans migrated from Mashi to present day Kavango. I argue that these accounts refer to specific clans and do not cover the history of other clans, which also moved from the same area to Kavango. If I accept Likuwa's (2005) argument about Kavango being a small place with abundant resources which was found by those who came earlier hunting an elephant, it could have been a motivating factor for other clans to move to the area. However, they are not mentioned and only the royal clans are mentioned with the exception of the *Vakandjadi* clan, which claims to have been the first inhabitants of the area.

Already a form of exclusion is evident among those who claim to have been part of the early migration legends. Eventually all the above groups came to settle in Kavango, but their narrative of origins changed over time. For example, the Vakwangali[43] and Vambunza are believed to have come from Mashi together with the other groups around 1750 or 1800 as narrated by Hompa Sitentu Mpasi of Kwangali. Instead of moving further south towards the Kavango River, they went westwards to what was known then as the *Handa* area close

---

[40] Interview was held with *Hompa* Maria Kandambo on 24 December 2006 at Gciriku.
[41] Cuito is an area in southern Angola believed in oral accounts to have been previously inhabited by the Vanyemba groups.
[42] Interview was held with *Hompa* Alfons Kaundu Mattias on 14 April 2007 at Sigone. Kaundu's legitimacy as a Hompa for the Vambunza has been contested recently. He is said to be a Nyemba, thus may have wrongly been installed.
[43] The Vakwangali royal clan is called the *Vakwasipika* which is the clan of the hyena.

to *Nyembaland* in present day south-eastern Angola. However, when one listens to other local migration legends from common people while considering the royal clan history,[44] it becomes evident that the current dominant narrative is that they all came from Makuzu gaMuntenda in present day southern Angola and not from Mashi, as claimed in other narratives. For example, Rudolf Ngondo a minister in the homeland administration and currently a senior member in the Ukwangali Traditional Authority does not speak of the two sisters who are believed to be the maternal ancestors of the Vakwangali and the Vambunza. In his view the Vakwangali and Vakwanyama settled together at Makuzu gaMuntenda. From there, as their names imply, the Vakwangali remained behind lying on their back (in a relaxed mode) while the Vakwanyama went on to hunt as they were fond of meat. Eventually the Vakwangali began to move along the river in search of fish. There is, however, a connection in terms of fish with the legend of the Vambunza as narrated by Hompa Alfons Mattias Kaundu, which may have resulted in the dispute between the two groups.

I need to reiterate that there is no direct mention of the Vanyemba in the above Vakwangali chronicles[45], although it is claimed by authors of *Ntunguru*,[46] (J. K. Kloppers and Damian Nakare, a local author) an early language text book for primary schools of Kavango in the 1980s, that they lived together before war broke out between them resulting in the further movement east of the then Vanyemba *Hompa* Ndumba yaTjimpulu. Shiremo Shampapi 2010 wrote about the relations between the Vanyemba and the Vagciriku in eastern Kavango between 1874-1924. He described them as relatively cordial despite the fights between Hompa Nyangana of the Vagciriku and Hompa Kativa kaMutuva of the Vanyemba. Hompa Ndumba yaTjimpulu who seems to have fought with the Vakwangali in the west appeared to have had good relations with the Vagciriku in the east as he was given a wife as a token of friendship by Hompa Nyangana during one of his visits. (Shiremo, 2010:67) Interestingly, the Vanyemba came to be excluded and denied any ancestral land or a *Hompa* in present day Kavango even though they had lived together with the other groups for a long period. Their ancestral land is believed to be in *Limbaranda* and *Monyemba* (Nyembaland), an area in the south east of present day Angola. One can place the above contestations of belonging in the context of access to local resources such a land rights.

---

[44] During his 31st anniversary as Hompa of the Vakwangali people, Daniel Sitentu Mpasi in his speech emphasized that the history of his people begins at Makuzu gaMuntenda.

[45] On the same occasion Hompa Sitentu Mpasi mentioned at some point they resided near the Vanyemba in what is present day Angola and did not give any other details about their way of life together.

[46] The book titled Ntunguru in the local Rukwangali was published by the South African *Inboorlingtaalburo* (native language bureau) and was to be used in homeland schools.

The above legends became solidified with the advent of successive colonial administrations especially after the Odendaal Plan. It is difficult to spot differences between the Vambunza and the Vakwangali presently as their languages were formalized to Rukwangali (the language of the latter) under the colonial administration. There are no longer any Vambunza people able to speak a form of Mbunza language.

At the culture festival I observed that the Vakwangali and Vambunza dances are similar. Both *Kambamba* and *Mutjokotjo* are common dances among the groups. One would only be able to differentiate between their origins from the lyrics sung which mostly mention the population group or Hompa. If there is no mention of such names, it remains difficult to make the distinction as the dances are so similar.

The Vagciriku, Vashambyu and Vambukushu, as well as the Vanyemba in the east of Kavango, are believed to have come from Mashi to settle in Kavango. The dominant narrative of migration as told by Hompa Maria Kandambo of the Vakankora clan in Gciriku is about the Vakankora clan from which the *Hompas* of the two groups, namely Vagciriku and Vashambyu, were born. The same legend is told by the Vashambyu and the Vagciriku. Interestingly, unlike other myths, they include the Vanyemba people as having travelled with them since their migration from Mashi. However, they only tell about the Vanyemba living with them when probed. As in the dominant narratives told in western Kavango, the Vanyemba people continue to exist only on the sidelines. As for the Vagciriku and Vashambyu (as with the Vakwangali and Vambunza groups) the boundaries between the two groups are blurred. The royal families of the two groups are all descendants of the same clan, namely the *Vakankora*. It is this clan that migrated from Mashi, settled in Kavango and eventually reigned over respective areas of settlement and people.

In the contemporary postcolonial discourse of the region, there is not much said about the San or Vanyemba. In the context of culture festivals in which the state imagines its citizens through representations, the San and Vanyemba as residents of Kavango are hardly represented at a formal level. For example, the two groups feature in no more than a paragraph in the culture booklet published by the state. Only the five groups namely the Vakwangali, Vambunza, Vashambyu, Vagciriku and Vambukushu are prominently featured and narrated. Despite these contestations, it is evident that other people settled in Kavango along the river banks and made the area home or country. (McKittrick, 2008:785) As a result, the majority of the people living in Kavango region today identify themselves through their association with ethnic groups within the geographical space of Kavango or as Vakavango, whose origins are elsewhere. This situation is, as I will show, largely due to the role of colonialism in Kavango, specifically that of the German and South African colonial administrations and the subsequent influence on people and how they imagined their culture.

Below I present some historical accounts from the German through to the South African colonial periods to show how they have impacted Kavango and its people through missionary activities, academic research and the system of separate development. I also refer to some postcolonial debates between local scholars and earlier authors to contextualize the contemporary and ongoing sanitization of the region's history in the national or public domain. There is little published about Kavango; the region is less well represented than other areas, even in high school post colonial history text books. I view the debates below as a means of locating the history of Kavango politically in the public domain.

Early German Colonial and Missionary Encounters

Although the region was difficult to access during most of the early colonial period, the German administration established a police post in Nkurenkuru in order to exert its presence and rule in the region. There is considerable evidence about early colonial activities such as trade and cooperation. For example, it is claimed in oral history that *Hompa* Kandjimi Hawanga of the Vakwangali in whose territory a police post was created in 1909 had a good working relationship with the German's colonial representatives. Such relations are specifically said to have been between Hompa Kandjimi Hawanga and Zawada, the German colonial representative. They had a signed memorandum of understanding. (Eckl, 2004) At the time of the First World War Hompa Kandjimi Hawanga personally fought on the German side against the Portuguese as Simon Kandere told me:

> Kandere: However our old people told us that he was brave and dangerous. When the Germans came to fight the mission of Nkurenkuru on the other side that belonged to the Portuguese, he (Kandjimi Hawanga) told them to wait and hold their fire while he was going on the other side for reconnaissance, because he knew them very well. So he went across and stood by the Portuguese weapons, as they went out of their camp they were all shot. Only the coloured Portuguese survived.
>
> Q: Does it mean that Hawanga assisted the Germans in their war?
>
> Kandere: Yes very much![47]

The narrator is a local elder who grew up in the Vakwangali palace of Hompa Kanuni. He worked with Native Commissioner Morris during the 1950s and is regarded by local people as knowledgeable about matters of Kavango history especially during the time of Native Commissioner Nakare and Morris. In eastern Kavango, trade between the *Hompas* (especially Nyangana in Gciriku and Diyeve in Mbukushu) and traders seem to have been

---

[47] Interview with Simon Kandera on 28 January 2007 at Safari, Rundu.

significant as shown in the travel letters of early traders such as Johan August Wahlberg during the period 1836-1856. (Preller, 1941:87-128; Hummel, 1992:156-158) Trade was not only limited to German traders, deals were also made with Afrikaners[48] and Portuguese who were mostly interested in slave and cattle trading as narrated by Kashera a local historian of the Vakandjadi clan below:

> Q: Was it the will of a slave to die with the chief?
>
> Kashera: No! It was by force, there was no freedom of speech. If you were hard headed, you would be sold to the Portuguese for slavery.
>
> Q: Now, did they also sell people for slavery around here in Kavango?
>
> Kashera: Hey, hey, my child, why do you even ask that question?
>
> Q: Tell us about who was sold as a slave and who came to buy the slaves and where they took them?
>
> Kashera: I know of another case of a Tjimbundu speaking person who came to buy cattle for the Portuguese on this side. One day when he came, he slept in the homestead of the headman Karambuka. That Tjumbundu man asked if anyone knew a person named Haikombo of Cuni, they told him that the people used to live at that village. He asked again if people knew a man known as Haikombo of Ngoro and they told him that Haikombo Ngoro was their grandfather who once lived at that place. He also told them that he was also a descendant of him because his grandmother was sold a long time ago for slavery to go that side. When they told him that all those people you are mentioning are our family members, he took the cattle of the Portuguese to Angola and quickly returned again to settle permanently on this side. He died on this side.[49]

This narrative shows that the view of German colonialism in Kavango should not only be limited to military activities; the activities of the missionaries were also important. The missionaries, whether consciously or not, helped to promote the colonial agenda. Kampungu 1966:75-104 gives a detailed history of missionary activities in what was then South West Africa. He presents a picture of the competition existing among the various missionary societies wanting to create stations in the territory[50]. The Catholic mission, unlike its Lutheran counterpart under the Finnish, did not fare well in the Kavango during the early stages of missionary activity. The Hompas in Kavango repeatedly refused them settlement. (Kampungu 1966) The situation could partly be attributed to the relationship between Hompa

---

[48] Preller (1941) gives a historical account of the Dorsland trekkers from Transvaal through Botswana to Angola during the 1800s.
[49] Interview with Djani Kashera on 20 January 2010 at Kambowo village.
[50] Kampungu (1966) quotes a letter from Pref. Nachtwey to the Superior General of the OMI Congregation in 1903 in which he states the importance of a second attempt to open a station before the Protestants precede them as it would be difficult to gain entry after them.

Kandjimi of the Vakwangali in Western Kavango area and the German colonialists. After relations deteriorated, the colonial administration sent a punitive expedition in 1903.

The Lutheran missionaries[51] did not encounter serious resistance in western Kavango after being received in Ovamboland from 1870-1889. After repeated expeditions, the Catholic missionaries were eventually allowed to set up a station at Andara in eastern Kavango during 1909 under the rectorship of Father Krist. This mission station was later abandoned due to disagreements[52] between the missionaries and Hompa Libebe of the Vambukushu. The next mission was built in Nyangana in eastern Kavango on 22 May 1910 after a successful expedition led by Fathers Joseph Gotthardt, August Bierfert and Brothers Georg Russ, Johannes Rau and Konrad Heckmann. (Kampungu 1966:105) The mission at Andara was resurrected in 1913 after repeated negotiations[53] and requests from Chief Libebe and the missionaries. (Kampungu, 1966:110) Other stations were built at Tondoro in Ukwangali and Bunya in Mbunza respectively.

In the Kavango missionaries were often the forerunners of the administrative occupation. This became more intense during the time of the South African administration, which took over the territory from the Germans in 1915 and administered it as a League of Nations mandatory territory. A case in point was the insistence of the native commissioner for the women of Kavango to discard their 'traditional' clothing and adopt the European style. The early Catholic missionaries followed by the Lutherans in Kavango are shown in much of the literature to have acted as colonial agents of the imperial German and South African authorities respectively. (Gibson et al. 1981:25, Mutorwa, 1994: 7, Likuwa, 2007:6). Likuwa 2007 in his response paper to Eckl, 2007 argued that the work of the missionaries to pacify the Africans and force them into devotion and submission served as a tool to clear the path for colonization. A founding father of Catholic mission scholarship, Schmidlin[54] wrote in 1913 (as quoted in Hunke 1996:10):

---

[51] Kampungu (1966:77-110) relates that the Finnish Missionary Society began work at Omandongo in 1870 after they had been accepted by the Ondonga chief, Shikongo. The foundation stations were at Omandongo, Olukonda, Uukwambi and Uukwanyama. Within the year of 1871 they had built five missions. Notable missionaries were Martin Rautanen (locally known as 'Nakambale') and Pettinen stationed at Olukonda, Nannula at Oniipa and Alex at Omulonga. The Lutheran Mission reached Kavango in 1923 and established a station at Nkurenkuru in 1929. Following that, stations were built at Rupara and Mupini in the Mbunza area. The fourth was at Mpungu.

[52] The disputes were brought about by the incident in which a missionary mistakenly shot a young Mbukushu man who was an interpreter and repeated trampling on royal graves by the mission oxen. These acts warranted a punishment, which the missionary regarded as unfair and he later decided to leave the area.

[53] Negotiations were centered on the return of guns, which were taken and kept by chief Libebe, from the earlier missionaries of previous expeditions who had died of disease in the area.

[54] J Schmidlin was a German Catholic priest.

> The mission is one that spiritually conquers our colonies and assimilates them internally. The state may have power to conquer and annex the protectorates at the external level; yet the deepest goal of colonial policy, the internal colonization, must be implemented with the help of the missions. The state could well enforce physical obedience through punishments and laws, yet it is the mission's duty to bring the natives to spiritual submission and devotion. In this context we may reverse the phrase pronounced by the secretary for colonies, Dr. Solf, at the Reichstag, 'to colonize is to do mission work' and to 'to do mission work is to colonize.

Despite repeated refusals by the *Hompas* in Kavango to allow missionaries into their 'countries', they later permitted them to built stations between 1909-1910 for the Catholic mission in eastern Kavango and in 1922 for the Finnish to work in western Kavango. (Mutorwa, 1994:6) The introduction of the new religion encouraged people to regard traditional religious beliefs as ungodly and as associated with paganism and evilness. (Mutorwa, 1994: 7) The missionaries were perceived by locals as different people with a strange culture. (ibid.) In his publication of the history of the Roman Catholic Church in Kavango, Mutorwa 1994 argued that mission work significantly altered the norms and values of the people of Kavango and influenced the world view of the Africans on religion and general well being. Lukas Dikuwa, who was just a young boy when the missionaries set up camp at Andara in Mbukushu narrates:

> Q: So then, if you already knew about God before they came, why did you accept the missionaries again?
>
> Dikuwa: That is what I am telling you. They said we do not know God in the same way as they knew him. So they wanted to lure us to be a part of their sin of having killed God. We told them, we know God already, they said no you do not, and God is like this and that. They wanted us to be part of their offence of having killed the son of God.
>
> Q: But, what benefits did the missionaries bring along to the people?
>
> Dikuwa: The only benefit is helping us to know what was going on in the world. The missionaries were the only ones who said that we should live peacefully together[55].

This exchange shows that teaching of submission to the Christian God and to the earthly rulers was emphasized. It suggests that the Kavango were seen as being different to their Ovambo counterparts. For example, people of Kavango have been represented in travel and official accounts as those who "lack self confidence and are less provocative[56]" while

---

[55] Interview with Lukas Dikuwa on 09 July 2009 in Mbukushu.
[56] Information about people of Kavango as accounted by a certain Laubschat (1902)and quoted by Eckl (2007:).

"their inclination to steal is less apparent.[57]" (Laubschat 1902, Bericht 32 as quoted by Eckl 2007:29) Harold Eedes, who was the Native Commissioner for Kavango during the 1930s, time and again recorded in his official documents "people of Kavango as being lazy and not willing to participate in contract labour[58]." (Laubschat 1902 Bericht 32 as quoted by Eckl 2007:30) The inhabitants of the region were regarded similarly to and often compared with their western neighbours of Ovambo by the authorities. Eckl 2007:30 who has reconstructed the official historical colonial account of the German administration argues that 'less important groups were subsumed under their more important neighbours.' However, he does not show in which aspects the importance is located.

Although the people of Kavango were presented as apprehensive and lazy in various published accounts, their resistance to invasion and missionary conversion has not been recorded. As Kampungu 1966 and Shiremo 2005 have shown a case in point is the conflict between *Hompa* Nyangana[59] of the Vagciriku and traders from Germany. This resulted in the confiscation of belongings, capture and even some deaths. The repeated refusal to give permission for German missionaries to enter and establish a mission in Ukwangali by *Hompa* Himarwa is another. (Kampungu, 1966:77-104)

Maria Fisch presents additional evidence in a history of the Roman Catholic Church in Shambyu in Kavango. She claims that the church and the administration of the time struggled to convince the "locals to rid of their traditional ways of life". (Fisch, 2005:66) Further evidence is to be found in the official correspondence between the native commissioner Harold Eedes and the Secretary for South West Africa, in which Eedes reports what was believed to be "child marriage and child prostitution[60]" in Kavango. In another related communication Native Commissioner Harold Eedes addressed the issue of female head-dress with the Roman Catholic priest as follows:

> As pointed out by Father Frohlich, there is no law which compels native women on accepting Christianity, to remove their head-dress. Missionaries could, however, use any influence they may have to induce native women to discard their filthy head-dress, and in this way the women would be able to, by this outward sign, show that they had accepted Christianity[61].

---

[57] bid. The same perception continues to be used by labour recruiting agencies during the latter years of apartheid and colonialism.
[58] See NAT,1/1/54/S/U-20/File 25; A PhD thesis by K L Likuwa on labour contract in Kavango (forthcoming), in which he deals with certain historical issues why the people of Kavango did not really see the need and reason to go on contract.
[59] For a detailed historiography of Hompa Nyangana, see Shiremo (2009).
[60] NAT1/1/54 File 25 Official Communication dated 1937/2/21
[61] NAT1/1/54 File 25 Official Communication dated 1937/2/21

Obviously, the missionaries found the situation difficult to deal with Father Frohlich responded to Native Commissioner Eedes:

> With reference to our conversation at Runtu in January 1937, I may be allowed to inform you that a girl of one of the nearest locations, who had put off her dirty headdress last year, now at her maturity went back to the old custom of wearing cords. Still more as the wish of the girl herself it was that of her father, mother and grandmother. In consequence also other girls are willing at their maturity to begin again with this habit[62].

The refusal of the locals to change their way of life as recorded in correspondence can be read as assertiveness against foreign influences. It is evident that the Native Commissioner was on a serious mission to change and thereby to civilize the people of Kavango in line with conventional Christian norms. Unlike his predecessor the Ovambo Native Commissioner, 'Cocky' Hahn,[63] who encouraged people in Ovamboland to display their traditions such as *efundula* for official spectacle and visitors, and "opposed attempts to promote Christianization, monogamy and the wearing of Western Clothes" (Hayes, 1998:80), Eedes[64] was not at all in favour of old customs. It is worth noting that there is no significant published research of the impact of colonial policies on local power relations, ideas of tradition, gender, and generation in Kavango to date except the work of Becker (2006) on comparative perspectives on gender and chieftaincy in Namibia.

The above historical accounts present evidence that the Kavango people were not lacking self confidence or unresponsive, as claimed by early visitors to the region. Instead, there might have been a difference in politics between Ovamboland and Kavango administrations (apart from personal styles and convictions of the officials). Ovambo was regarded as a major source of migrant labour, whereas Kavango was not. The above situations can be viewed within the historical context where Christian teaching and successive administrative coercion may well have contributed to the creation of negative perceptions about the people in Kavango, who were presented as being lazy; the truth may rather lie in their unwillingness to participate in work contracts as offered by the colonial administration.

While the missionaries were initially closely linked to colonialism they, together with the local inhabitants, later began to oppose the colonial activities. This was especially the case for the Lutheran missionaries, whose church was organized in a fused ethnic identity.

---

[62] NAT1/1/54 File 25 Official Communication dated 1937/2/21
[63] For detailed reading on activities of Cocky Hahn see Hayes (1998).
[64] Hahn, who was responsible for the two regions, is celebrated by some sections of the people in Kavango, as he is believed to have brought freedom for the common man against the traditional leaders of the time who were said to have been rude and difficult in their dealings with the subjects.

The people in Ovamboland and Kavango were brought together in a religious sense under the Finnish missionary banner OvamboKavango. The "OvamboKavango Church (ex Finnish mission) operated in the two northern homelands of Ovamboland and Kavango and the Evangelical Lutheran Church (ex Rhenish mission)" which worked in southern and central Namibia, jointly wrote an open letter in 1971 to the then South African administration attacking it for not fulfilling the United Nations mandate. (Hunke, 1996:63) The church in northern Namibia established and identified itself according to the geographic and ethnic population served by its work. The name OvamboKavango does not seem to suggest a hierarchy of any sort between the ethnic populations concerned.

In the remaining sections below, I outline the activities of the South African administration in Kavango with the specific focus on the proclamation of native reserves in the 1930s followed by the Odendaal Plan of the 1960s under which homelands were created in South West Africa. The Odendaal Plan created an important social space, namely the colonial culture festival, between the colonial administration and local people.

Kavango the Native Reserve

Colonial occupation, especially by South Africa in the later years, gravely disrupted traditional norms with local systems of control. As a result people were moved to new areas to make way for developments such as the creation of borders, appropriation of the system of tax payments and eventual adaptation to the practice of the Europeans. Local people were forced to modify their ways of life. At the same time, however, the South African administration purportedly supported local traditional structures.

What started as a method of control to regulate what was known as tribal trust funds[65] and the mobilization of black labour power in the white economy later culminated in a system of separate development and apartheid. The proclamation of Ovamboland as a Native Reserve for the sole use and occupation of the Ovambo in 1929 was followed in Kavango in 1937. By 1939 about seventeen reserves had been established. (Du Pisani, 1987:19) After colonial rule was imposed on the Kavango area in the early 20th century, colonial policy rezoned ethnic settlement areas in order to implement what became known as tribal trust funds during the 1930s[66]. Some of the Vambukushu people (the easternmost of the Kavango groups) were forcibly moved from the Western Caprivi Zipfel (east of the Kavango region)

---
[65] The trust fund was meant to collect tax revenue from the natives; it would also be used to run and manage reserve affairs. The practice was used by the authorities as a way of reducingthe excessive reliance of reserves on central coffers.
[66] NAT1/1/54 File 25 Official Communication dated 1937/2/21 Tribal Trust Fund: Okavango Native Territory

to the southern banks of the Kavango River. At the same time, the western border of Kavango was shifted eastwards in order to accommodate settlers from Ovamboland in the former neutral zone between the two territories. When the tribal trust funds were implemented, five tribal groups were officially gazetted as the original inhabitants of Kavango, namely the Vakwangali, Vambunza, Vashambyu, Vagciriku and the Vambukushu. Other groups living in the area, including those known as Vanyemba and Vachokwe, were declared recent arrivals from Portuguese West Africa (PWA), today's Angola. As a result groups like that of the San and Vanyemba are non-existent in the earlier literature of the region and the blame could squarely be placed at the feet of missionaries, colonial officers and anthropologists. (Lentz, 2000:107-115) The creation of the native reserve and subsequent formation of the tribal trust fund and the gazetting of the five tribes is crucial for understanding the contemporary contestations of those who belong in Kavango. Although the creation of Kavango as a reserve and the formation of the tribal trust fund were created solely for the management of the natives and collection of tax, the practice had serious psychological implications for the inhabitants of the region. My ethnography of the festival, which is the centre of investigation in this study, presents evidence of how people in Kavango imagine Kavango-ness according to the ideology, which underlies the construction of the notion of 'Kavango' during the colonial era. The creation of reserves and tribal trust funds preceded the Odendaal Plan of 1964. Professor Johannes Petrus van Schalkwyk Bruwer, who had undertaken a study tour of the territory in 1954, engineered the Plan at the University of Stellenbosch in the department of Volkekunde. (Gordon, 2005:26-30) The inclusion of *Volkekunde* in this discussion will illuminate the argument I made earlier in the chapter that academic research of the time informed colonial policies such as creation of the homelands.

Volkekunde Anthropology and Kavango

Anthropological studies of Namibia in general and Kavango specifically cannot be understood without mention of Professor Johannes Petrus Van Schalkwyk Bruwer. Bruwer was the *volkekundige* (Afrikaans: ethnologist) regarded as the expert by the South African state on the *volke* (peoples) of Namibia during its case at the International Court of Justice. The South African administration was taken to court by Liberia and Ethiopia for not having fulfilled its mandatory obligation as outlined by the League of Nations charter and demanded that its mandate be revoked. Bruwer acted as advisor to the South African government on South West Africa issues. His numerous suggestions would define and shape the territory in later years. His concern at the time was the development of the political situation inspired by SWAPO propaganda and the way it would affect the workings of the state and its image abroad.

Bruwer recommended the need to "mobilize goodwill and reiterated the need for a well-organized plan of development for the territory". (Gordon, 2005:32) He pleaded for the Commissioner General of the territory to be an experienced ethnologist who could liaise and promote the plan of development among the natives. He would later become the Commissioner General for South West Africa affair even sponsoring a number of students who undertook fieldwork in the densely populated northern areas of the Kavango and Ovambo regions. I briefly discuss three studies sponsored or co-supervised.

One of these studies by M J Olivier focused on the mandate of the territory and the role and management of the inhabitants by the South African state. He recommended the territory to remain under the mandate of South Africa until it was able to deal with its own affairs; however, he is not specific on the duration of the mandate period. In hindsight, he advocated for permanent mandate. (Olivier, 1961:413-416) Among his recommendations he advocated for the separate treatment of the native as set out in the Natural Administration Act of 1927. That was seen to *"beskerm Bantoe belange*[67]*".* (Olivier, 1961:416) As one of Professor Bruwer's earliest students, his thesis was very important in the legal sense as it informed administrative ideology at the time.

The next thesis was on the north-east of South West Africa by Johannes Lodewickus Bosch. Bosch's study (1964) focused on the matrilineal orientation of people in southern Africa. Still under the old anthropological research influence, Bosch did an ethno-historical study among the people of Shambyu in north-eastern Kavango not very far from Rundu town and recorded socio-historical information about the Vashambyu. His study presented the Shambyu as a distinct ethnic group in Kavango whose matrilineal organization was under threat of switching to patriliny. He argued that such changes were informed by outside influences such as Western languages and other social factors.

A study by Kampungu 1965 sponsored by the Roman Catholic Church focused on Kavango marriage customs. He paid specific attention to the culture of the Vakwangali. Kampungu was the first local university trained intellectual and a Catholic priest. He later served in the Kavango Legislative Assembly. In fact it is apparent that his and Bosch's works were done almost at the same time as is evident in certain correspondence between himself and N J van Warmelo, a South African government ethnologist, recorded in his unpublished thesis (Kampungu 1966:4) As a local intellectual his work is of particular importance as it

---

[67] "Protect the Bantu interests"

provides a wide ranging history of the territory (South West Africa) and its peoples and not only of the Vakwangali.

Kampungu's work was followed by Van Tonder's ethnological study in 1966. Van Tonder, like Bosch a student of Professor Bruwer, produced a study implicitly influenced by the theory of the cultural anthropologist, Herskovitz, which he used to vehemently criticize British Anthropology for "its lack of conformity in terminology such as social process, ethnography and ethnology". (Van Tonder, 1966:2-3) His study was undertaken among the Vambukushu in Kavango in order to inform the course of action which was sought by government and administration authorities of the time. He advocated for the retribalization of Africans which, he suggested, would enhance social cohesion and functionality.

A later publication on the "Kavango Peoples" published in 1981 by Gibson and colleagues appears to be a replication of the works of Bosch and Kampungu. Their comparative work emphasized the distinctness of their subjects of study by treating them as tribes. They argued that since there was less interference from outside influences, their culture also remained significantly unaltered. As such, they strove to reconstruct the unaltered Kavango culture and attempted to compare them. While their study focused on people on the lower Kavango River, they excluded the groups such as the Nyemba and Ngangela who were also resident in their area of research.

Both Bosch 1964 and Van Tonder 1966 were students of Professor Bruwer. Their work demonstrates the political agenda of the time as envisaged by Professor Bruwer and was conducted in conjunction with the state. These studies preceded the anticipated planning development and policy matters of the Odendaal Plan of separate development in South West Africa. All these studies emphasized the distinctness of tribe and its functionality during the political context of the time.

The category tribe and its uses and reference to the subject of anthropological study especially in Africa have been widely criticized. Archie Mafeje in 1971 criticized the notion of tribe including its usage and relegated it to an ideology of intent in his essay titled *The Ideol ogy of Tribalism*. He maintained that anthropologists may have been right in insisting that traditional or pre-colonial African societies large or small may have been tribal especially if the usage of the term tribe is restricted to specific forms of economic, political, and social organization that can be fixed in space and time. However, he argues that if the society has been penetrated by European colonialism that has successfully drawn it into a capitalist, economy and a world market it was a serious transgression to continue using the term. However, while Mafeje issued a harsh critique of the use of the concept 'tribe' in earlier anthropology, he did not adequately address the context where lay people and politicians use the term tribe in reference to identity and culture at the time of his essay writing. Lay people and governments do not care much for the anthropologist's dilemma with the concept and the term tribe; they will continue to use the term because it is a useful simplification to social processes as Peter Skalník 1988 argues. In his chapter almost twenty years later he argued that indeed tribe is a colonial category that has proved to be "particularly resilient in anthropology for the general public in the West and for the people to whom the term has been applied". (Skalnik, 1988:69) As such, Skalnik 1988 suggested that as anthropologists we formulate concepts whose usefulness could be tested in understanding and explaining social processes to the benefit of both science and public life.

The most notable research on the region is the work of Diescho 1983 which is an analysis of the Odendaal Commission of enquiry into South West Africa Affairs 1962-1963, with specific reference to its findings, recommendations and implementation in respect of Kavango. His work was followed by Mbambo 2002 who studied indigenous knowledge systems with the specific focus on traditional healing and its relation to religion among the Vagciriku in north eastern Kavango. Mbambo argues that traditional healing served a social purpose of belonging to the social structure of the Vagciriku. His thesis relies heavily on early volkekunde sources not seeming to appreciate the changing nature of social life among the subjects of his study.

Mattia Fumanti's study on creating youth elites in postcolonial Kavango is the latest critical anthropological engagement from the region. Fumanti 2003 critically analyzed the politics of elitism in various social spaces performed by the youth of Kavango, thus creating a sense of belonging and involves a great deal of performance. His work is a contemporary critical anthropological study in comparison to the earlier works of Van Tonder and Bosch of the 1960s.

Research and related activity were encouraged at the time of the creation of homelands authorities and their subsequent administration, specifically by the Department of Volkekunde of Stellenbosch University, the 'Afrikaanse Universiteit van die Witwatersrand' presumably the university known as Rand Afrikaanse Universiteit, (RAU), today. The University of Johannesburg also seems to have played a significant role in a circulated memo, which requested the collection and donation of artifacts for its museum through the magisterial districts of the 'Native Areas'. The collection request for artifacts was supposedly for educational and tourism purposes[68].

Specifically the theses by Bosch 1964 and Van Tonder 1966 and later the work of the German linguist Mohlig 1967 on Kavango without doubt assisted in the construction of the

---

[68] NAR/155 File N1/12/6 dated 1967/10/25 Official Communication from Afrikaanse Universiteit van die Witwatersrand

imagined colonial Kavango identity and nation as the following excerpt from the communication between the Native Commissioner and one researcher shows:

> Today I have the pleasure to send you a copy of my thesis under separate cover. I hope to be able to continue my investigations among the Dciriku in the near future and to forward further publications on the language and the culture of that interesting people.[69]

> We are working on developing the traditional tribal governments into self-rule for the whole of Okavango area. Your work, therefore, appears at a most appropriate time and will be of the greatest value. May I take the liberty to suggest that you also present copies of your thesis to the Dciriku Tribal Authority and the Chief Bantu Affairs Commissioner in Windhoek. The latter now has an Ethnologist, Mr Budack, on his staff. Mr. Budack shows great interest in the tribes of the Okavango and since he has to advise the Government in regard to cultural and traditional political matters, your work will benefit him greatly.[70]

The above letters were written at the time when the recommendations of the Odendaal Commission were being implemented. I have not been able to locate his thesis, but according to reviews it provides a description of Bantu language namely Dciriku, currently spelled Gciriku. He completed his thesis shortly before the official department of education was established in the homeland. (Westphal, 1970:294) Shortly after this a group of local *hompas* from various ethnic groups sought for the recognition and teaching of vernacular languages in school, an idea that was strongly encouraged by the state.[71] The demand by the *hompas* was treated as a necessity and addressed with urgency by the Native Commissioners. The authorities took advantage of the situation in demanding loyalty and allegiance in return[72].

Kavango After the Implementation of the Odendaal Plan

Later colonial activity, in particular the proposals of the Odendaal Commission for a system of separate development, was informed and shaped by earlier administrative mechanisms

---

[69] NAR/1/55 Letter dated 1967/10/29 to the Bantu Affairs Commissioner in Kavango from Dr. W Mohlig in Germany

[70] NAR/1/55 Letter dated 1967/11/09 to Dr. Mohlig in Germany from the Bantu Affairs Commissioner of Kavango

[71] NAR1/1/55 File N1/12/7/2 Letter dated 1968/05/11 to the Chief Bantu Affairs Commissioner detailing the demands of the Vagciriku King Shashipapo for recognition and teaching of Rugciriku in schools.

[72] NAR1/1/55 File N1/12/7/2 Letter dated 1968/05/11 to the Chief Bantu Affairs Commissioner detailing the demands of the Vagciriku King Shashipapo for recognition and teaching of Rugciriku in schools.

such as the Tribal Trust Fund of the 1930s. In the early 1960s, the Odendaal Commission propositioned that:

> As far as practical a homeland must be created for each population group, in which it alone would have residential, political and language rights to the exclusion of other population groups, so that each group would be able to develop towards self determination without any group dominating or being dominated by the other[73].

Following the Commission's recommendations, ethnic-based homelands were created in South West Africa with a political system of differentiation and exclusion.[74] During colonial Kavango five groups[75] were recognized by the administration as the only *real* inhabitants of the region, while others were generally regarded and treated as outsiders. Earlier studies that presented people as distinct and homogenous did not treat the situation differently when it came to Kavango, instead they emphasized uniqueness and difference as conceived by the administration of the time. (Bosch, 1964; Kampungu, 1965; Van Tonder, 1966; Mohlig[76] cited in Gibson, et al. 1981)

The above proclamation was aimed at controlling and regulating the movement of black contract labour. The South African policy of apartheid was introduced into SWA particularly in the areas of education, influx control, the Immorality Act, the Mixed Marriage Act, separate residential areas and amenities. The "introduction of ethnic administrative structures in the various homelands was introduced and strengthened through the implementation of ethnically based second tier governments". (Du Pisani, 1987:20) The legacy was based on the "outcome of the Odendaal Commission Report of 1964 which propagated the system of separate development and self government of the native nations in South West Africa". (Du Pisani, 1987:20) The legacy was a "decreed restructuring of institutions and ideology from the conventional colonial racial hierarchy of white and non-white into eleven statutory national groups' such as the Herero, the Kavango, the Damara" etc. (Gottschalk,

---

[73] NAR/1/155 File BB/0276 SWA- A Five Year Plan- for the development of the Native Areas
[74] For more details on the Odendaal Commission and the creation of the Kavango 'homeland', see Nambadi (2007), Likuwa (2005), and Karapo (2008). These historians have looked into the precolonial history of Kavango and its inhabitants, the colonial conquest and finally the conception of Kavango as a homeland and the role of traditional authorities.
[75] This happens dominantly after the implementation of the recommendations of the Odendaal Commission of 1962-1963 which suggested the restructuring of the colonial state ideology and institutions from the conventional colonial racial hierarchy of 'white' and 'non-white' into eleven statutory 'national groups' such as 'the Herero', 'the Kavango' etc. with '*intra national*' groups such Vakwangali, Vashambyu, etc. (Gottschalk, 1987:30)
[76] Mohlig's early work in Kavango is not readily available locally, however, he published a Rumanyo dictionary with a local author Karel Shiyaka Mberema in 2005.

1987:30) Gottschalk argued that the Odendaal Plan was in that context used to counteract the fast developing political activities of the time inside and outside the country.

Various other activities, for example, the deployment of "parastatal pseudo parties", such as *Ejuva* in Hereroland, *Etango* in Ovamboland and *Ezuva*[77] in Kavango, were used to counter the revolutionary politicization advocated by SWAPO. (Gottschalk, 1987:31) Teachers and students more particularly were the targets of *Ezuva*. Although activities of *Ezuva* are widely narrated by people in Kavango, few of those who participated were willing to speak about their experiences in the organization.

The Odendaal proposals would be meaningless unless legitimated, and as a result the Kavango Legislative Council was declared in 1970 with Rundu as its administrative district according to Act 54 of 1968. However, the council only received full powers three years later on 9 April 1973. As a semi-autonomous state it had its own Volk anthem and citizens were comprised of five population groupings, namely the Vambukushu, Vagciriku, Vashambyu, Vambunza and Vakwangali respectively. They were expected to register in order to become full members of the "Kavango Volk[78]". Legislation passed by the Legislative Council of Kavango, decreed that a member of the Kavango Volk[79] would be:

- Any black person born in Kavango before or after the legislation
- Any black person who has since settled in Kavango
- Any black person who could speak any of the Kavango languages
- Any black person who share the culture or have family relations in Kavango.

Upon registration they were to receive certificates with which they could claim belonging to the Kavango Volk. This classification was further characterized by criteria such as physical attributes or appearances; any person who was believed not to meet the above criteria was deemed not a member of the Kavango Volk and would thus be excluded or fined if found to be in the territory of Kavango. On 26 April 1974, Jannie De Wet, the then Commissioner-general of Native Affairs, handed over the flag[80] of the Kavango Volk to Prime Minister Alfons Majavero who later became hompa of the Vambukushu people in 1983. At the ceremony preceded by cultural dances the Commissioner-general said:

---

[77] *Ezuva, Ejuva* or *Etango* literally means 'sun'.
[78] NAR/1/155 File F002-JX10006- KAVANGUDI (1973 April) homeland official newspaper published by the Department of Information.
[79] NAR/1/155 File F002-JX10006- KAVANGUDI (1973 April)
[80] NAR/1/155 File F002-JX10006- KAVANGUDI (1974 April)

Here on the southern point of Afrika lives a Kavango Volk:

- A Volk with its own origins
- A Volk with its own traditions
- A Volk with its character
- A Volk with five tribes united in one mighty Kavango nation.

The administration of the time constructed Kavango as a nation comprised of five distinct tribes. This task, however, proved to be difficult for the administration of Kavango[81] especially when other population groups such as the San and Vanyemba were not legally acknowledged to be Kavango people, despite their historical ties to the land in question. The five groups whose settlement in the area had been officially acknowledged had their histories of origin and settlements along the Kavango River disputed in contemporary Kavango leading to the assumption that the identity of Kavango-ness would not be an amalgamation of these five tribes alone. I show later in chapter seven that such colonial identity constructions, which were internalized, became a subject of serious contestations in the post colonial Kavango region of Namibia.

The first signal of the local Kavango radio "*Ezi Radio Kavango*[82]" (This is Radio Kavango) was heard in 1977. The radio was created for purposes of information, education, entertainment and political propaganda[83]. Kavango as a homeland actively participated in the activities of the time, especially administratively. It identified itself through a national flag and anthem. The anthem presented the people of Kavango as a unique nation, which is situated near the Kavango River. In the anthem there is a metaphor of the river of darkness through which light breaks bringing hope. The nation on the banks of this river is presented as primitive and receiving light through hope which flows in the dark stream. It is this former colonially imagined nation and various forms of 'cultural' representation then and now which forms the crux of this study in the post colonial moment. During my research and stay in Kavango, I have not heard or seen people singing the Kavango Anthem.

---

[81] The possible exclusion or inclusion of the San was debated later in many sessions of the Kavango Legislative Council just before the universal suffrage was to be held in the homeland in the 1970s.
[82] NAR/1/55 File AP/7/1/1 Jaarverslag (Annual Report) 1978 Departement Van Onderwys- Kavango Regering
[83] The radio later becomes an important tool through which local 'culture' is contested by local inhabitants in contemporary Kavango as I show in chapter 8.

Kavango in Contemporary Discourse: A Historical Sanitization Project

The notion of Kavango-ness continues to be contested in contemporary Namibia at all levels of society. As I observed during my fieldwork such contestations seem to be oriented and rooted in matters related to access to resources and association to those in positions of power. Local authors on Kavango such as Shiremo (2005; 2007; 2010), Likuwa (2006; 2007), and Kavango Elders (2007) suggest it is important to understand current debates and the political standing of the region according to historical perspectives, which, they argue, has been influenced and shaped by various factors. Their focus is on the role of early European scholarship of history, ethnology and traders who visited the region during the initial stage of colonial conquest and the periods thereafter. They argue that historical records were misrepresented and biased. As such, they have contributed to the imagery of how Kavango is imagined in contemporary times.

This widely held perspective among the local academics and authors on the region was recently emphasized and debated after an article on the history of Kavango was published in 2007 in the Journal of Namibian Studies: "Reports from 'beyond the line': the accumulation of knowledge of Kavango and its peoples by the German colonial administration 1891-1911" by Andreas Eckl, a German historian. He has argued in his essay that the German colonial influence on the area was minimal and as such it can be argued that the region did not experience colonialism. Eckl (2007) emphasizes that Kavango was always a region which still had to be brought under control. His arguments were based on archival documents of early German colonial officials' journals and correspondence about the region. While his article presents various examples and evidence about the colonial activities in the area until 1915, he maintained that there was no influence which can really be argued to be colonial. The general deduction from Eckl's argument is that Kavango was not colonially subjugated, as were other parts of South West Africa in the police zone, because Germany had less interest in the area and its people in the economic and political sense. Although Eckl (2007) argues that German interest in Kavango was mostly limited to its economic value rather than political domination, his essay and sources [84] contain evidence to the contrary.

It was partly this essay that led to the conference[85] held in the Kavango region and sponsored by the National Archives with funds from the Archives of Anti-Colonial Resistance and the Liberation Struggle (AACRLS) themed "Recording and Restoring our Part in the Past". Two young local historians Romanus Shampapi Shiremo and Kletus Muhena Likuwa

---
[84] Debate between Shiremo, Likuwa and Fisch also contain sufficient evidence with regard to the colonial role of Germany in Kavango.
[85] I was also invited to present a paper in this conference. My paper was titled: 'Independence Day in Rundu, Northeastern Namibia: Representations of local and national culture'

whose presentations detailed documentary organized the conference and oral perspectives of the German colonial influence and argued that interactions and cordial relations existed with certain local chiefs and only became sour later in time. Eckl[86] was invited to present a response to the debate in the conference but did not attend. The role and influences of the German colonial presence during the late nineteenth century in Kavango became the focal point of the debate. Essays by local authors, showed that there was significant colonial interest in the area such as attempts to convert local people to Christianity and eventual use of labour services in the envisaged farming industry near the river. (Mutorwa, 1994; Shiremo, 2005; Likuwa, 2006; Shiremo, 2007; Shiremo, 2010)

Officially the area came under German colonial rule after 1886 when the German colonial administration signed an agreement with Portugal. (Hangula, 1991:118-124 as cited in Eckl, 2007) At present the German colonial role and impact in Kavango is being disputed, despite considerable evidence that the area had indeed been greatly affected by foreign influence from the first contacts of colonization. (Eckl, 2007:10-12)

The debate[87] about the colonial influence in Kavango did not spare the former state ethnologist, Dr. Maria Fisch. Fisch as the colonial ethnologist was widely regarded as an authoritative source on the culture of Kavango during the colonial time. The accuracy and scientific credibility of her work and the problems associated with this forms part of the ongoing debate between Fisch and historians from the Kavango region. One major bone of contention was the role and influence of German colonialism in the area of Kavango as debated by Eckl 2007, (see Shiremo and Likuwa 2007). The other issue was the more general question as to whether "whites can write our history?[88]" as contained in one of the letters from Likuwa who responded to the discussion between Shiremo and Fisch. Likuwa's letter to the debating parties advocated the objective representation of historical perspectives irrespective of whether the authors were white or black.

On the first point, while Eckl suggested that German colonialism had only had minimal colonial influence in the area, Shiremo 2007 and Likuwa 2007 argued that the influence was significant and has contributed to the current image of Kavango. This interaction was mainly between Fisch and Shiremo a historian from Kavango and it was in the form of letters. This communication[89] was sent to people perceived to be knowledgeable about matters

---

[86] According to the conference organizers he told them that he could not make it.
[87] The debate about colonial control and influence in Kavango had been ongoing between Shiremo and Fisch before the article by Eckl was published in 2007.
[88] The letter is dated 31 July 2006
[89] Correspondence of the debate and subsequent legal action between those concerned, primarily Shiremo and Fisch, were deposited in the National Archives of Namibia and are available for perusal.

of Kavango by the two actors referred to as Kavango Elders. The debate between Shiremo and Fisch in 2006 ended short of being taken to court for adjudication.

In his 2010 thesis on Kavango hompas and their relations with the early Germans, British and finally South Africans, Shiremo focuses on the reign of Hompa Nyangana of the Vagciriku and neighbouring kingdoms. He shows Hompa Nyangana to have been protective of his territory's sovereignty against outsiders and not a blood thirsty tyrant as he was presented in various travellers' accounts. Shiremo's investigation dealt with the relationship between Hompa Nyangana and Catholic missionaries who were invited to set up a mission station.

As an author on Kavango, I agree with local perspectives that the current imagination of Kavango is informed by earlier writing about the region. The role of academic authors in any historical context is of particular importance and those who write always have an agenda. However, the same can be said for the contemporary writings of the region. To date, the region remains excluded from the academic debate. History is integral in young democracies specifically in the context of creating national narratives of belonging. Even in this time of independence, the region is constantly struggling to locate itself within the national discourse of belonging and public history. A historical publication 'Trees never meet' in 1998 illuminates the above assertions. Although the project was meant to address research and the publication gap on Namibia, it created another dilemma. Notable absentees are histories of Kavango, Caprivi, and the San. Editors of the book were apologetic about this omission and presented the publication as a beginning only, however, no further publication has been forthcoming.

In the first half of the chapter I discussed the representation of local history in myths and legends and its appropriation by contemporary Kavango to signify contemporary notions of belonging and difference especially among the ethnic groups, which were previously officially recognized, and those that were not. Contestations of these historical narratives are not only limited to those who were not recognized, but operate within those groups that were recognized and claim to belong to the Kavango.

The above narratives show an imagined Kavango according to the Odendaal Report as land with its distinct population each with its own language and traditional practices. Various apparatus such as delimitation of borders, anthems, flags and subsequent sensitization through various 'cultural' activities such as festivals were aimed at reinforcing this notion. On the day of the flag, Kavango was presented as a distinct nation with unique traditions and character composed of (only) the five tribes. Such occasions of pomp and ceremony with full representation of colonial authority were used to emphasize the ideology of difference and awareness of unwanted communist influences from outside the borders of South

West Africa. Before and after Kavango was declared a homeland various expeditions of missionaries, traders, colonial officials and academics took place and my argument is that they had a great influence in the shaping of a Kavango identity. Missionary work supported colonial administration in terms of providing information about the natives and their way of life. The above discussion has demonstrated how the various administrative politics and historical social formation have influenced the Kavango and its people. In the following chapter, I discuss the making of the colonial sangfees and its transition towards the introduction of the postcolonial Annual National Culture Festival.

5 Sangfees, the Antecedent of the Postcolonial Annual National Culture Festival

The Making of the Colonial Festival: 'sangfees[1]'

In this chapter, I investigate the creation of the colonial festival formerly known as the sangfees in Kavango and the transition towards the introduction of the postcolonial Annual National Culture Festival in Namibia during 1995. Memory narratives and official archival sources reveal the colonial festival as a public discourse underlying the politics of difference and belonging that created a sense of distinctness among the people of Kavango. The new culture festival follows the colonial model of representation, although it is different in conception and ideology. The postcolonial festival was created in terms of a narrative that tolerates diversity in accordance with the constitutional democracy unlike the sangfees, which was meant to enhance the distinctness of the homeland population and its relationship to other Bantustan homelands of South West Africa. Significantly, the research data appears to show the festival in all historical contexts to be a social space where belonging and difference are expressed and represented through a process of performance. I emphasize that we should comprehend these notions of difference and belonging within the social and political contexts that created them.

Using the memory narratives of my research participants and archive sources to sketch the inception of the culture festival, which was officially known as the sangfees in colonial South West Africa, my discussion will focus on the late colonial Kavango homeland. I pay attention to the Department of Education and the Division of Youth in the homeland administration of Kavango as producers of the festival in order to show their role in the construction of the Kavango identity through cultural activities. I describe some of the activities, which were held at Maria Mwengere Camp[2] locally known as *Ekongoro*[3] during the late colonial period. Maria Mwengere Camp[4] was built on a prime 300ha piece of land near

---

[1] Sangfees literally translates as Song festival in English.
[2] The Department of Youth was responsible for the Maria Mwengere Camp. The name was changed to Maria Mwengere Culture Center during the postcolonial festival.
[3] Ekongoro is a mythical serpent, believed to live in the Kavango River. The word is locally used to refer to the rainbow. The contemporary notion of Ekongoro as a rainbow referred to the number of ethnic groups resident in Kavango.
[4] One of the senior culture officers who had worked at the centre for some time and whom I cannot identify asserts that it was the army which came up with the idea of requesting land from the hompa under the guise of organizing "youth activities" which were vaguely explained. The state's intention it can be argued was to construct a centre which would be used to launch political and

the stream of Ncua not far from the Kavango River donated in the late 1970s by Shambyu Hompa Maria Mwengere to the administration for the construction of a new building. It was locally believed that Ekongoro was a mythical water serpent living in that stream. However, there are conflicting accounts as to whether Hompa Maria Mwengere was approached by the Department of Education or the South African Army to provide the land. As I argue in the preceding chapter, this festival at Maria Mwengere Camp signified the type of Kavango-ness that the colonial administration envisaged. Here I argue that the colonial festival was a response to the fast-growing politics of struggle and emancipation led by the Swapo movement inside and across the border.

Secondly, I focus on the introduction of a postcolonial festival. I analyze the making of the postcolonial festival as a response to the public discourse of difference and belonging that emerged immediately after independence. People in Namibia expressed sentiments of difference and belonging in radio chat shows and other media. This expressed desire of difference and belonging was not in line with the popular "One Namibia, One Nation" slogan used before independence and shortly afterwards.

I argue that political issues such as the Basterland question in Rehoboth and a failed secession attempt in the Caprivi region in northeastern Namibia as well as access to resources served as important indicators about the need for the state to adjust its nationalism discourse from "One Namibia, One Nation", to "Unity in diversity". The two scenarios in independent Namibia are generally believed to be motivated by the politics of ethnicity. During the first decade of independence, certain sections of the population in the Caprivi (under the leadership of traditional and political leaders such as Chief Boniface Mamili of the Mafwe and Mishake Muyongo of the United Democratic Party) advocated the secession of the region from the rest of Namibia; their first military attempt was foiled by the state in 1998. In Rehoboth, the former Baster leaders under Kaptein Hans Diergaardt who served in the second tier local government within the colonial framework refused to be part of the new national government in 1990 and even went to court to prevent postcolonial state processes such as the constitution and new land delimitation. (KjÆret & Stokke, 2003; The New York Times, 1990; New Era, 2009; The Namibian, 2009) There are other social spaces in postcolonial Namibia where sentiments of belonging and association are expressed. For instance, Becker 2011 in her essay on commemorating heroes in Namibia reports that many of her interlocutors were concerned with the memorial association to ethnicity and regionalism. Her research focus was the Heroes' Acre built to celebrate and commemorate the heroes of Namibia. She argued that the war aftermath was not able to establish national symbols that

---

psychological warfare which would influence young people to turn against the SWAPO movement and its ideals.

would foster national identity. In her analysis Becker 2011 suggests that the postcolonial sites do not specifically represent Namibians from the central and southern regions of the country that had little direct experience of the armed struggle.

It is also evident that culture festivals were introduced as a result of the lucrative heritage industry gaining momentum during the 1990s. (Fairweather 2001 and the Comaroffs 2009). The postcolonial state encouraged its citizens to participate in the fast growing heritage industry, which was emerging alongside the tourism sector. Fairweather's (2006) focus on the northern regions of Namibia shows that cultural tourism required the articulation of local identities with reference to a global tourism market that sought to construct contemporary postcolonial subjects as dwelling in a homogenized traditional past.

The Department of Education Administration for Kavango

Under the pre-independence homeland dispensation, government departments with executive powers such as finance, works, home affairs, health and education were created in Kavango. The Department of Education was headed by Rudolph Ngondo a minister in the then homeland (multi-party) government and Louis Burger who served as his secretary. The Department of Education created a Youth[5] Division discussed below.

Ngondo[6] was also a prominent businessman and farmer in the region. Burger was the planner and educator whose ideals shaped the educational discourse of the time.

In 1974 the Kavango homeland administration issued a legislative directive[7] on the institution of a youth movement aimed at giving the youth an opportunity to know their (Volk) nation who, as result, would not be easily influenced by foreign factors. Activities such as weekend workshops where the youth would be taught needlework, nature conservation, woodwork, agriculture, traditional medicine, traditional dances and culture would be held. Bible studies and history purportedly to enhance the love of the Kavango nation and

---

[5] Mufune (2002:179) who writes in a postcolonial context suggests that youth is an elastic concept that is socially constructed. The social construction of 'youth' is determined by various rites and initiations which people undergo during their lifetime. In Namibia youth as a social category is used variably by those who are in positions of power. Although there are no clear indications of induction into age systems, the category youth in this context was used to refer to a portion of the population which fell under a particular age group. This particular population group had to be managed differently from the rest of the citizens because of its social character. Thus due to complexities of exact determination of a youth, it is fair to regard the latter as part of the negotiations and contestations of the cultural process. In the colonial context under discussion it was felt necessary to have legislation which would regulate activities of the youth.

[6] At the moment he is involved in matters of the Ukwangali Traditional Authority where he serves as chairman of the Traditional Council.

[7] NAR/1/55/ File F002-JX10006 KAVANGUDI (May 1974)

its culture were included. Most importantly, it was stipulated that youth be made aware of the negative influences of foreign 'cultures' and the importance of embracing and nurturing their own culture.

These activities were designed according to the perceived needs of each homeland; in this case Kavango and its people. The population in the homeland needed to be aware of their identity. Such awareness was created through teaching the youth to sing the Kavango Volkslied[8] (Kavango anthem) and appreciate other symbols such as the Kavango flag, which was meant to signify belonging and allegiance to the homeland. The Volkslied was sung at all official occasions. The Volkslied signified the Kavango River as a very important space, which brought hope of civilization to the people of the homeland and woke them from the slumber of doom. The singing of an anthem constructed an image of a distinct and separate people in Kavango, different from the rest of the population in the South West African territory. Other activities such as tribal[9] dances, nature conservation and woodwork created a sense of essentialism, primitiveness[10] and closeness to nature. The Bible and its teachings were seen by the authorities as a necessary instrument to secure the submission of the inhabitants, specifically the youth, to their parents and especially to the tribal authority and the state.

Through participation in tribal activities the youth would learn about the workings of their tribe and to respect its authorities. They were divided into three age categories: 7-11 juniors, 12-15 seniors and 16-20 year olds to be known as the Kavango Youth Organization. It was from the latter group that future soldiers, police officers, nature conservation officers and firemen were chosen.

The directive under discussion cannot be viewed in isolation from the political situation of the time. The period between 1970 and 1978 saw the SWAPO[11] movement intensify its propaganda and ideology of liberation and independence inside the country as the official year report of the administration in 1978 shows:

> Met die opbouende politieke onrus oor die grense was 'n vol program vir die jaar georganiseer. Saamtrekke is vanoor die hele gebied (gehou) waar die jeug dan vir 'n volle week onnderrig ontvang in onderwerpe soos gesondheid, nasionalisme, eerstehulp, padveiligheid, ens. Dit dien ook as saamtrekke vir groot sangfeeste wat op

---

[8] See the Kavango Volkslied in appendix.
[9] Authorities at the time refer to leaders of specific ethnic groups as tribal leaders, since then the term has been locally appropriated. In this study I use it in that context.
[10] See the Kavango Volkslied.
[11] SWAPO stands for South West Africa People's Organisation. It was a liberation movement which was transformed into a political party in 1989 just before the elections which preceded the independence of Namibia. It has since become known as the Swapo Party.

nasionale basis gehou word. Groot getalle ouers en belangstellendes woon hierdie feeste by en hierdie belangstelling is baie verblydend.[12]

(Given the tense political developments across the borders, a full year programme was prepared. Gatherings will be held in the whole territory where the youth will attend workshops and be taught on topics such as health, nationalism, first aid, road safety etc. These rallies will also serve as sangfees (festivals) which would be held nationally. Large numbers of parents and other interested people attend these festivals and this interest is pleasing.)

This period marked an exodus of young people leaving South West Africa for Angola to join SWAPO. The majority of young people in the homelands of South West Africa began to cross borders into neighbouring Angola, Zambia and Botswana to join the SWAPO movement[13]. The report above indicates the importance for the state to organize gatherings and workshops for the youth so that they were kept busy and did not become involved in political activities across the borders. One can suspect that the tense political situation referred to was (inter alia) the brutal 1978 massacre of people carried out at Cassinga, a SWAPO refugee camp in Angola.

The homeland administration designed a counter-process inside which included the introduction of festivals then referred to as sangfees at school level and other movements such as *Ezuva* with activities to target young people. The sangfees was of particular importance within that historical context as it became a social space through which the state advocated its political agenda. I argue, however, that the creation of the sangfees was not initiated without the involvement of local people. Local people at the time, especially those in the civil service and students, were encouraged to participate and support the sangfees. As Robert Mukoroli, a local artist and former employee of the Camp, and Irma Jericho a former student and teacher at the time said in an interview:

Kwa kaliro ira mpo yetu kuna kufa, makura lighano lyakurambwita mpo yetu lya tovalire. Lighano linya lya tovalile.[14]

(Our culture was seen to be dying, and it was a good idea to have culture performances and tradition revived. It was quite a good idea.)

Soos ek, ek het daar gegaan maar nie met die weermag nie. Ons het daar gegaan met onse skoolhoof. En ons het bybel studie en ander dinge gaan doen en vir die hele week daar gebly. Ons het bybels en gesang boekies saam gevat. Ons het ook nuwe

---

[12] NAR/1/55 File AP/7/1/1 Jaarverslag (Annual Report) 1978 Departement Van Onderwys- Kavango Regering
[13] NAR/1/55 File AP/7/1/2 Jaarverslag (Annual Report) 1978, Kavango Regering (TOP SECRET)
[14] Interview with Linyando Manfred Mukoroli, joined by Kletus Muhena Likuwa at Safari, Rundu, 16 January 2009.

liedere gaan leer. Ons het ook politiek gaan leer. Die jong seuns het gaan leer hoe om te paradeer.[15]

(Like myself, I went to the youth camp but not with the army. We went with our school principal. We did bible study and other activities and stayed there for a week period. We took our bibles and song books with and also learned new songs. We were also taught about the politics of the time. The young boys were trained how to parade.)

The above quotation shows how people in Kavango perceived the idea of the sangfees. Although the inception of the sangfees was an administrative idea, local people participated in its realization. That is why when the idea was initiated in the late 1970s to establish youth camps in the various tribal authorities traditional leaders supported the initiative. In hindsight I view it as a welcome step for the so-called traditional leaders[16] who then had became unpopular among the young people who felt supported and were loyal to the colonial administration. However, there was an official element of secrecy in this state project. For instance, young male students and teachers who went to the camps did not know that they were to receive paramilitary training. Participants encountered certain practices that were not communicated to them prior to their participation and it was these new revelations that raised suspicion among people. Local people thought and believed that if the younger ones went to the camps they would be taught what their culture was, that they would grow better as people with identity and a sense of belonging, as Karel Shiyaka told me: "The aim of organizing the youth and camps as we were told was to educate them about their traditional, ancestral culture, lest they forget their culture[17]".

The idea of creating awareness of difference and belonging was not confined to planning documents or directed only at the youth. Older people were targeted when they attended functions sanctioned by the state. The ceremony in question featured cultural performances, when the flag[18] of the Kavango Volk was unveiled and hoisted for the first time in 1974, Jannie de Wet, the then Commissioner-General of Native Affairs, had this to say:

Here on the southern point of Africa lives a Kavango Volk[19]:

– A Volk with its own origins

---

[15] Interview with Irma Jericho at Tutungeni, Rundu on 18 December 2008.
[16] When the various tribal governments/authorities were established local leaders were collectively referred to as chiefs or traditional leaders and not as kings or queens.
[17] Interview with Karel Mberema Shiyaka, Maria Mwengere Culture Centre, Rundu, 23 September 2008.
[18] The colour of the flag was green
[19] "Volk" is hard to translate into English. It is "people" (in the singular), as in "ethnic group", but also has the connotation of "nation".

- A Volk with its own traditions
- A Volk with its character
- A Volk with five tribes united in one mighty Kavango nation.

While cultural performances at gatherings such as the one referred to above were conceived by local people as an attempt to resurrect their "dead culture and tradition" and provide a learning experience for the young people, the authorities regarded the events as a social space in which it could express its ideas of belonging to the Kavango nation and homeland as imagined and created in the Odendaal Plan. For the young Jericho then, it was a school-related project in which the youth participated and enjoyed. Although the talk of the then Commissioner-general shows a picture of a distinct nation with its character, I think the authorities saw it as a ritual of association and belonging. However, it is the type of association and belonging that we should contextualize historically and politically. Rudolf Ngondo (at the time Minister of Education) interprets the commissioner-general's opening address as follows: "Nasinye sina kwa kere ekambadaro lyo kutura muntu omu gahamena.[20]" (It was an attempt to place people where they belonged.)

In the process, people would internalize the idea of belonging to a particular ethnic group, which was a required outcome as stated in the homeland's annual report for 1978. While local people and students participated in the state projects of homeland nationalism, there were those who shunned and defied these efforts. Two former students[21] of Rundu Secondary School at the time told me in a mocking manner that after the Cassinga massacre of 1978 (when SWAPO exiles were attacked by the South African forces), they secretly planned a commemorative demonstration at school. The Minister of Education came to address the students and urged them not to participate in the planned demonstration. In this gathering of the minister he asked the students: "Yilye gweni mwa diva ka kafire Kokasinga? Yilye? Mutumbureni paapa ngesi! Walye omuli vonga vonga moyininke yaana divilisa. Tengureni muze kosure mu la lironge![22]" (Who do you know that is related to you was killed in Kasinga? Who is it? Mention him now! Why do you want to involve yourself in matters which you do not know and do not concern you? Go back to school and study!)

The Youth Division was an important arm of the Department of Education. Young people were a very important population target especially during the mounting political tensions in South Africa (the administrative centre) and the South West African territory. The

---

[20] Interview held with Rudolf Ngondo, 15 January 2010 at Katjinakatji.
[21] I will not reveal names of these students here for ethical reasons.
[22] My research field notes.

administration designed a "Hearts-and-Minds" campaign that had secret roots in the army, as I will show in the discussion of Ezuva as one of the projects designed for that purpose.

Division of Youth and Culture Affairs

A Division of Youth and Culture affairs was created within the department of education headed by Elrich Pretorius who was assisted by Robert Mupiri from 1974 onwards. Pretorius, a white Afrikaner who had come to work as a teacher in Kavango homeland was later promoted to senior officer in the Division of Youth and Culture Affairs. He had received some university training in Volkekunde[23] and was also the son-in-law of Louis Burger, secretary of education in Kavango.

Mupiri, a qualified teacher, was appointed as youth officer. However, he was not given a teaching post at a secondary school in his tribal district Gciriku as he wished, because of his refusal to take up the position of youth officer to which the administration appointed him[24]. He stayed in the Division for six months and resigned to join the radio service of Suid Wes Afrika Uitsending Korporasie (SWAUK) in Kavango.

The first youth camp was built in Mbunza and named after Hompa Leevi Hakusembe; however, the centre of activities moved to *Ekongoro,* which was built in Shambyu on the outskirts of Rundu and named after Hompa Maria Mwengere of the Vashambyu people.

Three camps were then constructed in Ukwangali (named after Hompa Kandjimi Hauanga) in Gciriku (named after Hompa Linus Shashipapo) and in Mbukushu (named after Hompa Frans Dimbare). It appears that these camps were given the names of the traditional homeland leaders to give them significance among the local inhabitants. District leaders responsible for camps in various traditional areas were recruited and trained to manage the camp environments in their respective districts. District leaders had to facilitate teacher training and workshops on the activities of the sangfees such as the composition of songs for a *sangbundel*[25] (song collection).

The winning groups[26] appeared at the finals at Ekongoro in Rundu. The songs in the *sangbundel* were the Kavango anthem, Christian hymns and choir songs. The *sangbun-*

---

[23] Personal communication with Elrich Pretorius at Maria Mwengere Culture Centre Rundu during 2008.
[24] Inteview with Robert Mupiri at Tutungeni, Rundu on 19 October 2008.
[25] NAR/1/55 File AP/7/1/1 Jaarverslag (Annual Report) 1978 Departement Van Onderwys- Kavango Regering.
[26] My wife was one of the school children who came to Ekongoro at the time; she recounted some of the events especially towards the final years of colonialism in Namibia.

del also incorporated so-called traditional songs,[27] which participants sang in order to get points. It was the duty of the state official at the four camps, under the leadership of Elrich Pretorius, to collect and record songs and stories about the inhabitants of Kavango from people in their surroundings. The intention was to have a collection of traditional songs, which represented and reflected the image and style of the five so-called tribes in Kavango. The camp organized, competitions in the five 'tribal areas' from which the best items would be selected for display in the museum[28].

In 1978 the Maria Mwengere Camp was upgraded to a fully-fledged culture centre with a museum, botanical garden, dormitories, kitchen and dining hall, administrative office block and a house for the senior youth officer. The centre was run by Elrich Pretorius[29]. It later served as a sanctuary to house injured wild animals such as lions, hyenas, birds and reptiles. An amphitheatre with about 300 seats was erected. A stage on wheels was used for the choirs. The museum[30] housed a collection of traditional artifacts such as fish traps, baskets, snakes found in the Kavango, milk containers and clothing. The Kavango museum never really opened to the public. Its collection[31] started to slowly disappear as local people borrowed items without returning them. The officer in charge of the museum during 2008 intimated to me that the change in management after the departure of Pretorius and a purported lack of interest among the staff members contributed to the gradual disintegration of the museum[32].

Staff at the various camps were requested by the head of the camp to suggest and advise how a traditional Kavango homestead was to be erected in the museum[33]. They drew up a plan to present a Kavango homestead with key aspects of the five tribal groupings to serve as a model of the traditional Kavango house or village. These artifacts were catalogued and

---

[27] The officials at the centre selected the type of songs to be performed and bound them into the *sangbundel*.
[28] I will expand this discussion in chapter 6.
[29] By the time the camp became operational, Robert Mupiri, Pretorius' assistant, had already left the division.
[30] There were other museums countrywide at the time, documented by Schildkrout (1995), in towns such as Tsumeb, Rehoboth, Windhoek and Swakopmund; their display narratives included landscapes, colonial economy, natural minerals and local histories of the early white settlers. Some had ethnographic exhibits showing the "traditional" African culture displayed either in the ethnographic present or in conjunction with the stone tools suggesting the ancient sub-strata of human occupation in various regions.
[31] Several items were borrowed by local teachers who used the artifacts as teaching aids at schools. A museum in the Netherland borrowed items for exchange from the museum during my stay of research at Maria Mwengere Culture Centre. As I left the centre, preparations were being made to ship the artifacts.
[32] My field notes.
[33] Interview with Linyando Manfred Mukoroli, joined by Kletus Muhena Likuwa at Safari, Rundu, 16 January 2009.

the oral narratives collected during research were summarized succinctly in booklet form to provide visitors with an abstract idea of Kavango culture. The culture book[34] as it is officially known today contained background stories of the origin and settlement patterns of the five tribal groupings of Kavango. It was produced by the culture officer at Ekongoro and the model continues to be used in postcolonial Kavango.

The centre was operated according to ten laws of Ekongoro.[35] This document also contains the emblem of Ekongoro, a brown eagle with its prey engraved in the homeland colour of green. Beneath the eagle and its prey was the motto: "upampi moyirugana yaKavango" which literally means (to be hard working and committed in/to the works of Kavango). The laws were printed in Afrikaans. I give the English translation below:

1. A member of Ekongoro is a believer
2. He supports law and order
3. He is always honest and sincere
4. He is friendly and willing to help
5. He is hardworking and economical
6. He is a lover of nature
7. He respects the elders
8. He honours his nation's culture
9. He takes his studies seriously
10. He is friendly.

Anyone who wanted to be part of the Ekongoro activities had to conform to these principles. The rules were written in a masculine form. The legislative directive, which was passed during the 1970s about the possible creation of a youth movement, ties in with the idea of producing civil servants, police officers and soldiers who were predominantly male at the time. One can safely argue that females were not yet readily recruited into the state services especially the police and the army[36]. Rules 7 and 8 can be read in connection to the deteriorating relations between traditional leaders and the young people at that time. With the

---

[34] The currentbooklet, unlike its predecessor, includes the Vanyemba and Vachokwe and the San groups which were previously excluded. I will present a detailed discussion of the culture booklet in chapter 6.
[35] See copy of Laws of Ekongongoro in Appendix.
[36] The young men were encouraged to join the South African army or the homeland police services. For example, see the advert shown in the quarterly newspaper of the Department of Education edited by Pretorius the chief of the Youth Division. See archive doc: NAR1/1/55 File JX/0256 KAVANGO ONDERWYSNUUS (1983 December)

above infrastructure in place, the centre was open to the public and indeed attracted many visitors. Parents could bring their younger children to Ekongoro for weekend outings. They were also taken on a museum tour especially during the early days of its existence. Through these and related activities Ekongoro was made attractive to all.

Sangfees at Ekongoro

The most important activity at the centre was the performance of traditional dances and songs at the annual sangfees. Participants were the winners from schools in various "tribal areas". The performances were held in the form of a competition. A circular[37] was sent round annually to schools and district leaders at various camps urging them to attend the sangfees and containing details of the compulsory song items. The finals were held in the amphitheatre of the Maria Mwengere youth camp. The gathering at the amphitheatre was always large.

The dance was performed on stage before judges and spectators. The main judge was always the chief[38] of the Ekongoro camp. He had powers to change the ruling if he disagreed with the ruling of other judges. The Minister of Education or any senior administrative official of the homeland addressed the gathering. Senior community members with expert knowledge of local tradition and culture were at times invited to judge. There was prize money for the winning group. This money was donated by the local business community and ranged from R350 to R1000. The prize money was not spent or shared among the group members, because it was seen to change the perception and purpose of participating in the event. People would then participate in cultural activities for gain and not for the love of culture.[39] This was an interesting contrast to the postcolonial context where people are encouraged to sell "their[40]" culture and heritage, as I will show in the following chapters. The pivotal role played by the Department of Education in Kavango in making and

---

[37] Every group would perform a compulsory hymn; they received the lyrics in advance to practice. A duet, quartet, a traditional song/dance and finally an open item were also on the list of items to be performed.
[38] The young Elrich Pretorius served as the main judge at Ekongoro during one of the sangfees gatherings.
[39] Interview with Jan Bradley, Tutungeni, Rundu, 20 September 2008.
[40] The postcolonial state promotes cultural tourism by granting concessionsto local people in order to improve their cultural trade. The Ministries of Education, and Environment and Tourism play a particular role in this exercise. Lodges owned by local people and the state invite traditional dancing groups to perform for their overseas visitors for a fee. The construction of a cultural village is envisaged in the Mbunza traditional authority with funding support from the Millennium Challenge Account to be locally known as Munyondo gwaKapande. Proceeds from this cultural village will be shared among the community members who are part of the project.

strengthening local ideas of belonging through its activities at Ekongoro were not limited to the sangfees, but also broadcast through the media such as a quarterly newspaper and local radio. The Department of Education and its Division of Youth managed to bring the people of Kavango together in the space created for the sangfees and used the festival space to assert the imagined Kavango-ness, which it had constructed through collecting the histories and oral narratives of the Kavango people.

This type of festival took place in other parts of South West Africa such as in the Caprivi and Ovamboland[41]. An event of a similar nature was held in Caprivi, dating back to 1966. Bennett Kangumu, a local historian and academic, reflected on similar culture festivals held in Caprivi in relation to their appeal against the creation of homelands and subsequent conflicts between the Mafwe and Masubia ethnic groups. (New Era, 2006) I refer to this long-standing conflict[42] when I deal with the making of the postcolonial festivals. However, the account below shows that public perception of the sangfees between the last colonial period and the dawn of Namibia's political independence had shifted due to the suspected complementary covert activities of *ezuva*[43]. In the following years, around the mid-1980s the sangfees at Ekongoro became unpopular among the local attendees, because of some activities the organizers included in the usual programme as narrated by my research informant and translated below:

> Mberema: The soldiers from 202 Battalion also came to the sangfees. That was a big question. I remember that in 1985 there were two items on the program of the sangfees. One was what used to be called a quartet or duet, I am not so sure. It was sung by one white soldier with two black others. If I remembered, I could have brought the tape I recorded so that you can listen to it. I recorded it on the cassette. Even my son Hunke likes to listen to that song whenever he got into my car. The other one was a troupe of real soldiers in uniform and they sang that song shosholoza. They had picks in their hands and other implements as they sang. They were also on the programme.
>
> Michael: Was that the time when people started to realize that there was something else in the festival?[44]
>
> Mberema: Ya, ya ya. That was when we realized that there was something hidden. The second thing we realized was as I just narrated the events of 1985, that there

---

[41] See my discussion in chapter four on the earlier works of Professor Bruwer and his role as colonial officer in the Ovamboland just after the implementation of the Odendaal Plan.

[42] This conflict may not be a definite cause of the postcolonial secession attempts in the Caprivi region, but did exert some influence on it.

[43] Ezuva is a local Rukwangali word for sun. Ezuva as a name was given to the youth movement created by the South African Defence Force.

[44] Interview with Mr. Karel Mberema Shiyaka, Maria Mwengere Culture Centre, Rundu, 23 September 2008.

was a list circulated in 1984 from the office of education that all school principals, inspectors and officials had to go to one place across the river near Andara. There was a camp at which they would be trained as para-military. They also attended a workshop themed: 'We are fighting for genuine freedom' (independence). It meant that the freedom we were being told by people across the river (SWAPO) was not a real one. Thus the slogan 'we are fighting for the genuine freedom was used'.

It shows us that although the colonial sangfees was organized along the theme "to preserve the culture and tradition of Kavango" it was actually a political space where communication between authorities and homeland citizens was expressed through performances. In this space, the authority transmitted its message of propaganda, which discredited the SWAPO movement in exile, whilst emphasizing the authority of the soldiers present at the sangfees. I think this was also an attempt for the state to show that its forces were friendly to local people and hence could participate in civil activities, unlike their counterparts in exile.

Despite the discontent on how the sangfees was organized and what was included on the programme in Kavango, it continued unabated until Elrich Pretorius left the homeland between 1985 and 1986. The uneasiness about the festival was brought about by the inclusion of the army in the sangfees and the calculated introduction of ezuva, which I discuss in detail shortly. According to Pretorius[45] there was tension between him the army chiefs and senior education administrators. He claims that this refusal led to his removal as head of the camp. Karel Shiyaka Mberema a local historian who was also an inspector in the Department of Education confirmed Pretorius's assertions of the disagreements between him and the authorities.[46]

Claims by locals with regard to Pretorius removal tell a different story. Local teachers, some of them now retired told me that many parents of pupils were against these cultural activities at Ekongoro because of the army's involvement. His successor who shared the same last name also left after a short stint at the camp. Major activities at the centre halted and theft of property was reported at the time when the camp lacked leadership.

Ezuva for the 'Youth'

During the 1980s the war of liberation intensified and the spirit of freedom and independence was heightened. The administration focused its attention on the young people and mobilized them to join a movement known locally as ezuva. Ezuva refers to the sun in

---
[45] Personal communication with Elrich Pretorius at Maria Mwengere Culture Centre during 2008.
[46] Interview with Mr. Karel Mberema Shiyaka, Maria Mwengere Culture Centre, Rundu, 23 September 2008.

Rukwangali, a local dialect. Ezuva is casually defined by local people as "mbunga za yeeyi yovadinkantu[47]". Ezuva as a movement ran workshops on 'culture' for teachers and the youth of Kavango.

The making and purpose of Ezuva as recorded in the local newspaper, Muruli Nuusblad Vir Kavango in 1986 is supposedly to promote youth and "culture"[48] as the following statements of the movement show: "Kry die jeug aan jou kant, dan het jy die hele wereld.[49]"(Get the youth on your side, and then you have the whole world.) "Ons die jeug van Kavango kies vrede[50]." ("We the youth of Kavango choose peace.")

Such statements[51] were used in the official propaganda media such as newspapers and local radio to make the young people aware of the imminent election and 'freedom', which was being negotiated at another level of administration, and to encourage them not to throw away what the state had already worked hard for. The usage of Afrikaans and the tone of the message in the documents of Ezuva are of particular interest in this context. It sounds very similar to the South African notion of "diens plig[52]" or "volk diens[53]" which targeted young males and compelled them to join the army in order to defend and serve the "nation". In South Africa, the state mobilized and instructed the young men about the importance of the nation and the need to protect and belong[54]. A similar approach seems to have been applied to South West Africa, but according to homeland specifications, thus the insertion: "We the youth of Kavango choose peace[55]."

Ezuva seems to have been sanctioned as an unwritten secret policy, because I could not find anything relating to the movement in any official colonial documents. Secrecy surrounding ezuva made it a sensitive issue among those who participated in its activities especially in the leadership positions. I was told in confidence that indeed the army was involved in the operations of ezuva, albeit in the background. Those who attended the ezuva camps near Andara confided in me that it was only when they were at the camps that they realized that the army was involved, because they facilitated the training and workshops. Teachers and students in the homeland were the primary focus of the movement.

---

[47] It directly translates as "the group of things for the youth".
[48] NAR/1/1/55 File JX-0257 MURULI NUUSBLAD VIR KAVANGO (January 1986)
[49] Interview with Karel Mberema Shiyaka, Maria Mwengere Culture Centre, Rundu, 23 September 2008.
[50] NAR/1/1/55 File JX-0257 MURULI NUUSBLAD VIR KAVANGO (December 1984)
[51] NAR/1/1/55 File JX-0257 MURULI NUUSBLAD VIR KAVANGO (January 1986)
[52] "Diens plig" is Afrikaans equivalent for "compulsory service".
[53] "Volk diens" is Afrikaans equivalent for "nation/national service"
[54] There are widespread websites about "diens plig' and "volk diens" with stories written by South African men who served in the South African army.
[55] NAR/1/1/55 File JX-0257 MURULI NUUSBLAD VIR KAVANGO (December 1984)

During my research, it was not easy to obtain information on ezuva. Searching through pictures in the local archive of the Ministry of Information in Rundu, I innocently asked the senior information officer whether he knew anything about ezuva. He denied knowledge about the activities of the movement and referred me to another person locally known to have been a member of ezuva. On another occasion while searching newspapers[56] about Kavango homeland in the national archive, to my surprise I came across a picture of the Kavango homeland executive committee of ezuva in which he is shown to have been the chairperson.

Because people who were in the local management of ezuva still do not feel at liberty to speak about it, I could only speculate that they fear victimization and the loss of their jobs should information about their activities become public. When I raised the matter with a former member of the Kavango Legislative Council, he was not willing to speak about it on record. However, he confirmed that the military personnel organized ezuva with the assistance of a psychologist from South Africa and the purpose was indeed to influence the youth to side with the activities of the state. Many people who participated in the activities of ezuva, especially those I spoke to, shared the details of their daily itinerary when they went on field trips. Participants went on field trips where they had bible readings, played hide and seek games in the bush while dressed in paramilitary uniforms. On the last day of the trip they were made to take an oath of allegiance to ezuva.

It is not clear how Ezuva and the Division of Youth cooperated, because there are no official records. However, local narratives about the activities of ezuva and Ekongoro sangfees appear intertwined and it is difficult to separate the two. Discontent among the local people in Kavango is claimed to have everything to do with the manner in which the sangfees was conducted during the 1980s and its murky relations with ezuva. Obviously the involvement of soldiers in the activities of Ekongoro and those of ezuva could be a factor in understanding the unhappiness of the local people.

Jan Bradley became the last senior administrator at Ekongoro during 1987. He did a lot of research in Kavango, which later shaped Maria Mwengere Culture Camp especially the reintroduction of a postcolonial cultural festival. He refers to himself as an ethnologist. When Jan Bradley took over at Ekongoro in 1987, the young people were no longer interested in singing choir songs or items other than performing 'traditional' dances. 202 Battalion members mostly performed the categories such as the choir, duet and quartet. This category was removed from the list of categories performing at the sangfees, because of the stigma it had as promotion for the soldiers. Instead Bradley spent most of his energy

---

[56] NAR/1/1/55 File JX-0257 MURULI NUUSBLAD VIR KAVANGO (January 1986)

and time on reviving the traditional dances and remobilizing people to participate, the task proved to be very difficult to implement especially when one takes the political context in to consideration[57].

There was mounting pressure from local people to stop the activities at Ekongoro that had been deliberately fused with those of ezuva and the army. The secrecy and lack of ownership of youth activities at the time make the whole issue about ezuva and the sangfees complex. The above events gave the activities of Ekongoro including the sangfees an unfavourable political status leading to its demise and eventual abolishment during the last years of political struggle. The role of the army participating in the sangfees was no longer viewed as that of a protector. I thus argue that the youth movement was systematically organized under the guise of song festivals and various workshops to counter SWAPO propaganda while supplying strategic human personnel for the administration such as the army and police. This newly created situation was seemingly a measure to curb the exodus of young people across the borders and joining SWAPO abroad. Although the sangfees was discontinued at independence, it was not long before it was reintroduced and reclaimed, albeit with a renewed meaning as Sam Nujoma attested below during our interview[58]

> I realized and saw already that our traditional cultures have been undermined and they were not even talked about. It was even prohibited, if the authority became aware that you spoke about issues dealing with Hendrik Witbooi, Maharero, Mandume or even Iipumbu yaTshilongo who fought the Boer administration, they could lock you up or even kill you. So I realized that we needed a Ministry that will deal with and develop our culture through doing research.

The interview excerpt shows claims to give new meaning to making a national narrative of the liberation history of Namibia and creating what could be viewed as a national culture of belonging. In this case, the state revived the culture festival, which would fill the void that was left by its predecessor, the sangfees. The postcolonial culture festival was not significantly different from the sangfees as a model. However, it has a different purpose and meaning.

Postcolonial Annual Culture Festivals

At independence festivals and all related activities which were seen to promote division or remind people of the country's ugly past were discontinued by the new national administration. However, five years into independence activities promoting ethnic identities such as

---

[57] Interview with Jan Bradley at Tutungeni 20 September 2008.
[58] Interview with Sam Nujoma, Office of the Founding President, Windhoek, 25 November 2009.

local traditional initiations, heritage tourism and festivals gained prominence in both the public sphere and official discourse. (Becker, 2004) There has been a trend in postcolonial African states to shun ethnicity, tradition and culture in the early periods of independence only to embrace them later in their quest for nation building. Tradition and culture were associated with backwardness and seen as an obstacle for progress; from the 1990s the situation changed. (Bayart, 2005; Eyoh, 1998)

These postcolonial festivals differ in conception and ideology. While both the colonial and postcolonial festivals were meant to preserve culture and heritage, under post-colonialism the hosting of the event signified "social cohesion and dialogue in the democratic process" as expressed by various many state representatives[59]. However, this is just the state discourse. In order to make sense of the making of the postcolonial festivals, as with the colonial ones, we need to clearly investigate the context in which they are made and the possible factors which may have influenced their making. In the Namibian context I pointed to the issue of secession attempts in two regions of the country that were in the making during the early years of independence. Later political events such as the need for the commemoration of heroes and development of the heritage industry, as suggested by Becker (2004, 2008, and 2011) and Fairweather (2001, 2006), may have influenced the recent culture festivals. Most importantly, I think it also reflects what people were saying in the media and in other social settings. In Namibia, the radio programs such as the national chat show in English, Ewi lya Manguluka[60] (Free Voice) and Mudukuli (Expose) are attempts by the national media to provide a platform for callers to express ideas about nation building and democracy. I suggest that the festival was introduced by the state to counter divisive tendencies. What is interesting is the manner in which ideas, previously deemed divisive, were now incorporated into the new national narrative of unity in diversity. This was a narrative that would tolerate and enhance ideas of diversity in a context of democracy.

Becker 2004 and 2007 shows that new developments in Namibia during the mid 1990s included the tentative embrace and references to local, traditional practices in contrast to their earlier reluctance to do so. Another aspect of her theory is, as the memory of the colonial regime's use of cultural difference began to wane, that debates over the values of the national and local community increasingly embraced notions of tradition and heritage. One

---

[59] Some of the recent statements made by the Minister of Youth and Culture at the institutional cultural festival (Polytechnic of Namibia), that "it is important to celebrate the diversity of our culture", New Era 09 August 2006.
[60] The two programs National Chat Show and Ewi lya Manguluka have been taken off air countless times as they were generally deemed by politicians and the public to spread ideas of tribalism and regionalism.

needs to look at the dynamics of global politics, such as the media and movement of people, as suggested by Appadurai 1996. Becker's report on the re-introduction of *efundula*[61] in northern former Ovamboland during the period 1995 and 1996 (screened on national television) is of particular importance in gaining an understanding of the postcolonial Namibian discourse of preserving tradition and culture. She has argued that the new national public discourse mirrored shifting local strategies. Local people began to speak about culture in various contexts. Appadurai and Ian Fairweather (2001) saw the inclusion and screening of the initiation ritual on TV, as well as regular regional and national cultural festivals organized by government, as a means to engender national unity through the incorporation of distinct local cultures. Fairweather (2001:4) has further argued that these nostalgic expressions are a response to the developing industry in cultural heritage.

The influence of the media and the movement of people in many forms such as refugees, expatriates and tourists may have led to an increasing consciousness of national identity developing among Namibians and their leaders. Several television productions from neighbouring regions such as Kabanana in Zambia screened on national TV in the early 1990s portrayed the pride of various characters that embraced their traditional way of life while settling in cosmopolitan areas. Another television production on national TV was a film from Ghana, which was given prominence in the local discourse of witchcraft. The sense of identity and pride portrayed by people who came to Namibia to work or visit could be one of the factors that may have contributed to the local desire for a national or individual identity. Appadurai (1996) has written about the influence of ethno and mediascapes in global networks and their operations that become socialized and localized through complex and deliberate practices of performances, representation and action. I argue that these complex and deliberate practices did not guarantee the sole role of the nation state in the politics.

In another context, Guss 2000 observed how transformed cultural landscapes in Venezuela focused on the reappearance and appropriation of what used to be contaminated visions of a primitive paradise, as alternatives to modernity. His insights are important in understanding the unexpected 'reclamation of culture' in postcolonial Namibia. Guss observed the celebration of San Juan, one of the oldest of all church festivals in Venezuela. Using concepts such as creolization (Hannerz 1992) and public culture (Appadurai 1996) he argued that forms of previously condemned behaviour, once released from the airtight environments said to have produced them, are now being granted new meanings and even more complex lives. These forms not only dissolve into the "market-driven global cultural

---

[61] Efundula is a female initiation ritual practiced in the northern regions of Namibia. The practice was discouraged during the early colonial time, especially by the missionaries as being evil and not in line with Christian teachings.

landscape, but enlarge its semantic fields, where meanings of the said forms are multiplied" (Guss 2000:4).

In Namibia, the postcolonial state introduced the Annual National Culture Festivals (ANCF) in 1995 which was produced by the directorate of National Heritage and Culture Programmes (NHCP). The directorate has culture offices led by senior culture officers in all thirteen regions of the country. In the context of Kavango, groups from the region participate in culture festivals both locally and internationally. However, in these festival contexts, groups were identified as Kavango groups and not as individuals. Their participation in the culture festival produced by the state has yielded countless trophies and accolades for the region. Due to these achievements and perhaps within the more general historical imagination of it being a backward and distinct area, the Kavango region has earned the reputation of being the true custodians of 'traditional culture' and being the 'hub of culture' in the country.

The NHCP invites groups that have excelled during the annual national culture festivals to participate in official engagements and international culture festivals. Groups from the Kavango region have participated in many such festivals especially outside the country because of their winning record in the national culture festivals. However, the outstanding performance of the region and its participation at the international level was not without its fair share of controversy with accusations of nepotism from officials at the directorate featured in the local media[62].

The Namibian post colonial situation cannot be understood in isolation from the global politics of difference and belonging, or ongoing contemporary politics of cultural difference and regionalism in Namibia[63]. Nor should the problems related to the politics of ethnicity on the African continent be ignored. These have, at times, resulted in situations where life and property were lost in conflicts fuelled with ethnic tensions. (Bayart, 2005; Geschiere, 2009)

I thus argue that the postcolonial reclaiming of tradition and culture by the state helps to enhance national identity and the idea of belonging. The postcolonial state realized the importance of tradition and culture as a crucial resource in carrying out its nationalism project.

Unlike colonial festivals and in addition to the current state-sponsored festivals, some cultural festivals are independently held in other regions of Namibia. These festivals are context driven and are shaped by local histories. In that context Kossler (2007) has argued that the mnemoscape on a national scale is fragmented and memorialization practices differ

---

[62] See Informante newspaper 11 February 2010. Complaints were also aired on the national radio program the 9th hour. The radio program is a phone-in program on topical issues.
[63] After a decade and half of Namibian independence a new wave of political parties emerged from various regions in the country. A party was also formed in Kavango region. Most of the parties were denounced by the ruling Swapo Party as promoting regionalism and tribalism.

between those that are state sponsored and those that are not. He further argues that among other memorial activities, annual celebrations or festivals are of particular importance as they take cues from key events such as colonial wars and the resilience of Namibian communities. These festivals are independently organized, but may be supported by the state in many ways, albeit not in monetary terms.

Amongst the festivals held in Namibia, the Witbooi Festival at Gibeon in the south-central Hardap region, the /Ae //Gams Festival in the capital Windhoek, the Damara Annual Cultural Festival in Erongo in the western part of the country, the well-known annual commemorations of the Herero Otjiserandu ('troop players') at Okahandja and the Lusata in Caprivi region are some of the commonly held festivals. The Herero Otjiserandu was a social space in which to express nationalist aspirations and commemorate the homecoming of the late Samuel Maharero, chief of the Vaherero since 1924, while the Witbooi festivals commemorate the death of Nama chief Kaptein Hendrik Witbooi who was killed by German soldiers during the Nama-Herero uprising of 1905. (Dierks, 2003)

The University of Namibia, Polytechnic of Namibia and various teachers colleges[64] hold annual culture festivals. These are about showcasing 'culture' and are seemingly held to create diversity awareness among students at tertiary institutions. This awareness is not only focused on the local diversity, it includes international associations. (Polynews, 2011) For the purpose of this discussion I briefly detail the making of the two festivals, namely the /Ae//Gams Festival and The Witbooi Festival.

Since 2001 the /Ae //Gams Festival[65] has been organized and sponsored by the City of Windhoek in conjunction with the private sector. This weeklong festival, dubbed "a tourist gaze" by the City of Windhoek, takes place during the month September, which is officially the beginning of the tourist season in Namibia[66]. Besides inviting local culture groups and artists to showcase their talent to the tourists and local people, international culture groups are also invited to participate. The festival provides a panoramic view of Namibian cultures creating an identity for tourists that they can expect to encounter during their visit. Usually the head of state or the prime minister officiates during the launch of event.

The Witbooi festival is held annually during November at Gibeon. This historic event can be traced back to the 1930s. (Kossler, 2003) The Khowesen traditional authority, which constitutes the Witbooi clan, together with other stakeholders, organize the festival. The event is held to celebrate the heroic deeds (and death) of the Nama Kaptein Hendrik Wit-

---

[64] All the teachers colleges have since been incorporated into the University of Namibia.
[65] Interview with Selma Negumbo the tourism officer at the centre of tourism, City of Windhoek in September 2008
[66] Interview with Selma Negumbo at City of Windhoek 29 October 2008.

booi against the early colonial settlers in the area. The event is characterized by horse riders wearing hats covered in a white cloth to symbolize the officially adopted image of Kaptein Hendrik Witbooi. The march consisted of the national police and military brass band, the vehicle carrying the Chief Hendrik Witbooi and horse riders. The sister of the chief narrates the history of the Khowesen. Water is taken from the fountain and shared among the people who are gathered to symbolize its founding by the predecessors. This festival is an elaborate one; it begins on Friday at the gathering at the fountain and ends with a church service on Sunday. The Witbooi festival presents a local narrative of heroic resistance against the colonial German authority. This gathering can be interpreted as an extended celebration of heroes that are nationally observed, but in this context it is given a local meaning and perspective. Kossler 2007 argues that although the Witbooi festival is a clearly marked occasion, the voiced concerns of the community transcend to the leadership. In the process the leadership attempts to address problems of land reform and restitution of communal land.

I use Stuart Hall's (1996) perspective of new times and Guss' (2000) investigation of the San Juan celebration to explain the above unexpected introduction and shape of various culture festivals within a changing political era. This introduction of state-sponsored culture festivals should be interpreted as a new time where social and political changes shape the material and cultural conditions of existence including the context in which they occur. Colonially invented culture festivals are re-appropriated and old notions such as protecting the native and his culture, which placed Africans in a backward position, are given fresher perspectives of modernity through the reinvention of tradition, and development of ownership.

In Kavango specifically it appears that the reintroduction of the postcolonial culture festival opened a space of local intra-identity assertion and contestation. This emerging identity contestation is what locates the region within the national body politic. Kavango participated in all the Annual National Culture Festivals, winning on three occasions. The Kavango region has on many occasions represented Namibia at various international events. Such outstanding performance led to the region being seen by other people especially through the media, as a cultural hub where culture is properly preserved and showcased.

I argue that at a local level the postcolonial culture festival creates a space for the making and remaking of new ideas of belonging and differentiation through performance. Local identities that were initially suppressed during colonial Kavango have started to emerge. At present we see how various identities that were previously officially recognized become contested and given new meanings in this new space. The constitution guarantees the right of expression and association and has in this way opened new spaces where such identities are asserted and expressed. One example is the unexpected assertion and awareness of the Nyemba identity, which did not have a place in the public sphere after the implementation of the Odendaal Commission and throughout the colonial occupation. Another is the envisaged construction of the Cultural Village at Kapako in Mbunza traditional area, initiated by a group of young people with the aim of creating employment in the constituency and showcasing the culture and tradition of the Vambunza in Kavango. (New Era, 2010)

During the early phase of my research there were various public debates in the local radio about the need to introduce Runyemba[67] as a language in the education curriculum. The above instance was coupled with a demand from some Vanyemba headmen who serve under Hompa Matumbo Ribebe of Vashambyu that they be allowed to have their own hompa. These demands were not favourably received especially by the Shambyu Traditional Authority, which removed the entire Vanyemba headmen as a result. The bone of contention was how they could demand a chief if they did not even own land in Kavango. Although oral historical sources show that the Vanyemba were believed to have migrated from several areas in Southern Angola into Kavango but for various reasons[68] they are not recognized as 'real' locals. These and related issues are germane to my study.

Currently, there are clear signs of the development of a Nyemba awareness on Face Book, the social network site. A group of young Nyemba adults have created a network on Face Book called "Vanyemba Vangangela[69]" which has attracted many followers previously condemned. On this site there is brief information about the Vanyemba which is rather academic in nature. It would be interesting to find out the source from which they derive information. Conversations on this network are of a general nature and vary from topic to topic. Although the writing is in Runyemba, it is significantly fused with English and Afrikaans terms, which are appropriated as slang in the language. I have discussed this tendency elsewhere, where I have demonstrated how the young people in the History Club of Rundu Senior Secondary School switched and coded their language with English and Afrikaans. (Akuupa 2006) The contact details and information about the head office is said to be Kaisosi in Rundu. The Kaisosi settlement in Rundu is locally believed to be dominantly inhabited by the Vanyemba. It is situated in eastern Rundu not very far from the University of the Namibia Rundu Campus. At the time of her study in 1991, Brinkman suggests the total population of Kaisosi to be about 4855, with 50% counted as Nyemba.

Interestingly, Brinkman (1991) has classified the population group in question into two categories namely: *vandambo* (familiar) and *vatywayuki* (refugees). Those who are believed

---

[67] Runyemba is a generic word to refer to the languages spoken by the Vanyemba people.
[68] I have elaborated the issue of migration including the Vanyemba in detail in chapter 4.
[69] I thank Kletus Muhena Likuwa for alerting me to this face book platform.

to have settled along the Kavango River and came across for longer periods before they migrated to the Namibian side, are referred to as vandambo while those who came to settle in Kavango during the war in Angola are referred to as vatywayuki. I take issue with her, because the notion of *vandambo* or *undambo* of Vanyemba cannot only be read in terms of the period of the war. The Vanyemba and other groups in Kavango have been living in the Mbunda area long before they came to settle along the river[70]. The area north of Kavango River, which stretches from western Kavango until Mbukushu going northwards, is known as the Mbunda area or Limbaranda by the Kavango people. Hompa Maria Mwengere, for example, often visited her relatives in Limbaranda, the place they initially settled before moving southwards and eventually crossing the Kavango River. Those who are likely to be classified as vatywayuki are the Vimbundu who are not known to even share the same historical origin as Kavango people, including the Vanyemba. These are people who formed part of the unforeseen exodus and who arrived at the river banks in 1975 after the outbreak of the civil war in Angola. I refer to the exodus as unforeseen because, despite numerous measures which the Portuguese authorities and their southern counterparts had in place to control movement of people, it came as a surprise[71]. However, the South West African authorities moved these refugees to a camp outside Rundu in order to prevent their assimilation with the local inhabitants.

Another perspective on the complex issue of the Vanyemba as *vandambo* or *vatywayuki* is to use the local notion of othering: *ugeni*. *Ugeni* can be literally translated as stranger, and he or she who is regarded as a stranger in local terms is *mugeni* (singular) or *vageni* (plural). I would view differentiation in Kavango in the context of *ugeni* especially when it is directed at the Vanyemba. Bearing Brinkmann's perspective in mind, the Vanyemba are not necessarily seen as *vatywayuki*, but as *vageni* as they have not run or fled persecution as is the case of those who would be referred to as *vatywayuki*, who fled in order to settle in Kavango. They are and have always been part of those perceived as 'real' Vakavango since time immemorial but, despite their shared history, have always been regarded as strangers. This differentiation, therefore, has to be understood within the various historical contexts through which the Vanyemba together with other groups in Kavango have lived. Generally, it seems that the people in Kavango settled on either side of the river. They would cross the river because of a dispute in a family and community and return later when the situation had stabilized. Sometimes people crossed the river to seek grazing for their animals. There is also a long history of intermarriage between the Vanyemba who stayed along the river and the people on the south of the river, as a result of which kinship ties developed on both

---

[70] Interview with Shidonankuru at Ndiyona 24 December 2006.
[71] NAR/1/155

sides of the river. As a result of this intricate relationship, one cannot neatly distinguish who is a Nyemba and who is not.

The above discussion demonstrates that the importance of asserting identity in any political process. During colonial South West Africa, the administration of the time emphasized various ethnic identities as distinct and united them against others. In the process they invented the sangfees as a space where people could display their distinct identity. Through the principle of divide and rule this political process was successful in its own way, especially by synthesizing difference and the sense of belonging to various ethnic groups. This project was invented in line with the early recommendations of separate development i.e. the creation of Bantustans or homelands and closely guided by the Odendaal Commission of 1962-1963. The subsequent creation of the homeland state and its machinery strengthened and legitimated the imagined Kavango identity, which seemed to differ from other ethnic groups in South West Africa. In order to realize their objectives, the South African colonial administration organized the sangfees as a social space through which it could easily construct the colonial idea of Kavango-ness. Although the sangfees was organized and intended for the youth and protection of traditional cultures, it impacted on the wider population of the region in various ways, especially on the contestation of Kavango-ness during the postcolonial period.

To a certain extent this 'colonial unity' became the bedrock from which contemporary identities have sprung and are now asserted and negotiated in Namibia. Finally, I argue that the sangfees tradition is a colonial invention that was later re-invented with new meanings in postcolonial Namibia in order to contribute to the national discourse of unity in diversity. In the following chapter, I present and discuss the ethnography of the museum at Maria Mwengere Culture Centre in Kavango. I pay attention to the postcolonial festival booklet as produced by the state and the subsequent national dialogue and narrative as they reverberated through song.

6 Kavango Cultural Identity in Postcolonial Namibia

Reclaiming Colonial Ethnicity in a Postcolonial Context

In this chapter I present the ethnography of Maria Mwengere Culture Center with specific focus on the Kavango Museum as a space in which local culture in Kavango is officially appropriated and produced in the postcolonial context. In this context I pay particular attention to the management of the museum at the centre and the perceptions of culture officials of the capacity of the museum to produce and transmit local 'culture' in the region.

I analyze the concept of the state commissioning the postcolonial culture booklet (which is presented during the culture festival to the judges and festival participants) and its content. During the circuit, regional and national festival rounds, officials who are responsible for culture programs nationwide encourage festival participants to produce and compile booklets in which they present their culture and tradition from their own perspective. Participants in various groups prepare their booklets, especially during the circuit and regional festival contexts, and material presented by the groups that qualify for the national level is officially compiled in a single master narrative.

In his exploration of nationalist discourse in Quebec, Canada, Handler 1988 concluded that fairs and festivals contain modes of objectification. Elements of what is perceived to be culture are treated as indicators of identity. When such indicators are absent in what is represented or imagined as culture, it becomes contested. (see chapter 8) In the following discussion I present incidents that I argue to be modes of objectification (to borrow from Handler). Specifically, I am interested in what began as a colonial project to represent the inhabitants of Kavango and later appropriated during the postcolonial period and represented in what is now officially termed a "culture booklet" at the Maria Mwengere Culture Centre[1] as an attempt by the state to create post apartheid nationhood. The culture booklet, that the Namibian state inherited from the colonial dispensation, has become an important means and resource through which it re-imagines colonial identities and, by contrast, emphasizes an ethnicized Namibian-ness. I argue that although the state is involved in the production of national identity through projects such as museums, heritage hunts and the construction of culture villages, it does not operate in isolation from its citizens. Heritage in contemporary Namibia is understood as that which "connects us" to the past (i.e. prior to successive

---

[1] The Maria Mwengere Culture Centre was initially known as the Maria Mwengere Culture Camp or Ekongoro. The name has since been changed, however local people continue to refer to it as Ekongoro.

occupations by South Africa, Britain and Germany); it incorporates tangible and intangible cultural materials.

The museum at Maria Mwengere Culture Center is not open to the public. Officially, the museum and its culture booklet are believed to store and preserve the cultures of Kavango people. The format, content and the changing nature of the culture booklet and the museum activities are central to my analysis in this chapter. The ability and extent to which citizens (participants and public audiences) were involved in representing and interpreting national culture from their perspective while making the culture booklet was interesting. While festival participants represented and interpreted their culture and tradition through songs and drama in the booklet, content in song and drama shows that at least to a certain extent participants presented their culture as evolving and not fixed as represented in the museum narrative.

The dance and melody is essentialized in concept, while song content is constructionist in approach. The content of the songs and drama is also of an advocacy nature. As I have observed, the focus of songs composed and sung by the cultural groups are context-driven. Thus the content of songs differed significantly from one area to another in the region, and in the national context. Participating groups know that through representation of song, dance or drama they create awareness, caution, advocate, praise and criticism through that particular medium. I argue that while the people and their culture are imagined as fixed by the state in the context of museum representation, participants in the festival not only view the culture booklet as an object in which local identity is asserted, but also as a space for dialogue specifically directed at those who represent the state and the general audience.

Earlier studies on the perceptions and production of national cultures in postcolonial Africa (Flint 2006, Askew 2000 and Van Binsbergen 1994) have demonstrated how the state participates in what is perceived to be the production of national culture in postcolonial Africa. Such participation in the production of national culture is realized in the form of sponsorship of cultural troupes, organizing arts performances and competitions. While these authors generally argue that such participation of the state entails the production of national culture, Van Binsbergen 1994, in his investigation of the Kazanga Festival in Central Western Zambia, argues that such demonstrations should be seen as instances in which cultural reconstruction with emphasis on ethnicity radically transform local historical cultural forms towards a global idiom of performance, inequality and possibly the commodification or folklorisation of culture. Contrary to Van Binsbergen's argument on ethnicity as cultural mediation and social transformation, Flint's focus on the Kuomboka Festival in Western Zambia presents a different set of dynamics displaying inner ethnic contradictions and challenges in representation of the past history and heritage of the Lozi people. Although the above two festivals are locally organized by the traditional chiefs and people, they have attracted the state's attention in the processes of culture "retrieval" (Sonyika, 1990:114) and this has since influenced such activities.

Askew 2002 through her documentation and analysis of specific dances organized under the auspices of the National Arts and Language Competitions in Tanzania shows how the state and public produce and display national culture. She recorded and explained the contexts of the various songs and dances of the groups she observed in different social spaces outside the orbit of the state, such as weddings. However, her analysis emphasizes the role and dynamics of state involvement in production of the dances and the music productions, rather than the public. Askew, unlike Van Binsbergen 1994 who brings out a nuanced analysis of ethnicity politics of Zambia mentions how the dances assert ethnic identities in support of state nationalist projects. He has shown how the festival attendees influenced the making of the Kazanga Festival through their specific participation in the event. In the section below I discuss the perceptions of the state agencies on how it (the state) not only produces an imagined national culture for its citizens, but also participates in the assertion of ethnicity through the production of the culture booklet and other activities, for example the museum.

On the Search for 'Tradition' and 'Culture' in Namibia

During their first five-year term the Namibian government embarked on a national awareness campaign to preserve and promote tradition and culture. Through the medium of television, the state-funded Namibian Broadcasting Corporation (NBC) aired traditional weddings, dances and food in culture magazines such as Tutaleni[2], Boma Namibia, Kalanami and more recently Culture Paradise. During the 2008 Annual National Culture Festival in Kavango the production team of Culture Paradise was there to record the proceedings. The producer explained:

> It is important for people to know who the Kavango or the Ovambo are. And this we can make possible when we record such activities and ask elders to explain certain things such as clothing, utensils and rituals[3]"

The producer[4] Kandali Nangolo, described how the production team followed culture festivals country-wide in order to collect material.

---

[2] Tutaleni means "Let us see".
[3] Personal communication with Kandali Nangolo at the Annual National Culture Festival held in Kavango during 2008 December.
[4] My fieldwork notes.

On radio, three hours are scheduled daily to "feature aspects of Namibian culture with the aim of promoting the national ideal of unity in diversity and thus the ultimate object of building a One Namibia, One Nation[5]." Producers invite people deemed knowledgeable on 'traditional' subjects such as birth, burial and wedding rituals; and interview them live on radio. During these discussions local culture is mostly presented as fixed. These programs though, do not give a platform to the audience to call in and participate in the discussion. The above intentions of the national broadcaster are evidently similar to those expressed in the national culture policy, which came out in 2001- as discussed in chapters four and five.

The above quote by Nangolo, an employee of the national broadcaster, can be understood in the context in which cultural characteristics supposedly mark the distinctive "differences" of population groups in Namibia. (Akuupa, 2010:103) Her assertions imply that traditional culture as recorded at the festival is essential and fixed. The search and promotion of Namibian tradition and culture by the state is not only limited to radio and television programmes, it is implemented through directorates in the Ministry of Youth, National Service, Sport and Culture (MYNSC). The two directorates, namely those of Arts and National Heritage and Culture Programmes are responsible for matters related to art and heritage. The directorates have established offices in the thirteen regions of the country.

MYNSC not only organizes culture festivals it supports a project known as the Heritage Hunt implemented by the Museum Association of Namibia (MAN). MAN receives funding from the state to run and facilitate museum projects nationally. One of these is the "heritage hunt" campaign, which identifies sites and graves to be turned into national memorial monuments. In this project MAN has successfully utilized history students to form clubs at high schools nationally and do research on heritage sites through a competition known as SCAM-X (School and Museum Exhibition).

In Kavango the history club under the mentorship of Kletus Likuwa was selected to participate during 2007. Their exhibition portrayed cultural and memorial sites and unknown graves of SWAPO fighters in the region. The group took pictures of unmarked Swapo resting places in the area of Mbukushu in eastern Kavango that had been pointed out by local people in the area, as well as early colonial landmarks, such as the official house-cum-office of native commissioner, Harold Eedes.

Regional governments have also, at times, encouraged people to embark on a "heritage hunt" for sites to be included in the government gazette and marketed for human development. I suggest this should read "cultural tourism", which has become a favoured economic

---

[5] Namibia Broadcasting Corporation: National Radio Grid 2010 obtained from www.nbc.om.na 2011/08/11.

activity of the national state. Its potential to generate income for the communities has been recognized by the state and resulted in such initiatives in its media marketing campaigns. As the governor of the Kavango region said in his speech at the Kavango Regional Culture festival:

> Finally, ladies and gentleman I would like to use the opportunity to call upon the Directorate of National Heritage and Culture Programs to identify important heritage and cultural sites in Kavango particularly and Namibia in general for the fulfillment of the culture policy. Culture and heritage should be regarded as an important aspect in human development; we want to see a nation that is proud of its culture, a nation that has identity and promotes its culture.[6]

The call by the regional governor of Kavango shows how heritage hunting at the regional context is emphasized for the purpose of enhancing a regional ethnic identity, which I have referred to earlier as Kavango-ness. The narrative shows how the national state has embarked on a well-devised national project of cultural awareness through strategic projects at schools, exhibitions, festivals, radio and television broadcasts. However, as I have observed throughout my fieldwork, such official pronouncements on how to preserve culture and tradition are appropriated variously in all thirteen political regions. It depends on those who officiate during the festivals, judging from the content of speeches[7].

Kavango Museum

The Kavango Museum was never opened to the public. Many people I have spoken to have not even bothered to find out where the museum is situated although they may have heard that it is at Ekongoro. My observation during my stay at Maria Mwengere Culture Centre was that the museum was not regarded as the best tool to promote and perhaps brand local cultures. Below I discuss how the culture policy of the state privileged traditional dances devised for and performed at the festival rather than develop the museum.

I met with Thomas Shapi, the senior culture officer at the Centre who introduced me to his colleagues. Shapi outlined the projects at the centre in the following manner:

> Shapi: Mr. Akuupa, we have a lot of things going at our centre. We have a project of collecting stories about our traditional rituals in the community. It has been quiet for some time now, because we are very busy with other things such as the festivals and meetings. We are doing research so that we can assist our groups in the festival with

---
[6] Speech by John Thighuru the Regional Governor of Kavango Region, delivered during the Kavango Regional Culture Festival held at Maria Mwengere Culture Centre in Rundu during 13 September 2008.
[7] See my discussion in chapters 7 and 8.

information for their presentations. We also have a museum that has never opened to date. We need someone to assist the official responsible for the museum. I do not know what is happening with those senior people in the ministry, because they keep on promising that they will hire somebody to run the museum and that is still to be seen. Myself, I am very busy with many other things, but I will support any idea related to the museum. So see in which area you can also assist us. Mrs. Kazanga you are responsible for the museum, you can ask Mr. Akuupa to help you in what he can. If you want to collect stories about the rituals you can just request for a car and a driver so that you can be taken there to do interviews. We can think of how we can sort out other issues such as the S&T for the driver. Donaveltha, ask Saraphina to clean that other office for Mr. Akuupa[8].

My immediate impression of the environment was that this was a good place to work, because of the senior officer's approach and description of the centre activities. I was welcomed wholeheartedly and there was a clear sense of direction at the centre. From my understanding of the statement by the senior culture officer, he implied that my services would be required in the dealings of the museum and collection of oral narratives in the villages.

After the meeting was adjourned, Valesca (Mrs. Kazanga) convened another meeting in her office so that we could deliberate on how to get the museum off the ground. Valesca is a qualified teacher who has since left her teaching job to take up employment in the directorate. She told me on one occasion[9] that it was because of her love for traditional dances that she decided to join the NCHP directorate. She is a member and leader of a cultural group Tukulikeni[10], which performs in the youth category. She is not a qualified museum curator but has attended various workshops on museum management, organized by MAN.

The museum building was in a dilapidated state. At the entrance was a box full of cards used to catalogue the artifacts inside the building. As you entered on the immediate left you saw dirty display glasses with few artifacts such as bottled snakes found in Kavango, *marudeve*[11] and *vihiho*[12]. On the right hand side, there is an elevated space made of cement and covered with sand. This space formed a large part of the building area and was where the envisaged traditional Kavango homestead[13] was planned but never constructed. Instead other artifacts such as fish traps, pestle and mortars, milk containers, baskets, wood, countless clay pots, calabashes, reed mats, storage containers, chicken containers, bows and

---

[8] My fieldwork notes
[9] My fieldwork notes.
[10] Tukulikeni is a Rukwangali expression for 'lets grow' in the literal sense.
[11] Marudeve (sing: rudeve) is clothing made of reeds which grow along the Kavango River. The reeds are cut into pieces and joined together with a string and tied around the waist like a skirt.
[12] Vihiho (sing: sihiho) is a form of female headgear. It is a long snarl that hangs down to the female's shoulders and is made of tree inner bark.
[13] See my discussion in the previous chapter with Linyando Manfred Mukoroli.

arrows, hoes, and spirit distillers were arranged according to type on the sand floor. I also noted objects that were important during the homeland administration, namely the mace and pulpit although in a broken state. However, these artifacts were very dusty since no one was willing to go and clean inside as one of the cleaning staff intimated to me. She told me that the place was too frightening to work in it[14].

The museum was conceived to be part of the Centre (then only a camp) during its construction the late 1970s. It was a move which would encourage people to protect and know their tradition and cultures. This would then create and emphasize ideas and feelings of distinctness among the inhabitants of the homeland[15]. The ideology of the time was to present museum artifacts as fixed traditional reference points as stated in the homeland culture policy. The idea behind the intention of one day having the museum open seemed to be the same as the colonial one as Valesca expressed once that: "if the museum opens, people will be able to see and know the Vakavango tradition[16]."

The museum was not affiliated to the Museum Association of Namibia (MAN) an umbrella body that assists various other museums with resources and the training of personnel. Valesca wanted us to request funding from the directorate so that we could register the museum with MAN. She also suggested a regional drive to procure items for the collection because insects were gradually damaging the existing collection.

We finally drafted a submission letter to the office of the Director of the NHCP, Dr. Diaz to inform him of the intent to open the museum to public and requested the N$200.00 fee required to register the museum with MAN and possible renovation of the building. The senior culture officer who signed the letter appeared skeptical about our efforts. We revived the former local board of governors of the museum so that they could continue the project. Despite the two or three meetings we had with the board on how to proceed, they too appeared skeptical as to whether this attempt would get the museum off the ground.

For a month we did not receive any response to our submission to head office. Valesca was not happy at all as she complained on the way to her office:

> I knew the director was never interested in the museum, he just said I should call the deputy director at the office of national museums as they are the ones to deal with museums. I don't know what it is lacking, this museum belongs to Maria Mwengere and it does not fall under the jurisdiction of national museums. They must give us the money.[17]

---

[14] My fieldwork notes.
[15] See my discussion in chapter four and five.
[16] My fieldwork notes.
[17] My fieldwork notes

From the report that Valesca gave me it appeared as if there was no clear indication of jurisdiction over the museum. In my personal interaction with the director of NHCP, he had told me that the museum was to be treated like any other in the country and that it should benefit from the Museum Association of Namibia (MAN). MAN receives funding from government in order to "build capacity[18]" in museum management nationally. The impression from my communication[19] with the director was that the museum in Kavango should benefit from MAN since his ministry provided financial support to it. However, the question of it being an independent entity like other museums in the country or a part of the centre seemed to be one of the issues forestalling its operation. At present it seems no one at higher management level is willing to take responsibility for the museum, let alone the centre.

The museum story did not end there. I suggested that we focus on the Museum Association of Namibia. Two executive members in the MAN committee namely the Vice Chair Aaron Nambadi and voting executive Kletus Likuwa are residents of Kavango. My informal e-mail conversation with Nambadi follows:

> Q: Another question since you are in an influential position now: what can you do for the region's museum?
>
> A: My friend, there are only two problems with the regional museum first, the officials and the politics of that house (office). Secondly the requirements for the positions are higher in relation to remuneration
>
> Q: I know. Can you arrange for some funding then and probably get someone who can train those officials?
>
> A: Yes I can, but take note that MAN has already contributed N$40 000 for two Planning Workshops, so it will be difficult to ask them again, but it is possible. What do you think of the Kavango Museum; I'm sure you spent some time in the Kavango and what is your input, especially with the senior officer?[20]

My interaction with the vice-chair of the museum association, albeit in various contexts did not yield the required results. The two executives also sounded discouraged by the unresponsiveness of the centre's management. No action had been taken after the two workshops Nambadi referred to. One of the major aspects of the workshop was to train the curator on how to manage the museum and catalogue artifacts. It appears there was no officially appointed curator at the time, so no one could implement what was offered at the workshop. For the rest of my time at the centre the museum was not registered with MAN, as there was no N$200 forthcoming from the directorate. Although the centre collected money through

---

[18] MAN- Three Year Development Plan 2009.
[19] My fieldwork notes
[20] Electronic mail communication with the Vice Chair of MAN on 19 October 2009.

various services it rendered to the community, it seemed the senior official was not keen to part with money and always referred the museum official to the over-elaborate standing orders for utilizing state funds. Despite the above obstacles, Valesca has been determined to make the museum work, as demonstrated below.

In one of our meetings[21] we resolved to have the Kavango traditional homestead constructed in its initially intended space at the museum. The matter was brought up during the second last preparatory meeting[22] for the festival. It was presented for discussion but received scant attention. Valesca was eventually given only enough money to complete two homesteads.

After two months at the office, I requested permission to do interviews in the two villages in the east. The senior culture officer instructed his driver to take me to the villages, but not without adding what I should not forget to ask.

"Shapi: Mr. Akuupa, do not forget to ask about the rituals as well.

Michael: Ok, sure! But which rituals specifically?[23]"

Shapi's main emphasis was on research and anthology and not really the museum.

When regional culture festivals have taken place and participants to the nationals are confirmed, some officials go out on field trips to visit and coach various culture groups. They meet with the groups during their rehearsals and explain to them what is expected of them, how they should keep time and prepare their aids during presentations. Such trips do not encounter funding objections as do the museum's requests. Even my request was granted subject to a reminder of what the centre needed most from my short trips.

The accounts above show the bureaucratic dealings with regard to the museum and the perception of the officials at Maria Mwengere Culture Centre of what seemed to brand best in the context of production, preservation and display of local tradition and culture. The focus of the discussion was more on the state officials as there was seemingly no resident involvement noted in the affairs of the museum except that of the dormant board. It is evident from the observations above that although state representatives and agencies advocate for museums to be treated as a method of preserving culture, various local offices might prefer other methods that supposedly brand better. Schildkrout 1995 argues that museums in Africa have only played a minor role in defining national identity and, unlike festival attendance, visiting museums is not a "ritual of citizenship" as it has been for a long time in

---

[21] My fieldwork notes
[22] Minutes dated 10 November 2008: The 14th Annual National Culture Festival Preparation Committee meeting held at Maria Mwengere Culture Centre.
[23] My fieldwork notes

Europe and the United States. Nevertheless, new postcolonial African countries continue to use museums to make politically useful memories within the context of the state and the above accounts are just some of the many struggles museums in Africa encounter in the construction of national identity and culture.

Few local people in Rundu and at the centre speak about the museum and the need to utilize it as a tool to conserve their much-discussed 'culture'. When the official responsible for the museum requested money to buy something, she was told many stories about lack of money even though the centre operates on a sufficient cash flow generated by other means. In fact the ministry[24] had previously tried to recruit a museum curator, but had not been successful as there are very few curators in Namibia and the salary was low compared to other museums nationally. Towards the end of last year after the salary structure was improved did they finally appoint a curator, Helvi Mbwalala. Mbwalala is a university graduate whose major subjects were in tourism. Her immediate plan was to have the museum building renovated before embarking on the restoration and collection of new artifacts. However, when I visited the centre this year during the July holidays, she faced the same difficulties that Valesca had encountered.

The above issues are complex, and it will be perhaps uncritical to refer to them as problems or the 'struggle' involved in museum development in Kavango as Schildkrout 1995 does. Museums in other parts of the country flourish, especially in the northern regions such as the Nakambale run by the Lutheran church, in Kavango. It seems that privately run museums do better than those for which the state is responsible. This can perhaps be attributed to the marketing and public relations strategy used by private museums. There are two fully- fledged museums in the Oshikoto region, at Olukonda and Tsumeb. Neither museum belongs to the state. These museums have become strategic economic resources for those locals with an interest in such initiatives. These initiatives seem to be informed by a fast-emerging cultural tourism industry reinforced by the state discourse of social development.

I argued earlier that a museum is perceived by officials and may be local townspeople to be ineffective in promoting and preserving local culture and tradition. This is confirmed by what I call the 'cold relations' between the leadership and officials of the Maria Mwengere Culture Centre and the national association of museums. However, I can take it further and say that the lack of interest in the Kavango museum also expresses the desire not to reclaim the legacy of local colonial history. The situation should thus be viewed as a subtle revolt against the colonial history by those who ran the centre.

---

[24] In 2006 when I was still busy studying for a Masters degree at the University of the Western Cape, Shapi asked me informally whether I was not interested in that position.

Maria Mwengere Culture Centre: 'The Culture Booklet: An Instrument of Objectification'

The idea of the booklet emerged during the colonial South West Africa period, when it was commonly held that the culture of the native should be captured and stored in museums for ethnographic presentations, and the tourist gaze and finally for the production of colonial unity. The relation between the museum and the culture booklet needs to be understood in the context of homeland politics and the Odendaal initiative, which in turn was influenced by Volkekunde studies. Volkekunde emphasized the distinctness and retribalisation of the native. (Olivier 1961, Bosch 1964 and Van Tonder 1966). Thus the collection of so-called traditional artifacts in the museum and recording thereof was seen by the state as a way to preserve the pristine cultures they found (or were perhaps attempting to re-ignite?). The earlier relation between the museum and the culture booklet was essentialist in nature and, as such, created the tourist spectacle of a fixed traditional way of life of people in Kavango. The practice was similar in neighbouring Ovamboland.

The administrative officers at Maria Mwengere Culture Centre collected and recorded traditional songs, oral histories and did research on tradition and culture of the people in Kavango. The songs were bound into what was known as a *sangbundel*[25] containing choir songs, choruses and the Kavango anthem. These histories of origins, migrations and cultures of various 'officially' recognized population groups were bound into a booklet by the state and were informed by contemporary academic research[26] in the region.

The current culture booklet consists of a front page, which has the name of the group or school participating in the culture festival, the year, and any decoration in picture form that symbolizes the group. The second page has the historical background of the group and the list of names of participants. Then follow the songs and drama acts, written in local languages and explained in English. The background of the song and how it is sung and danced is outlined. The songs are organized in three phases namely the entrance song, the main song or drama (often the drama is preceded and closed with a song) and finally the exit song.

The groups organize and prepare their own booklets independently which are submitted to the judges. The judges then use the culture booklet in order to assess the performance.

In postcolonial Kavango, the booklet has been reinvented, reorganized and given new meaning. The current booklet contains the five previously recognized ethnic groups in Kavango and in addition the Vanyemba and the San. Although it emphasizes local ethnic differences, it contains a nationalist narrative of inclusion. Most importantly, local people who

---

[25] NAR/1/55 File AP/7/1/1 Jaarverslag (Annual Report) 1978 Departement Van Onderwys- Kavango Regering.
[26] See my discussion about sponsored colonial and independent academic research in chapter four.

participate in the festival create the culture booklet themselves. During the Annual National Culture Festivals the regional culture offices compile what I call a master cover narrative of the history and cultures of ethnic groups identified as Vakavango in Namibia. This master narrative gives the judges a bird's-eye view of various presentations from the region.

When such a narrative is prepared, leaders of various cultural groups are not represented and, as I have noted, the narrative has remained the same over time, apart from minimal changes. The officials do not edit the songs. That is why I argue that, because the narrative has not being changed for some time, the state presents Kavango-ness as fixed in all these festival encounters. While the state constructs ethnic identities as fixed in its master cover narrative, the public through participants, acknowledges differences and changes in their idea of Kavango-ness. They contribute to such a process in the way they compose and present songs and dances in their culture booklets. As it appears, the above is a process that fixes boundaries. However, I show below that it is quite a fluid process especially if we take into consideration the participation of local groups in the making of the culture booklet.

I was repeatedly told that cultural groups create their own culture booklets. During my time in the field, I was not able to encounter a group making a booklet. Every time I went to visit a group whether at school or anywhere in the region, they always had their booklets. I only noticed later that the groups actually have what I call *databases* in the form of computers and books in which their songs and drama plays were stored. Group leaders produced and managed these databases. Many groups used school facilities such as computer printers to produce their culture booklets. They drew songs from their databases and only occasionally changed the content in order to address a particular context in the festival. I was informed during my interviews at the schools I visited that it was teachers who compiled the culture booklets, but they also relied on local people for content material[27]. I have, however, been able to observe how the group Tukulikeni complied and bound songs for their culture booklet in the regional festival of 2008.

Tukulikeni is a local cultural group that competes in the youth category of the festival. Valesca, the official responsible for the museum at the centre, also takes part in it. She was the group leader at the time. Valesca printed songs from the computer file and the group would then rehearse those songs for the regional festival. These songs are filed in the official computer by the employee who takes part in cultural dances. The songs were downloaded from the computer and bound in a booklet. This observation is interesting in the sense that a particular group member was almost autonomously able to select items.

---

[27] See my discussion in chapter seven.

As I have observed, local people make and remake their culture through text and images that they capture in the culture booklet. The compilation of songs and dances in a booklet contains extensive social communication between performers/participants who represent the electorate, and the state. For the local people, the culture booklet creates a focal space for political advocacy, identity politics, social awareness and the celebration of nationhood in the region.

The discussion above focused mainly on the Maria Mwengere Culture Centre as a space in which the colonial state produced and articulated histories/identities of the local people of Kavango through the compilation and promotion of the culture booklet, the collection of oral stories, songs and research on various musical instruments and traditional implements in the region. In contemporary culture festivals the culture booklet is presented as a tool to assist the judges to do a better job. This ethnography, however, shows that the state uses the culture booklet to construct the identity of its citizens in what I call regional ethnicities in various political regions; while participants apply it to present culture as they imagine and see it with their own eyes. Contents in the culture booklet convey imagery of the population groups in Kavango as bounded and separate, while the song and drama contents[28] show otherwise. This aspect of the culture booklet can be understood within the context of the colonial idea of the quest for exploration of Kavango tradition and culture and how this has been re-appropriated in the postcolonial time.

Jan Bradley, one of my research informants and a former state ethnologist, who headed the Maria Mwengere Culture Centre towards the end of colonial political administration, made the following statement during our interview: "You know an Afrikaner is fanatic about his culture, until today.[29]"

He implied above that because Afrikaners conserve their culture, those who worked at the centre before him had ensured that the people of Kavango were rooted in activities of their culture, by participating in the organized activities[30]. It seems the idea was that everyone should preserve and protect 'their' culture, like the Afrikaner did at the time when the apartheid ideology was conceived (Sharp, 1988). Also Afrikaners who worked at the centre, including himself, made sure that the supposed culture of the Kavango people was well recorded and documented because they wanted to maintain originality and respect for local traditional dances and culture. They used notions of authenticity.

---

[28] See my discussion in chapter seven.
[29] Interview with Jan Bradley at Tutungeni, Rundu, 20 September 2008
[30] I note that Bradley's idea of culture is essentialist and I present them as such in order to make sense of the discussion.

There seems to have been a general fear and anxiety at that time of various outside influences. Van Tonder has alluded to the above perspective in his study of Kavango during 1966:

"Natural segregation between different ethnic groups and races seen as separate homelands with adequate land from which to develop into an independent economic and political unit, is a justified balanced process."

Van Tonder went on to debunk the idea of the detribalization of the native in favour of retribalization:

> To advocate or force detribalization and integration, or even potential integration, on different ethnic groups who have nothing in common, not even the colour of their skins, is to advocate perpetual dependence and conflict, domination, racial discrimination, upper and lower social strata, an unequal distribution of rights and privileges, and also duties and responsibilities. (1966:19)

Although Van Tonder concluded the above from the functional perspective of the Kavango society after the implementation of the Odendaal Plan, the implication was that of a retribalized[31] and conservative society that regarded itself as different. Thus it was very important to record the culture of the native in the above context as well as the context of Bradley's essentialist idea of culture and tradition.

The development of the booklet began with the formulation of the judges' sheet of the adjudicators. As Jan Bradley explains the process below:

> I have drawn up a performance guide for the judges how to judge and what to judge; for all the judges. Then I had a workshop at Ekongoro and we discussed every point. And then it was judged by performance, the clothing, and meaning of the story. That's why we won! The Kavango group, because I introduced all the traditional dances perfectly in a booklet. And then the evening before the dances I issued a booklet to every judge from the other regions. You need to have an initiative attitude. Tomorrow when you start every judge was following the dances of the Kavango dances and they could understand perfectly well. You must remember that you have a Vambo speaking judge, a Kwangali speaking judge, you've got a Nama and they don't know the Kavango dances and the Kavango also do not know their dances. I felt it was my responsibility to introduce the Kavango dances to the judges, otherwise how do you judge? After that the Minister of Youth and Culture John Mutorwa then requested that every region must introduce a kind of script like that for understanding. That played a tremendous role in reconciliation[32].

---

[31] I have shown in chapter two that earlier native commissioners of the region especially after Cocky Hahn were not in favour of retribalized natives in Kavango, unlike in the former Ovamboland.

[32] Interview with Jan Bradley at Tutungeni, Rundu, 20 September 2008

The initial colonial motive for the culture book was to store the culture and traditional dances of the Kavango as Jan Bradley and Elrich Pretorius[33] claimed. Supposedly the culture booklet is produced to convey a sense and idea of culture and traditional dances of various groups to the judges during the festivals. What is interesting is Bradley's view that judges from other regions did not know anything about the various culture dances and so needed to be oriented so that they could award marks fairly. Clearly in this context there seem to be a representation of 'culture' in a fixed manner. The other interesting point is the request of the former Minister of Youth and Sport, John Mutorwa, that each region presents a script about their cultures so that they could be better understood in the festival contest. That moment marked the reinvention and re-appropriation of the culture booklet by the directorate. I mentioned earlier that the idea of the culture booklet was a colonial invention. However, the culture booklet or *sangbundel* did not achieve its success and acclaim at the time it was invented, it only became popular during the early phases of independence when the culture festivals were reintroduced.

The other pertinent issue about the culture booklet is its mediation. When I spoke to Bradley, he indicated that he prepared the information of the regional booklet himself and only presented the idea in a series of workshops. By contrast, current culture groups produce the booklets themselves without any involvement from the officials at Ekongoro. It is also worth noting that most booklets I have studied are prepared along intra ethnic contexts such that the groups or schools in Mbunza area supposedly present the Mbunza culture, or Shambyu or Ukwangali etc. However, when the groups participate in the national finals, the culture office covers all the scripts submitted by the groups with an overall official history of the Kavango and their dances. As a result, the region is presented as a unified fixed ethnic entity during the finals.

The booklet can be viewed as having served the same purpose during the two historical moments. However, in both moments the culture booklet created contexts in which the identity of the Kavango was defined and emphasized. As in contemporary times, during the colonial era the participants in the culture festival did not have the liberty to prepare booklets on their own. In postcolonial Kavango, on the other hand, the participants in the festival are allowed to define for themselves who they are and present songs and drama of their choice. While the various groups are able to freely decide what to include in the booklet and how they see themselves, the regional office creates the regional identity and a narrative portraying the people of Kavango as riparian. This regional identity is presented as fixed in the national context. When presenters enact the various performances at the festival, they

---

[33] My personal communication with Elrich Pretorius at Maria Mwengere Culture Centre in Rundu during 2008.

are read by judges within the context of the culture booklet. Judges award the points according to what they read and see in relation to the culture booklet.

Their acts are further influenced by expectations that are listed on the judge's sheet. While the groups present and emphasizes the various local inner ethnicities at the regional festival, the culture office asserts the regional ethnic identity at the national event. The above activities at the Maria Mwengere Culture Centre make it a space were local culture is retrieved to borrow Soyinka's (1990) term from historical silos, remade, disseminated by state officials and consumed by the public audience who attend culture festivals. The officials at the centre objectify songs, dances and drama in culture booklets and present them as belonging to particular groups at the festivals.

Do we see ethnicity at play in this context? I argue that there is ethnicity in action. However, this ethnicity must be contextually defined and divorced from the primordial view of ethnicity as inscribed in shared biology, ancestral history and innate disposition, as argued by Cohen (1974:xii) cited by Comaroff and Comaroff 2009 in their seminal Ethnicity, INC. In this case, I use ethnicities in a constructionist perspective where those who claim it, do so in order to subjectively assert difference of identity. During the national festival, regional ethnicity is of particular importance as it forms part of the wider diverse audience which must to be united in order to have a nation. Unlike the stages of the festival that are internal to the region, at the national festival presenters are no longer Mbunza or Gciriku, but Kavango and it is this that identifies them from amongst the many other ethnic groups that comprise the Namibian nation. Thus ethnicity in this context manifests itself as a general category as well as a specific identity. It is an identity that people and the state produce in their quest to address various social matters such as solving problems, to enhance and defend their positions, to justify their actions, to establish meanings, to achieve understanding, or to otherwise negotiate their way through the world in which they live. (Cornell &Hartmann, 1998: xviii) While I argue that ethnicity is made and asserted through the culture booklet, the approaches of the actors vary, but the distinctions are blurred. Like the master cover narrative, which the state constructs, it seems implicitly that the culture is fixed, essential and unchanging, and as such is regarded by officials as the reference point that judges can use in order to award marks 'correctly'. Local people also seem to have the same perception of culture and its representation. However, their drama-play presentations especially signify contemporaneity[34].

In the culture booklet there is a clear distinction between and assertion of the various population groups resident in the region. It depends whether the group originated from

---

[34] See discussion in chapter seven.

Mbukushu, Gciriku, Shambyu or Mbunza and Kwangali area. I have shown in earlier chapters that these five groups were officially recognized as the original tribes resident in Kavango, while the San and Vanyemba were not recognized as Kavango groups during colonial times. Up until today the Vanyemba and San are presented as not having an ancestral place in the region although most of the songs in the booklets are written and performed in *Runyemba*[35]. Many Kavango dances continue to be hotly contested locally, especially when a connection is made to what is believed to be the Vanyemba culture or tradition. (Akuupa, 2010) However, the most interesting observation is the classification of the above five groups into two categories where Mbunza and Kwangali due to their geographical location are regarded as the west, whilst the Shambyu, Gciriku, and Mbukushu make up the east. This categorization is a complex one especially when it comes to issues of regional development, party politics and appointments to positions of influence at the regional and national government as I show in the next section.

With regard to the lyrical content in songs and drama, I observed that these were influenced and defined by issues in areas where the groups originated. In the next section I discuss how the culture booklet is used as an advocacy and communication tool for social dialogue regarding rights and resources among the officials who represent the state, audience and participants at the festival. I argue that the culture booklet as represented in the cultural festival is a socio-political space through which social dialogue is enacted.

"Culture Booklet": A Resource of Advocacy

Earlier I stated that a culture festival is viewed as a vital resource for nation-building by the state. In order to understand the state-sponsored culture festival as an important resource of nation-building for the state is not to read it holistically but through the various small segments that comprise it. To focus instead on the dominant role of the state during the event, I analyze the festival with a particular focus on the songs and dances in the culture booklet, the audience response and various cultural representations.

In this section I shift my analysis of the culture booklet from being an object of identity construction and assertion to a medium of dialogue and advocacy. I pay attention to the content of the culture booklet, namely the songs and dances, in order to show how participants in the festival use it as a resource and medium through which to address local issues. Songs

---

[35] Runyemba is a generic word used to refer to dialects spoken by the population group identified/classified as the Vanyemba. I have discussed the 'question' of Nyemba-ness in detail in chapter five and chapter eight.

and drama present an opportunity to deal with social issues that people are grappling with, as indicated below by the teachers at Sauyemwa Junior Primary School:[36]

> We go there to give news messages! There should be a message in any song or act. People should present or practice dances so that audience can see and know how a particular dance is done. However, the purpose is not about dancing only, but to give a message. Even a long time ago people did not just gather to dance for entertainment, they sang about things which had happened. In that manner they are able to go and tell people about what happened. They gave messages about everything good or bad. So we are also emulating what happened long time ago in our songs. We observe what is going on and sing about it. Sometimes we look at what we need to be done for us and direct our message to the people who can do such things for us. We ask; what do children want? How are the leaders working with the people? So that is what we formulate into a message and direct it to those it is intended for.

Looking at the manner in which various songs and drama contained in a culture booklet is contextualized, and the interview excerpt above, it is evident that this booklet is issue-driven. As Issues range from identity politics, HIV/Aids, service delivery and regional disputes to praises of the leader. Cultural groups use the songs to ask their leaders to do things for them. There is a message communicated between the audience, performers, judges and state representatives through song and dance. Although the message in the song is contemporary, the manner through which it is spread is believed by the teachers at the schools and grandparents to be traditional. In my discussion with the teachers there is a sense of nostalgia-construction which expresses the desire for a sense of rootedness in rural tradition as argued by Fairweather 2003 in the context of heritage contestations between villagers and cosmopolitan citizens at Olukonda in Northern Namibia.

When the festival takes place at the regional and national level, the stage of performance is centered between various audiences, which I categorize as follows: a public audience composed of local people who come to view the dances at the festival and the political audience that is formally invited by the organizers to attend the gathering and legitimize it as a state ritual. Political audiences are there to represent the state. Last, but not least, there is an adjudicating audience that must judge the acts according to the guide[37] provided for by the organizers. The participants are also part of the audience, but here I want to portray them as presenters of what is being witnessed and communicated in the performance: the message!

---

[36] Interview with Magdaleena Pessa Kasera, Theresia Sikongo, Anastasia Mufenda and Helena Nasini, they are teachers responsible for culture at Sauyemwa Junior Primary School, 20 January 2009.

[37] The judges also use a score sheet and a guideline on what to look for in the enactment prepared by the Directorate which directs them how to allocate marks in order to determine the winner.

The above categorization can also be understood in the context of front stage[38] as perceived by Goffman 1959. Goffman 1959 suggests that when an act of performance is prepared and presented to an audience in a mediated context it is done front-stage. What takes place is consistent and contains generalized ways to explain the situation or roles the actors are playing, to the observing audience.

There are dynamics that are context driven among audiences and determine how they respond to performances. Important is the language[39] of presentation and also the message contained in the songs. When the festival is held regionally those present, especially the political and the public audiences, are able to easily comprehend what is going on in song and dances, because they are conversant with the language used. The representation of dances is not likely to be viewed at face value, because the language in which it is presented is understandable to most, if not all, audiences. The message is not likely to be distorted by other factors encountered during translation. However, translation becomes necessary at national level. Certain songs contain messages that are deemed sensitive, especially so when they are presented in particular contexts. These messages can be classified as resources to demand, complain, caution, praise and ridicule.

The other dynamic deals with those who compose the songs. The majority of participants in the festival are pupils and high school students who have been coached by teachers. Teachers compose songs that are mostly about social issues such as health, education, though they may be more overtly political. One prominent issue in the culture booklets during the festivals of 2008 was the dispute about grazing land in the Ukwangali traditional Authority[40].

From 2005 until late 2008 tensions brewed between cattle herders from the former Ovamboland who settled (illegally) in the western Kavango district of the Ukwangali Traditional Authority in western Kavango. Several herders from Oshikoto and Ohangwena region in the Ondonga and Oukwanyama traditional areas respectively had for some time been allowed by the Ukwangali Traditional authority to graze their cattle in western Kavango. All was in order until those who had grazing rights began to invite others to bring their cattle to graze and settle in western Kavango illegally[41]. The cattle reportedly belonged

---

[38] For an extensive analysis of this notion see chapter seven.
[39] I refer to the overtly used language.
[40] Since Namibian independence institutions formerly known as tribal authorities were changed to traditional councils/authorities as the enactment of the Council of Traditional Leaders' Act of 1997.
[41] In order to understand this problem of illegal grazing and settlement of people from former Ovamboland in Kavango, one needs to pay attention to what happened historically. I have discussed earlier how the South African administration resettled people in their quest to create colonial tribal trust funds. As official records show the Kavango territory has been moved twice

to politicians and senior civil service officials such as Ministers and regional councilors from the former Ovamboland. The situation angered Hompa Sitentu Mpasi, who ordered the herders to vacate and leave the area. Despite repeated attempts to make the herders leave, they remained. The Ukwangali Traditional Authority resorted to civil justice and as result the herders were served with court orders to leave. The police enforced the order. Below are the cautionary songs that were performed during the 2008 festivals when grazing in Ukwangali was a thorny issue:

Vakavango pindukeni[42] - Kavango people wake up (Translation)

People of Kavango wake up, they took your land.
People of Kavango wake up, they took your land.
Our five leaders unite with one heart/mind.
Together with the headmen and councillors.

Evhu Lyaukwangali[43] - The Ukwangali land (Translation)

They took the land of Ukwangali, oh my goodness!
oh my goodness!
They took
Chameleon change into collar band

During the 2008 circuit and regional culture festivals, participants from the west,[44] as they are locally referred to by their counterparts in Eastern Kavango, presented the above songs with lyrics about the grazing saga in Western Kavango. These songs were a warning directed to all residents of Kavango[45] to be wary of those who wanted to grab their land. The lyrics ridiculed those who were given rights to graze in the area and likened them to chameleons which change colour and camouflage their presence.

---

in order to accommodate people from Uukwanyama in the area known as Mpungu. As a result there has been a higher concentration of people from the former Ovamboland in that area. Those who have settled in Mpungu then invited their kin to join them.

[42] The song is composed by Musese Junior Se condary School in Ukwangali. It is translated by the author.

[43] The song is composed by Kananana Primary School in Ukwangali. It is translated by the author.

[44] I mentioned the distinction between westerners and easterners in Kavango earlier in the discussion. It is a based on the geographic locations of ethnic groups; it is commonly used when people from either side are appointed to prominent positions by the head of state. There appears to be an overt competition over high positions among the traditional authorities. The more people you have at central government position from your traditional authority,(it is believed) the more influence there is from your area and your needs are more likely to be addressed.

[45] The issue still remains complex and sensitive at the moment and national leaders have since become involved in seeking a permanent solution. The head of state became involved by urging the Council of Traditional Leaders which advises him on issues of traditional authorities to seek a solution to avoid instability. (The Namibian, 23 November 2005; The Namibian, 23 June 2008)

When both songs above were presented at the regional festival the public and the political audience cheered loudly[46]. When the songs were presented at the national culture festival the response was not the same. The section on the stand which accommodated the Kavango region during the national finals responded in the same way as during the regional culture festival. While they cheered loudly and stamped their feet the rest of the audience just watched. I observed that there was no significant response from the VIP tent that accommodated the political audience representing both the regional and central governments. The silent response could stem from various communication factors such as the language barriers mentioned above, or perhaps their possible association with the politicians whose cattle grazed in the disputed area. At the national culture festival, political audiences especially those that represent the central government, may not be conversant with the language of presentation and had to rely on translations. In such a circumstance, they view the presentation as it is performed without understanding the linguistic content and may regard it as merely an exciting cultural performance. The message might also have been distorted if any of them had asked for a translation of the item being presented. I have observed that many times translations are done when drama is presented. Usually the local political leader or senior civil servant would lean to the visitor and say something when the drama unfolds and on rare occasions when the participants are dancing. However, the reason could also be that many of the political elite were actually involved in the issue. The songs caution people in Kavango about the imminent danger of losing land to their neighbours whom they had offered to assist during their time of need. Another group, Rupara Combined Junior Secondary School from western Kavango composed a song titled: "Vakavango mwaha rara evhu lyetu lina piti." (People of Kavango wake up, they have taken our land.)

Their culture booklet, which is handwritten,[47] explains the song in English as follows:

> This is a song that was composed two years ago by the Vakwangali tribe, due to the problem that they had that their land was intended to be given to other people. So they decided to give their complaints through different songs, this was one of them. It is addressing the Kavango people to be awake and work as a team, work to get their land back[48].

In this time which is perceived to be a period of difficulty, local politics that suggest ethnic differences are put aside, and the unity of Kavango-ness is mobilized by traditional leaders including headman and councilors who serve in the regional government, in order to deal

---

[46] In contrast to when a song about HIV/Aids was sung.
[47] It seems that to some groups the manner of how the culture booklet was prepared did not matter as long as the message was delivered.
[48] The song was composed by Rupara Combined School Junior Secondary in Ukwangali in 2008.

with the problem that threatens the region. In this context the west and east dichotomy too does not matter for the time being; people become united as a "cultural community" striving for a common goal. (Kymlicka. 1989:135) However, it does not mean that people have forgotten their local differences. They are fully aware and "conscious of their cultural differences". (Bauman, 1971:35)

The song below was composed and presented by Sauyemwa Junior Primary School (Mbunza Traditional Authority). The song praises the culture festival organizers at the regional level with the specific mention of Thomas Shapi the senior culture officer at Maria Mwengere Culture Centre and Diaz Ndango the director of National Heritage and Culture Programmes (NACP) for uniting people of Kavango with all the other ethnic groups in the country. Despite the imminent threat to stability in the region caused by grazing tensions, groups also composed songs of praise calling for national unity. The song urges the unity of ethnic groups represented by various regions at the festivals.

> **Tunapanda**[49] - We are happy (Translation)
>
> We are happy that you culture organizers united us
> We are happy that you culture organizers united us
> In Kavango
> We are happy that you united us
> Tate (Mr.) Shapi
> At the higher level (national)
> We are happy that you united us
> We are happy that you united us
> Tate (Mr.) Ndango
> We are happy that you culture organizers united us
> We are happy that you united us
> We are happy that you culture organizers united us
> We the Damara are happy that you united us
> We the Wambo are happy that you united us
> We the Herero are happy that you united us
> We the Kavango are happy that you united us
> We are all happy that you united us.

Another concern in Kavango during the time of my research was the road infrastructure between Rundu and Nkurenkuru[50]. The road network from Windhoek via Rundu in Kavango to Katima Mulilo in Caprivi is tarred and provides a vital economic link between Namibia and other Southern African Development Community (SADC) countries, namely Zambia,

---

[49] Song composed by Sauyemwa Junior Primary School in Mbunza during 2008. It is translated by the author.
[50] Nkurenkuru was recently proclaimed as a town. It is close to the Katwitwi border post.

Botswana, Zambia, Zimbabwe and the Democratic Republic of Congo (DRC). Angola has been a strategic business partner since the end of civil war. Most of the exports to Angola go through Helao Nafidi[51] a town at the border in Ohangwena region. In Kavango, Rundu and Nkurenkuru towns became business hubs that serviced provinces in southern Angola. However, there was no proper road network linking Rundu and Nkurenkuru. Despite the potential economic opportunities existing between the two countries, the lack of road infrastructure between Rundu, the administrative capital of the region, and Nkurenkuru has always been an issue among local people. Medical referrals made from Nankudu hospital in Nkurenkuru district were of particular concern. In many instances the patient died on the way because ambulances could not travel fast enough due to the dangerous condition of the road. In 2004, the state promised to build a new road linking Nkurenkuru to Rundu, but the project only realized in December 2007. (The Namibian, 18 July 2007) At the time of the circuit festival in 2008 the same group composed a song below which they presented to thank not the central government, but the local councillors and traditional chiefs for their success.

Teya twalilira[52] - The tarred road we yearned for (Translation)

They have started to built the tarred road we yearn for
Fame be upon the chiefs, thanks to the councillors
Driver, you can dance now, for you will have a smooth ride.

This achievement is locally viewed not as a success of the central government, but rather one for which the regional council and traditional authorities should be thanked. Unfair distribution of resources in Namibia has become seriously pronounced especially after establishment of two new political parties namely, Rally for Democracy and Progress (RDP) and All People's Party (APP) during late 2007. People who were previously senior members of the ruling party Swapo created the two political parties. The president of the RDP party, Hidipo Hamutenya, was no longer a favorite within the ruling party had also lost his position in the Nujoma cabinet and only returned later as an ordinary member of parliament. The APP president Ignatius Shihwameni from Kavango was once a member of the ruling party before he joined the first postcolonial opposition party the Congress of Democrats (COD) in 1999 by Ben Ulenga who had also been a member of the ruling party. Their election manifestos[53] (including that of the ruling party) all pledge to address the issue of resource distribution. The matter of fair resource distribution nationally was and is still prominent in both the print and electronic media.

---

[51] The new official name for the new town around the Oshikango border post.
[52] Song composed by Sauyemwa Junior Primary School in Mbunza 2008. It is translated by author.
[53] www.swapoparty.org.na, www.rdp.org.na, www.hellonam.com/party-manifestos date accessed 10 May 2010.

Sauyemwa Junior Primary School composed the song for the 2008 culture festival and presented the same song during its participation in the annual national culture festival. The song appreciates "development" locally termed *ekuliko,* which is brought to the region. The public audience responded to such a song with excitement and they also sang and danced together with the participants. Organizers had a difficult time to remove individuals from the public audience who kept on running on stage during the presentation of the song.

Moving further east from western Mbunza, focus in the songs shifts from issues such as conflict and development in the region to education and showcasing what I refer to as the essentialized tradition and culture of the Kavango. The songs create and emphasize Kavango identity time and again, as below:

Hadye wo hana kungena?[54] - Who is it that enters? (Translation)

Who is entering the playground?
Diyana is entering
To show their culture
We are Kavango
We are Kavango
We love each other
We are united
Let us show our cultural dance.

Other songs have content about Kavango food and how it is produced, about traditional huts and how they are made. Hunting is central in many songs from the east.

Below is a hunting song sung in Runyemba. The issue of the Nyemba songs presented in the festival is that they are contested as not being representative of Kavango. The Vanyemba identity as a sub-category of Kavango is of particular importance in the postcolonial politics of belonging. The Vanyemba identity is represented as somewhat unwanted in the local discourse on Kavango-ness. Yet awareness of Nyemba-ness as an integral part of Kavango is quite significant. Despite contestations and the exclusion of the Vanyemba in mainstream Kavango identity, songs in Nyemba continue to dominate many culture booklets I have analyzed.

Ndji nyanga lihuli[55] - The song is succinctly translated in the booklet as follows:

I'm taking the gun and follow my friends who went hunting. My friend Ndjelenga of Mulyata and Kalenga of Nduva. Rucara is moving slowly[56].

---

[54] Song composed and translated by Diyana Combined School in Mbukushu.
[55] The song is composed by Rucara Combined School in Gciriku.
[56] Rugara Combined School p.4

The other issue which features in the songs from the east is creating awareness among the youth about HIV/Aids. The 'youth' are constantly reminded about the danger of HIV/Aids and they are urged to be obedient and listen to their elders. The song also addresses the common issue of young girls who fall pregnant while still in school. It seems that, as in the colonial time, youth remains an important focus in the postcolonial discourse of nation-building.

> **Vanantjoka**[57] - The song is succinctly translated in their booklet as follows:
> Youth should listen to their parents; they are getting pregnant and dying of HIV/Aids[58].

The song seems to fit in a common moral discourse about youth in contemporary Namibia. Generally, when politicians address gatherings they always have something to say to the youth or about them. They urge the youth to be obedient and refrain from activities that are deemed destructive.

The above discussion shows how various population groups in the thirteen regions are ethnicized by regional governments through projects such as heritage hunting, museums and conservation before they are presented as a unified entity during national festival encounters. The most interesting matter here is how ethnicization is appropriated in postcolonial Namibia through the 'culture booklet'. Firstly, the regional governments of Namibia are closely demarcated according to ethnic orientation in a way that reasserts the already existing state of affairs. Ethnicity is appropriated in many ways and is contextually consumed. Discussion in this regard is dealt with extensively by the Comaroffs in their Ethnicity Inc (2009). The Namibian state has realized the economic potential inherent in selling culture and since its reintroduction of culture festivals has encouraged people in all the thirteen regions to rise to the opportunity and embrace its economic benefits. People in regional areas have formed cooperatives to operate guided tours to museums, heritage sites and cultural villages.

Song lyrics address a range of issues, apart from current affairs. At the time of my research grazing was an issue in my Kavango research site. The issue of grazing featured significantly in the songs and drama presentations in various culture booklets, especially those from western Kavango. Another common theme in the culture booklets was the communication of 'morality' to the youth warning them against risky behaviour in terms of their sexual health. Most of the songs I collected urge the youth to desist from alcohol consumption and unprotected sexual practices. Accordingly, I have argued that the culture booklet

---

[57] The song is composed by Rucara Combined School
[58] Rucara Combined School p.7

was not only used to construct the postcolonial Namibian identity but, indeed, acted as an advocacy tool targeting the state and its citizens. The museum, the idea of the culture booklet, and songs contained in the booklet are of particular importance in order to understand the postcolonial making of nationhood. These aspects cannot be dealt with in isolation especially if one is to understand how the ideas of belonging rooted in the notion of 'culture' are formulated and asserted.

The next chapter explores how lay-people and cultural groups in Kavango make "their" culture through participation in the state-sponsored cultural festival.

7 Namibian Identity Through Dance

"Making the Nation": The Role of Local People in the Festival

During my stay at the Maria Mwengere Culture Centre, I observed the festival at various levels of preparation and visited spaces where some of the local cultural groups met for rehearsals, a process referred to in Rukwangali as *maliyombiliso*, or *makuyombilito* in Rumanyo. Local cultural groups in Kavango, as in other regions of the country, take part in the composition of songs, choreography, directing dances and writing dramatic plays for the festival. Festival themes arise out of these rehearsals and are influenced by lay people.

During rehearsals, groups decide on the themes and dances to showcase[1] as one would say in English, or "ku likida mpo" (to show culture) in Rukwangali. Participants believe that what is produced during these sessions is rooted in essentialist notions of tradition and culture- locally referred to as "mpo zetu"[2] (lit. our culture/tradition). The notions are used interchangeably in the festival, as in other social contexts. Although tradition and culture are represented as fixed in various fields of the festival, the concept is deemed by some to be dynamic. Those who officiate during the gatherings mostly define culture from the anthropological perspective[3].

Culture booklets[4] are presented to the judges shortly before the performance. It is the performance of dances and drama that later become the subject of interaction at the festival, especially in the category of *kulinyanyukisa*[5] when it is presented in full view of judges and audience. At all levels of the festival there is a section known as *kulinyanyukisa*. This category is all about entertainment. This category is only available during the festival itself and those who present it do not earn points towards the competitions at the festival.

---

[1] The act of public performance in the festival context is locally referred to as showcasing, as are performances perceived to be representations of cultures that are showcased to the public.
[2] See my explanation on the workings and usage of the notion of *mpo zetu* in chapter one. Mpo zetu or Our tradition/culture in Kavango refers to old things. It is those old things that are believed to be carried from one generation to the next in order to preserve the being of people.
[3] See quotation from transcripts of the speech read by the Inspector of Education in the discussion.
[4] I have dealt with the culture booklet in the previous chapter, and argued that the state uses it in order to enforce and reconstruct local ethnicities, because of its power to mediate the context in which culture is constructed and legitimized. In the same vein I also argue that, although these cultural constructions occur in the context created and largely influenced by the state, festival participants and local audiences also take part in the processes.
[5] Lit. make ourselves happy or to entertain. The act of kulinyanyukisa is contextual. People can linyanyukisa themselves at anytime of the day. In fact rehearsal can also be regarded as kulinyanyukisa, because people are entertaining themselves. However, in the context of my study I am engaging it as an official category in the making of the festival.

This chapter addresses two issues, namely *maliyombiliso* and *kulinyanyukisa*. Using Goffman's dramaturgical theory perspective, I present categories of *maliyombiliso* as the back stage and *kulinyanyukisa* as the front stage of the festival. With ethnographic evidence I attempt to show the limitations, strengths and taken-for-granted understanding of performance especially when one attempts to analyze ritual performances while only being exposed to a single aspect of the performance and not its entire transitional aspect.

Local cultural groups create their festival submissions through preparation of the culture booklets. I describe and discuss the rehearsal as a process of making the festival after observing two groups, namely Mayana Combined School and Ukumwe Culture Dance Group, as well as referring to interviews I conducted with group members and leaders of various other cultural groups. The contribution and participation of local people in the activities of the various culture groups in the festival context makes them active role-players in the processes of nation-building as mediated and envisaged by the state. I argue that local people participate and contribute to making the festival as active citizens whose involvement has an intended outcome[6]. Carola Lentz 2001 in Ghana observed the Kakube and Kobine festivals and demonstrated how local cultural presentations in the event had significant national dimensions in Ghana's politics of nationhood. What is evidently different between her study and mine is that the festivals she studied were sanctioned by independent bodies who contended for the right to host these events. In my context, festivals were sanctioned and hosted by the State and this in itself created a different set of dynamics.

Performance of cultural groups at various levels invariably generates social interactions between audiences, judges and performers. I present and discuss the various interactions with a specific focus on the drum performance of Unongo Cultural Group in the Mpungu circuit and the Shiperu dance of Kapata Cultural Group during the regional competition, in the section referred to as *kulinyanyukisa*. I show that the interactions in the festival are not mainly about contestations and negotiations of what constitute the [proper] Kavango traditional dances and performances, but are also a celebration of regional and national belonging. Unlike the rehearsal sessions where such contestations could only be played out among those in the performance (namely the dancers and group leaders), the festival interaction involves those who come to watch, perform and organize. I argue that the festival creates a focal environment for communicating topical social issues. Thus, I view performance as a process of practice.

---

[6] Local people's participation in the making of the festival beside celebration is issue driven. They view the festival as a space where social issues could be interacted.

My overall intention in this discussion is to show how local people participate in the making of the festival and explore the dynamic transition that exists between the two aspects of the festival, namely the relations between what happens on the back stage, and on the front stage. In this context I will again rely on Goffman's dramaturgical perspective to locate the festival rehearsal in what he referred to as back stage and the actual festival on the front stage in order to show that performances that are showcased in the culture festival are perceived as *social reality* by the actors concerned. Goffman 1959:22-43 distinguishes between the two stages. He proposes that when the performer and the audience are present, performance takes place in front stage. The dramaturgical performance is consistent and contains generalized ways to explain the situation or role the actor is playing to the observing audiences. In the back stage only performers are present. The performers can step out of character without fear of disrupting the performance. When performers are on the back stage, they are nonetheless in another performance - that of a loyal member. However, back stages remain relative, existing in relation to specific audiences.

I feel that Goffman's theory has limitations, for example he does not recognize the ability of performers to manipulate the performance, especially when it is appreciated by the audience. I contend that the interface between the two stages is not fixed. However, his theory is useful in the context of the performance in that the performer communicates and explains the role to the audience. As my ethnography will show, the performer communicates aspects of real life to the audience and it is these aspects of lived experience that enliven the performance. The experienced life is rehearsed into a story during *makuyombilito* (back stage) and it is told in the front stage of the festival in its various contexts such as *kulinyanyukisa*. In using the two stages by Goffman, I do not imply in any way that what happens in the festival is staged rather than real. Rather, I have used his back and front stage notion to separate the two categories and understand the transition within.

The interaction between back and front stage can be understood in terms of Bourdieu's sense of habitus, field and capital. In his essay on the possibility of a disinterested act, Bourdieu 1998:75-76 has shown why it is difficult to measure that which people do and their motivation for their actions. It should not be assumed that people (or actors) are rational, that they are right to act as they do, or even that reason is what directs, guides or orients their actions. Human interaction postulates a complexity that can only be understood through multiple social scientific lenses.

Theoretically the chapter engages the theory of performance as conceptually conceived in the discipline and as an analytical tool especially by Turner 1979 and Bauman 1986. In anthropological terms performance is broadly understood as presentation of symbolic systems through living bodies as well as mediating objects[7]. As a concept[8] of analysis it is understood to be well suited to investigate aesthetic strategies, sensorial and embodied styles that are employed to authorize authenticity in contestations over gendered- and embodied identity, and citizenship in the contemporary world. Although I concur with such perspectives, I aim to show, (as argued by Hughes Freeland 1998 in the introduction to the collection of essays Ritual Performance) that there is the danger of misreading performances and allowing the symbolic to dominate the functional, if we in the social sciences do not appreciate performances as social processes that constitute practices. If we do not see them as social practices, maintains Schieffelin 1998, performances seem to be robbed of life and power, especially when distanced within discussions that are concerned largely with meaning. Schieffelin has argued that in anthropology performance has largely been used to refer to particular symbolic or aesthetic activities that are enacted as intentional expressive productions in established genres. His perspective is set against the marked boundedness of what he calls produced enactments. He suggests that we have largely ignored fundamental epistemological issues and we need to see performance beyond the text, embracing the action thereof that creates presence and presents vivid realities that can amuse or terrify.

Below, I give a brief background on traditional[9] dances on which the contemporary cultural dances are modelled in order to present an idea of how the current dance performances and perceptions of culture in the festival context are perceived.

A Note on 'Kavango' Traditional Dances

The traditional dance is an important component of the state sponsored culture festival. Although traditional dances are believed to be ethnically-bounded, anybody can actually dance them, as I demonstrate in the next chapter. I also present a scenario in which white students from Noordgrens Secondary School represent what is performed as Kavango dances. In this discussion I demonstrate that these dances are modeled on what is imagined to be traditional. As I observed, melodies and dances are presented as timeless, while lyrics

---

[7] Becker (2011) anthropology conference panel proposal. Similar perspectives are also expressed by Ebron, 2002 and Askew, 2002.
[8] Becker (2011) anthropology conference panel proposal. Similar perspectives are also expressed by Ebron, 2002 and Askew, 2002.
[9] I speak of the dances at the state-sponsored festival as 'traditional dances' as they are referred to as such by festival participants and some organizers including spectators. These dances are deemed traditional, because they are believed to have been carried over from past generations and thus believed to have never changed, although the metamorphosis of the dances is clearly evident.

are adjusted to social contexts. Dance moves are significantly modified. The originality of dance and song was highly contested, especially when they were presented by people who are believed to be Nyemba. What interested me most was the uncritical stance of the audiences when 'traditional' dances and songs were represented by White and Coloured children during a festival. This is important if one is to understand local notions of belonging in Kavango.

The performances are centered on traditional ritual dances, stories and old time riddles[10]. The dances in eastern Kavango (*Kambembe, Rengo, Shikavedi, Thiperu* and *Nyambi* respectively) are common among the Vagciriku, Vashambyu and the Vambukushu while *Mutjokotjo, Ukambe, Uyambi, Epera* and *Kambamba* are popular in the west among the Vakwangali and the Vambunza, and *Mahamba* is popular among the Vanyemba. The Vakavango dances are led by three drums, typically one bass and two tenors, the clapping of hands and singing by men and women. These dances were performed by the people of Kavango for celebration and thanksgiving after good harvests, deaths, rituals of passing and healing and as commentary on any social situation of note. Ngondo explained how dances and songs were historically conceived among the people of Kavango:[11]

> Yes, it's true that singing entails events that have happened and even long time ago that is how it was. For example if you listen to some of the traditional songs on radio you will notice that most of the songs they sang in Ukwangali are those of Epera dance. In this Epera dance songs you hear lyrics which praise certain people. What it means is that these are events they have seen and observed so all the songs are composed according to the life events people have observed. That is how it has been! The big thing here is that if one does not have a clear knowledge of the people nor the culture and its technique of talk you will not understand anything. I can tell now and today that if people began to sing about the song of how 'Kandere failed to operate the tractor of the secondary school' how many of us will know what is meant? Some will think that maybe Kandere was given a job of driving a tractor at the secondary school and could not manage to start it. Many will not understand what is meant at all, but the song has a meaning and only those who know its composition context will grasp what is being sung. Songs are spaces of expression.

The above excerpt shows that the composition of songs in what is conceived to be traditional dances spoke about social events that were deemed interesting in those contexts. The songs sung during the culture festival could create opportunities of interaction about open

---

[10] Bosch (1964) has recorded some of the 'traditional' dances, stories, riddles and tales of the VaShambyu in Kavango. Later Fisch (2008) also recorded some of these dances especially the hunting songs from the east of Kavango. The songs, dances, stories and tales are recorded as "tradisionele aspekte van die Shambui" by Bosch (1964).

[11] Interview with Rudolf Ngondo at Katjinakatji, 15 January 2010.

or concealed social subjects. The songs are believed to be interactive depictions of social events representing an image of the singers and their origins.

In contemporary Kavango, representations of a particular group are looked at in terms of how the songs are sung, the style of dance, the pitch of the drum and ability of the drummer to excite the listener and get them to cheer, dance and sing along or present tokens of appreciation to either the drummer or dancer. It is the style of dance, the song, the drum sound, and the costumes that demonstrate uniqueness. Events that are depicted in song are those that contain satire or village humour, conflicts that beg for intervention, praise for those who have excelled, and ridicule for those who are believed to have dragged the community's reputation into disrepute. Songs and dances in Kavango have changed according to prevailing social contexts[12]. They have mainly been influenced by political and economic conditions which are then embedded in song contents.

To date, all cultural groups from eastern Kavango perform the *Kambembe* dance during the cultural festival. *Kambembe* was performed when a member of the ruling clan had fallen ill or when a national disaster seemed imminent. It was the only ritual ceremony amongst the people of Kavango that [*at times*] required human sacrifice. (Fisch 2008:261) (my italics) When *Kambembe* was proclaimed all people in the vicinity were required to participate. Male and female dancers wore *marudeve* and they moved forward and backward, slowly stamping their feet and alternatively jolting their shoulders. Three drums were beaten and the rest of the participants sang while clapping their hands.

The dance was centered on the royal dancer who wielded a spear and uttered the words "*lilye mupika ndi ngombe*[13]" while dancing. This is how Shidonankuru remembers the *Kambembe* dance in her legend of the origin of Vakavango and their dances:[14]

> The Kambembe dance was acquired at Mpupa when we settled and cultivated there. What do you think existed there at Mpupa? There were people who lived underneath the waters. One would hear the sound 'wuuwu-were-were-were' of the waters sliding on stones. Then when we migrated downward Mulyata, Ngara, Nyumba and Shimwemwe settled at Mpupa. They only rested there; it was not their intention to settle yet. Then the wife of Shimwemwe cultivated a plot. One day she was picked up and taken underneath the waters. So, all that time when they used to hear the sound of drums 'Wuuwu-wuuwu' it was from people who lived there. So, the wife was picked up and taken to the depth of the waters and stayed there for three weeks to be trained. She learnt all the songs and how they played the drum. Then she was

---

[12] See my discussion in chapter six on festival songs.
[13] Lit. "The spear can either eat a commoner or cattle."
[14] Interview by Kletus Muhena Likuwa and Michael Uusiku Akuupa with Shidona Kamutuva, Gumma village, 27June 2008.

given a spear and told 'go back now'. She was brought out of the water and she came into the palace. She said 'listen to the Kambembe dance I got from that side'. So then they began the dance and she taught them and said 'there is Kambembe dance underneath there'. She had a reed-like spear. Now, in the beginning, do you think there was such a thing that the spear should kill a cow and then a human? They never used to kill a cow on the occasion! They would be approaching while someone like me Shidonankuru was seated uncomfortably and when they were about to conclude the dance they just passed the spear over your nostrils and there you died. That is how it all began with Kambembe dance. You think during Kambembe dance the spear was pierced into you? No, it just passed over your nostril and you died, it was a magical spear. Later the woman took that spear and handed it over to the royals. It was the royal people thereafter who danced the Kambembe dance. That spear was passed on to generations and even my grandfather King Nyangana finally got it after which it got lost. And nowadays it is a cow that is killed at Kambembe royal dance but in the beginning it was a human being.

Shidonankuru's[15] detailed explanation provides one perspective on how the Kambembe dance came about. It is believed to have been invented by people who lived on the riverbed beneath water and possessed supernatural qualities and were thus deemed magical. The words in songs for the Kambembe dance *"lilye mupika ndi ngombe"* referred to the likelihood and imminence of death of either a human commoner, or a head of cattle from a spear. Shidona's narrative of the ritual killing is different from the one presented by Fisch 2008:261 who recorded without going in to detail that the dance in question involved human death. Unlike Fisch who presented the Kambembe ritual as characterized by the killing of human beings or commoners, Shidonankuru's perspective is that of witchcraft. Her narrative shows that people were not actually stabbed with the spear. Rather, commoners could die when it was merely moved in the direction of their nose. That person could die instantly from the magical powers of the spear. The above dances have been part of the Vakavango ritual ceremonies since the 18th and 19th century. In the 1920s the colonial administration banned certain ceremonies, principally those with aspects of human sacrifice such as the Kambembe dance. (Fisch: 2008)

Shikavedi, another common dance, was used as a healing dance as treatment for evil spirits and other bodily ailments. When *Shikavedi* was performed it was confidently believed that the ancestors would neutralize the cause of illness. It was also performed for hippo hunters before they embarked upon a hunting trip. Dancers move their shoulders back and forth with their heels lifted, while moving their feet forward.

---

[15] Shidonankuru is a daughter of King Kamutuva of the Vagciriku. Due to her advanced age and social status as an elder she is considered by local people in her area as knowledgeable about the history of the Vagciriku and royal affairs.

Rengo and *Nyambi* dances were common among the Vambukushu people who populate the easternmost part of Kavango. It is similar to the healing dance of the Vanyemba known as *Mahamba,* and is said to have been adopted from the Vanyemba who are locally renowned for their strong healing powers. The *Nyambi* dance is used to heal illnesses related to 'emotional-neurotic disorder' as Fisch 2008:267 refers to it in conventional medical terms.

Rengo, a festival dance specific to the Vambukushu people, portrays rainmaking rituals. The rainmaking ritual has three stages known as *Kashandura, Dikumbwata* and *Thindongo*. The dance is characterized by long strides and extraordinary gyrations of the waist. (Fisch, 2008)

Dances that are common in western Kavango among the Vakwangali and Vambunza such as *Mutjokotjo, Epera, Ukambe* and *Kambamba,* are celebratory in nature. These dances are characterized by the clapping of hands and led by drumbeats. The dance styles of *Mutjokotjo, Kambamba* and *Ukambe* are very similar in composition, consisting of a male dancer situated between two females who are performing in front of other dancers forming a half-moon shape.

What makes *Mujokotjo* different from the other dances is that in the dance the male dancer is expected to direct a funny look at the faces of both female dancers. They in turn respond to the gesture. However, *Ukambe,* which is the dance of a horse, is performed in a horse-like galloping style slightly different from the other dances. The male dancer between the two female dancers move their legs in a galloping horse style with their heads and necks turning in various directions, so as to imitate the horse. The *Kambamba* dance is performed by one male dancer between the two female dancers with their feet moving back and forth while jolting shoulders in both directions. This style of moving shoulders is locally referred to as *kumhyaka.*

The various forms of dance serve as models for contemporary culture dances in Kavango, which are performed at the state sponsored culture festivals and any gatherings that warrant 'traditional' entertainment. Following on Max Gluckmans 1940 analysis[16] of a social situation and Geertz 1973 notion of thick description[17] in ethnographic research, I will show that 'rehearsal' creativity of 'traditional' dances, song and drama is not only produced

---

[16] The descriptions I provide in this chapter are not recorded on a single day; they are social events I observed over a period of time during my field research. However, I am using them to abstract the social relationships which happen in the making of the festival.

[17] I use thick descriptions in order to interpret and search meaning. Thick descriptions have general relevance and present a sociological mind with bodied stuff on which to feed on. He has argued in his introductory essay of *Interpretation of Cultures* that the important thing about the anthropologist's findings is their complex specificness and circumstantiality.

and mediated by school teachers and officials in the rehearsal and festival context, but is also created by local people who may not be directly involved. I present rehearsal events at a local school at Mayana and Ukumwe Cultural Dance Group followed by the festival performance of Unongo and Kapata Cultural Groups in the section of *kulinyanyukisa* respectively in order to demonstrate the type of social interaction these performances generate.

These rehearsed experiences are part of the social reality dealing with in real life events. In some instances the material used during the preparation for the festivals at primary schools was taught to children by their parents at home. The teachers later included the songs in their culture booklets, which were then presented during the festival.

When the rehearsed performances were brought into direct contact with the audience and other stakeholders at the festival, they ignited a social interaction that generated discourses of protectionism and reciprocity to issues communicated in the performance. While the materials presented during rehearsals and the festivals were local in nature, they were highly significant in the national context. Eventually when regions battled it out during the nationals, they brought local material to a social space that was mediated at the national level.

Rehearsal Performances

At Mayana Primary School

I was able to observe the rehearsal sessions of Mayana Primary School, where my wife is also a teacher. Mayana Primary School is situated about 28 kilometres east of Rundu in the Shambyu Traditional Authority area. It is a relatively large primary school that caters for about 550 children living in the adjacent villages including those from across the river (border) in Angola. The majorities of the inhabitants of Mayana village are Vanyemba[18] and have family on both sides of the river. They move freely in terms of settlement across the river, depending on the climate. Most of the families at the village are subsistence farmers. They cultivate millet, tend cattle and goats and catch fish. Their livelihood is supported by their ekoro who work and live in Rundu or elsewhere in the country. There are pockets of Vagcu/Vaduni or San inhabitants in the area whose children attend the school at Mayana.

The school has participated in various circuit culture festivals previously but has never before reached the regional culture festival level. My wife, Maria, with her colleagues is responsible for culture at the school. They compose songs, write the plays, and design the cul-

---

[18] Bosch (1964) recorded the settlement patterns and various inhabitants in Shambyu area. Already he had shown that the Vanyemba were in a majority then, rather than the, supposedly, original Vashambyu inhabitants in the area of concern.

ture booklet. The groups usually rehearse for a week just before the festival. The rehearsal of the school cultural group takes place immediately after class watched by the rest of the children from under a giant camel-thorn tree behind the class buildings.

The process of selecting participant performers is elaborate. All learners[19] at the school perform in trials according to class level and those who are seen to meet the standards are selected by the school's culture teacher. A preliminary mini-cultural dance competition is organized to select those who demonstrate knowledge of cultural dances.

The performers brought drums, costumes and other aids required for the rehearsal. There was the usual disorganization until Lucia shouted, "*Mweneni one*[20]*!*" There was silence and she began to read out the names of those who would rehearse, to go and get dressed in the costumes and take position in the half-moon shaped line. As they took their positions, Maria rearranged them according to their tonal range. There were three boys who would each beat the drum, eight girl dancers and five boy dancers. Judging by their appearance their ages ranged from 7 to 16. Their clothing was not as elaborate as one would find in the actual festival context. The boys wore their costumes (locally known as *marudeve*) over the school uniforms. The girls also wore their *marudeve* over their uniform skirts, and they donned the *vihiho*, the female head gear.

On the side Lucia urged the spectators (the other children) to move further out and watch the proceedings from a short distance. She also gave a short instructional talk to encourage the participants and explained the activities of the rehearsal as follows[21].

> Listen up very carefully! You will be required to sing three songs and perform one play. Whenever you sing, it must be loud so that the audience and judges can hear you clearly. You will perform one Kambembe dance, Mahamba and Shiperu dances respectively. And again when you dance you must do it very well so that you can get good marks. Is it clear? Which songs did you learn from home?

After this very clear instruction, one girl who is a lead performer approached the drummer. As the lead singer and performer she would direct the performance. After some pause, the lead drum sounded followed by the other two other drums. It was a test tune. The two teachers stood and observed how the expected dance would unfold. I stood with the rest of the learners who did not go home and stayed to witness the dances. All of a sudden the girl started to sing the song with drummers reciprocating the melody. The rest of the group

---

[19] Although the school levels are indicated to be lower and upper primary one does not necessarily find children under the age of fourteen as it normally should be. The children's ages vary and it is not surprising to find a sixteen year old child at this school. This age pattern can be attributed to children beginning school late say at the age of ten.
[20] Lit. Keep quite you all!
[21] My fieldnotes

clapped and moved their shoulders to and fro, flowing with the rhythm of the drums. The dance involves the turning of shoulders in anti-clockwise directions with movements of the waist and buttocks in circles, backwards and forwards. The song Ngombo as sung by the Vanyemba a long time ago was about the war of Mbambo:[22]

> The war is coming
> The war of Mbambo is coming very soon
> The diviner professed that the war is coming
> The war is coming soon

As the group members danced giving each other turns to enter the stage other spectators joined in the song and clapped their hands. After the performance the group reorganized and prepared to perform a play about a man who is married to a very clever woman. This woman wanted to have control over her husband's activities. If her plan succeeded it would mean her mother-in-law, whom she saw as meddling in her marital affairs, would be under her control. She went to seek help from the local healer. The healer, renowned for making potent medicine, gave her some to take home. The next morning as per the prescription she started to apply the medicine while her husband was still in the hut, by taking a sip from the concoction and spitting it out to the east and western side of the homestead while calling his name. Her sister-in-law spotted her and ran to her mother's homestead to report the matter. Upon hearing such news, the mother-in-law quickly went to her son's house to confront her daughter-in-law only to find her son sitting outside his hut basking in the sun. She first scolded him for being so tame unlike other men in the village. She told him that his wife had consulted a healer and that she had applied medicine around the house early in the morning. The son was forced to chase his wife away and make her cross the river in a canoe filled with her belongings. As I will show this play and its meaning were derived from local social interaction. During the play the small crowd of learners laughed as they anticipated certain sections of the unfolding drama. As the drumming began they danced moving their shoulders up and down and their legs forward at a fast pace while holding the small axes; they moved in the direction of the drummers and then ended the dance. At the end of the dance we all clapped.

On this occasion the teachers did not teach them anything other than give instruction on how to sing the songs and how to dance in order to get good marks from the judges and to generate audience response.

Below I present my observation of the Ukumwe Culture Dance Group during their preparatory sessions before the Annual National Culture Festival, where the group would

---

[22] The song is translated as such in the culture booklet of the Mayana Primary School.

perform for entertainment purposes in order to show how this well-respected adult dance group relied on the group members and their wealth of experience for producing a performance, unlike the school group that had to rely on parental input.

At Swapo Regional Office

Ukumwe[23] Culture Dance Group is composed of several members who defected from the Kambundu[24] Culture Dance Group as well as seven women from the regional Swapo Women's Council branch. It is composed of government employees among others who all belong to the Swapo Party[25] in the region. I observed that it was mostly women in this group who were self-employed and not the men. The majority of men in the group made a living working in their fields and keeping livestock in the surrounding villages. For the festival activities they commuted from their villages to Rundu. They rehearsed often, but this specific occasion was in preparation for their role at the festival.

The group, from which they originally split, the Kambundu Culture Dance Group, was one of the early culture groups formed during 1995 when the post-colonial state government began to reintroduce culture festivals nationally. What began as the Roman Catholic Church choir group later became a strong cultural dance group in the early phases of the state's reintroduction of culture festivals in Namibia. After an international trip, misunderstandings within the group led to a split and the creation of the Ukumwe Culture Dance Group. The misunderstandings were not openly discussed but it appears that they came about after certain individuals wanted to monopolize the group and run it as if it were a private entity. It transpired during the interview that certain people were refused entry to the group, because they did not belong to the Shambyu community, who were believed to be the majority. The newly-created group was named Ukumwe (unity) and was open to anyone in the region.

Later I learned that the group was keen to form joint ventures with profitable bodies and appoint a promoter to arrange performances. The majority of the group members were either self-employed or jobless and their income had to be supplemented with money from these paid performances.

The group had requested an official exemption from the festival competition, because it had excelled many times at all levels of competition. Members felt that there was more they could do than just to compete in the festival. Two of the group leaders wanted to be teachers

---

[23] The name Ukumwe which means "unity" was given to the group after its split from Kambundu.
[24] The group is named after Rebekka Kambundu the headwomen of the Rundu area under the Shambyu Traditional Authority. She belongs to the Vashambyu royal clan and was also a member of the group in the initial stages of the group.
[25] Swapo Party is the name of the ruling party in Namibia.

of culture in the region. As a result, the group would perform only for entertainment and important government occasions such as the welcoming of dignitaries, inaugurations of institutions and, occasionally, for tourists at various lodges in the region.

Consequently the group had assumed the role of 'teacher of culture and tradition[26]' although this was unofficial in the festival context. It made Sam Nuyoma, then head of State, its patron. The group performed for the queen and king of Spain on their visit to Windhoek in 1999, in Libya during the African Union Summit, as well as in Germany, Botswana and Zambia. Finally, it won the Kavango regional festival and the Annual National Culture Festival twice in 1998 and 1999. The above accolades have caused it to be recognized as the 'proper' representative of Kavango tradition and culture although it has also been criticized locally in the media and other social spheres. People in the local media[27] felt that there were other groups in the region that did a better job than Ukumwe, but they were not duly recognized or allowed to represent the region or country on as many arts platforms. During my fieldwork I have not heard of any other group that has gone the route of Ukumwe.

Ukumwe practices its dances and songs at the local Swapo office. The practice takes place every day after work. One afternoon I attended a practice with Tamwa Mbambo.[28] Although it was expected of the members to wear their costumes, it was not compulsory. They all dressed although not in full costume as they would in the festival. There were seven female and seven male dancers. This session was opened with a prayer by a female performer asking for guidance and wisdom in the rehearsal and future endeavours. After the prayer, the group members deliberated on the specific songs and drama they wanted to practice. They actually found it difficult to select from their extensive pool of songs and drama themes. It appears to have been tougher for the group members to agree on the drama theme than on the songs, because themes needed to convey a sensible message and in the process teach the tradition and culture of the Vakavango to the people attending the event. There was always contestation among group members as to which message they should use for their theme.

Eventually they agreed on the various themes: women in Kavango catching fish, the hunting ceremony, and finally the message of love and happiness. Two of the three songs they had in line of preparation were sung in Runyemba, the other was in Rukwangali. One of the songs sang in Runyemba was identical to the one practiced by the school children at Mayana Primary School. I was the only audience at the rehearsals.

---

[26] My fieldwork notes.
[27] My fieldwork notes.
[28] Tamwa Mbambo works for the regional culture office. He organizes various activities of the group, such as performance bookings and travel arrangements.

The group formed a half moon circle with drummers taking their position on the other end facing the dancers. Tamwa Mbambo began the greeting song titled: "Lombe lomba tusikalomba lisesa kulimwangane." (Hello, we are asking for permission from you all gathered here to allow us to dance.)

The whole group responded by clapping hands and beating drum to the lead singer. As the lead singer enters the centre of the semi-circle all other dancers swiftly move their hips and shoulders. At the end of the greeting song the group reorganizes to set the scene depicting women who have caught fish in the river. The performance was well handled with little flaws such as a female dancer who started to dance before the drum beat signal. There was laughter from the group, which continued to perform the final item of the practice, the Runyemba song, Ngombo.

The practice was very short, it lasted less than an hour compared to what I had observed at Mayana Primary School, which was over two hours. I will reflect below on the ethnography at the school and that at the Swapo office in order to demonstrate how local lay people contribute to the making of the festival through their material or intellectual contribution, a process that makes them active agents in the state project of nation-building, even if it takes place back stage.

Festival Making: Exploring Local Participation and Influences in the Discourse of Nation-Building

In order to make sense of the above rehearsal activity and the production of performances, I have categorized these as events at the back stage of the festival. In this context, events happen out of sight. Although events are rehearsed unseen, it is the process that makes it a practice of note. In this context the role of local citizens who are not directly involved in the festival may not be visible, except on occasions when teachers and group leaders of a particular school or group invite local people to come and assist or show them how certain dances or songs are done. In certain instances such assistance comes with a small fee, locally regarded as a token of appreciation.

Although this back of the stage activity is not the same as that described by Goffman, it included significant elements described by Goffman as the "back stage". The performance in the rehearsal is raw and it contains a lot of impurities. The rehearsal at the school setup had an audience other than performers and teachers. Other school learners were present and I as a researcher comprised an audience that may have influenced the rehearsal performance in various ways. The children who knew the dances and songs participated and that could have impacted on the process. Having knowledge of the content is another factor providing evidence of the social reality portrayed in the rehearsal. The children are primarily spectators, however, their connection to and knowledge of the social discourse make them active participants in the event and in the process the act is enlivened. The songs and dances that are performed are about real life situations as I demonstrate below, with an example of witchcraft.

When I spoke to the children at school, especially those who participated in the rehearsal, they said they had learned[29] the dances from their parents at home. The learning does not happen in a class-like environment and neither do parents summon children to a session of learning dances and songs. Instances of performance happened in ordinary daily activities such as when people drank alcoholic drinks, when they worked or even during their time of relaxation. One person always began to clap hands to a particular tune, the rest joined in and before you knew it there was a big performance going on. Children are always nearby when these activities happen and as a result imitate their elders.

The process of storytelling and riddles was learnt differently though. In many of my visits to the villages in Kavango and even in my own house I have observed how children keenly listened to *masimo*[30] especially after dinner is served and everyone is relaxed. *Masimo* is a local word that in the literal sense means story-telling. As I have observed, *masimo* is a favourite past-time for children. Usually *masimo* are narrated by elders in the family and not by children. It is these interactions in the home set-up that make the invisible ordinary citizens participants in the festival and its generation.

The composition of the various groups in relation to the communities in which they originate as well as social issues are important. Mayana Primary School is a relatively small group that is not very prominent or known in the wider circles of the festival as it has not progressed to any other level than the circuit. Why the school has not moved beyond the level of circuit festivals throughout the years of its participation could be attributed to its creativity or lack thereof and the production of its materials.

The teachers at Mayana did not appear to be fully involved in many aspects of producing the school's cultural group. During the rehearsal, the only task of the teachers seemed to be to gather and organize the children, but they did not seem to have prepared what learners were going to perform. They relied on what the performers knew or had learned from their parents at home. The ethnography shows that children practiced what they had learned from their parents at home. They appeared to know the songs and the drama lines

---

[29] My field notes
[30] Doing masimo is an art which requires skills in telling and narrating. It is that art which keep listeners in suspense, captivated and wanting to hear more of the masimo. If the masimo narrator is not skillful it becomes too boring.

well, and knew how to perform particular dances. It was not performers only who reacted to the type of songs, but the spectators as well who had to be restrained by the teachers so as not to interrupt those on stage. The ability of the children from the same area to sing and perform certain dances shows how local people influence ideas of what is believed to be or to constitute local tradition and culture.

From the song and theme of their drama presentation we can also deduce the social discourse of the community from which the performers originate. There had been talk of witchcraft among the community of Mayana for quite some time during my fieldwork. This type of witchcraft locally known as *wandjongoka* was rumoured to be prevalent in the area. *Wandjongoka* is a type of witchcraft that can loosely be interpreted as 'to tame' and is believed to be used by women who want to have control over their husbands' abilities and emotions, resulting in a total dislike of his kin and acquaintances. As a social issue it is regarded as so important. In the context of the play, it does not mean that those who are believed to practice witchcraft are unknown; identity is deliberately concealed so that the play and song can serve their purpose to entertain and educate. The practice of singing about life events and concealing identities of those involved concurs with Ngondo's perspective below in my interview with him: "What it means is that, these are events they have seen and observed, so all the songs are composed according to the life events that people have observed. That is how it has been!

When I asked Lucia the teacher responsible for culture what they taught the children and what influenced their production she explained:

> We ask the children to learn songs from their parents. You know especially grandparents know how to tell old stories about how people lived. You know we are very young and we do not know these things very well. They also know the tradition and culture very well. We only sometimes change the words, but the song melodies remain the traditional ones[31].

The teacher's expectation of children parents and grandparents helps to illuminate the role and influence of local people in the activities of the state-sponsored festival. In the context of the rehearsal I have just described, there was no obvious new input from the teachers. However, some of their contributions were implicit in the various administrative roles and responsibility. Teachers of culture are randomly selected by the school management. Expertise in matters related to culture is not a necessity. They may not necessarily have been enthusiastic about the task but in this case being young made them think that they were not well equipped to transfer ideas of culture to the children than the elders. This is due to

---

[31] My field notes

a perception of culture being about old things transferred from one generation to the next. Also, there are inner politics[32] among teachers especially about the particular roles they play at school and how these may benefit their own growth.

However, the role of teachers and their enthusiasm may differ as I learned through my interview with the teacher responsible for culture at Dr. Alpo Mbamba Junior Secondary School, Jonas Ihemba. He has been responsible for culture at the school since 2003, longer than many other teachers. His group has won many times in the junior secondary category. As I observed, it was the only school that appeared outstanding in terms of costume and choreography, on stage and off stage. When I spoke to him about his involvement in culture, it became obvious how he has taken on the culture aspect at school and made it his own project:

> Ihemba: You see myself also I like this culture. Although the policy says the schools must participate, I also like the culture. I see it as important, I also want to take part and I like culture. And I have to win. That is just my own arrangement.
>
> Michael: Do you compose the songs?
>
> Ihemba: Songs are, they are not the easy things to compose. I can remember that since I started this role of culture, I can compose even up to fifty songs myself. And one of my friends who is not here usually helps me to do it. We were just trying to make our own songs. So what makes us to compose songs? Some of the songs have been sung previously and each song must have a meaning. In order to make a song, you must look at the situation, I mean current situation. What is happening there? In my case I look at nowadays life, what is happening and educational things so that we can teach our youngsters or nation. The only tough thing we face is the melody; sometimes you have the words, but not the melody.

Unlike his colleagues who thought that it was wise to rely on local elders' input as they were knowledgeable in local culture, Ihemba expressed his love for culture and the importance of winning in the festival. He composed songs for the group. There is an important underlying difference in the manner how culture is conceived by the teachers at Mayana and Alpo Mbamba. The former understand culture in the essentialised terms as being fixed and transferred from one generation to the next. While in the latter, culture is conceived to be relative to the current situation. In this context one should not necessarily conclude that the teachers at Mayana were slack or disinterested. I also believe that there could be underlying complex matters influencing their thoughts on the government business of culture.

All teachers who deal with culture in all schools had a responsibility to have the costumes made for their groups, to write themes for the plays, finances, and create a reference

---

[32] For reasons of confidentiality, I will not dwell into this matter currently.

archive for future groups. Teachers at various schools also consulted local elders to assist them with how certain dances were performed, costumes designed and songs sung. However, in certain instances these consultations come at a cost. One of the teachers at Sauyemwa Junior Primary School bemoaned the situation:[33]

> Elders do not want to assist us fully. Say, if you ask someone to come and teach the children how to play the drum, that person would want to be paid every time he comes. The other difficulty is the movement of children from one school to the next yearly [in the process skills are lost]. In the process the whole exercise becomes expensive. If you decide to call someone to come and teach the children how to perform a particular dance, he or she would always ask for money. So things become very difficult. The other problem is since people became Christians they seem to have buried tradition. Culture is only starting again after it was introduced at schools. Some people know the tradition, but they would be scared to teach or show it lest they be suspected of being a pagan. For some their focus is on the money only and they ask very high prices.

While there is evidence of elders who assist various culture groups for free, there are those who would not assist without being rewarded for their work. The act of payment[34] to those who contribute to culture was criticized earlier during the time of the colonial festival (the *sangfees*) on the grounds that payment would hamper the "original" and "genuine" transfer of "traditional" knowledge to be displayed in the festival context[35]. In the context of the interview, however, money and Christianity were believed to hamper the cultural 'life'. For the purpose of this discussion, the teachers' sentiments at Mayana and Sauyemwa Primary Schools about the role and participation of local people in the festival activities showed their direct involvement, although it did require some form of reward. The issue of culture as social capital was also of importance in the interview excerpt. While teachers expected local elders to come to their schools and give dance lessons without being paid, the 'culture experts' expect reward in the form of money. During the colonial period monetary rewards were seen as an unwanted influence that would dilute the native culture; in contemporary times it is widely regarded as a source of income.

---

[33] Interview with Magdalena Pessa Kasera, Theresia Sikongo, Anastasia Mufenda and Helena Nasini Hafeni; they are teachers responsible for culture at Sauyemwa Junior Primary School, 20 January 2009.
[34] I have noted earlier in chapter 5 that unlike the colonial government which discouraged people to make money out of culture trade, the postcolonial government in its policy directives encourages citizens to better their lives by selling their culture. In this context culture is used as a resource which has a potential to improve living conditions if it is fully explored.
[35] This perspective has been shared by Bradley during our interview on 20 September 2008 in Rundu. See in chapter five.

The situation of school groups is different from groups that are well established and nationally recognized, such as Ukumwe Traditional Dance Group. Ukumwe is composed of adults from various social backgrounds. One member of the group is in the employ of the local regional culture office while some are either self-employed or work in the sewing project run by the Swapo Women's Council at the local Swapo office where rehearsals takes place. The membership of the group is steady and has remained the same since its creation.

The members' diverse social connections have contributed to the group's popularity, which has in turn helped it to become the group most frequently invited to perform at Swapo and State events. Most importantly, the group had Sam Nujoma[36] as its patron. In addition Tamwa Mbambo, a group member, has considerable influence in the local and national circles which deals with culture. He is believed to be an exceptional dancer locally and is regarded as a very important asset by the other group members.

Since its creation the Ukumwe Culture Dance Group has been seen as an alternative to the Kambundu Culture Dance Group,[37] which was viewed as discriminatory by local people, because it only recruited people from the regional Vanyemba. Discussions of what led to the split were concealed for fear of the consequences. The secrecy[38] and fear did not surprise me, because of the significant political influence at local level of certain Kambundu individuals. Furthermore, those who were excluded were not seen to be part of the Vashambyu majority.[39] Ukumwe, however, was locally believed to be inclusive of all people who viewed themselves as Vakavango and had knowledge of the "traditions and cultures, plus the desire to preserve the Kavango culture and norms for future generations[40]". However, it is an unwritten requirement to belong to the ruling party if you want to be a member of the group.

The group rehearsal was systematic and short. The group did not seem to struggle in putting together a theme which they drew from from traditional oral sources that include tales, riddles and historical legends and is not limited to songs as told by the elders. How-

---

[36] See the culture booklet of Ukumwe, in the section which deals with the background of the group.
[37] Earlier, I spoke about the secrecy about the split of the Kambundu Culture Dance Group and the sudden creation of the Ukumwe Culture Dance Group. Members of the respective groups have not been willing to share the details. However, I heard how people spoke about the politics within Kambundu and Ukumwe in other social contexts such as at the bars, the festivals and in local media.
[38] I will not detail this matter, because of its sensitivity. Even after a decade people do not freely speak about it.
[39] Refer to chapter 4 where I discuss the historical legends about the emergence of early Kavango and its inhabitants.
[40] Excerpt from the introductory statement of Ukumwe Culture Dance Group presented during the Annual National Culture Festival in 2008. Sam Nujoma is the first head of state of Namibia, under whose leadership the festivals were reintroduced.

ever, apart from the themes that the group rehearsed, at least some of the dance songs like *Ngombo* were identical to some of those I had heard performed by the schoolchildren. It illustrates that all groups I spoke about drew their material primarily from 'oral archives' that are believed to be transferred from one generation to the next. Like the school group, Ukumwe does not live in isolation from the local community and, as a result, the contribution of individual group members to the production of their material is influenced by outsiders - an impact that is indirect, but nonetheless significant. The discussion above demonstrates an interesting dynamic in the state-sponsored culture festival, which is considered local in terms of involvement, content and participation, but which is significant in the purported national discourse of unity-in-diversity and nation-building.

My next focus is on the interaction between festival goers, performers and state organizers. I present events of the Mpungu circuit and Kavango regional festivals as front stage[41] respectively to demonstrate that the festival becomes a social space were local notions of what constitutes Kavango 'culture' and Namibian nationality are contested, especially after those in attendance have viewed the presentations. Most importantly, events that occur in the festival front stage are highly mediated, unlike those in the rehearsals. Although the festival front stage is mediated, it does not necessarily mean that there are rigid boundaries that prevent the audience and performers from behaving or acting in a particular manner. I show that the festival is a space where belonging and nationhood is celebrated through audience interaction and participation in the cultural performance and the singing of national anthems.

Mpungu Circuit and Kavango Regional Festivals

The festival stage is of particular interest in our understanding of how people perceive what happens as social reality and not some staged activity. Following on from Goffman's (1959) notion of performance in the presentation of the self, I use performance on the front stage to suggest and refer to the activity of individuals, which occurs during a period marked by their continuous presence before an audience. It is thus appropriate to refer to such performance as front stage as it regularly functions in a fixed fashion to define the situation for those who observe the performance. As Goffman has argued, the front then becomes the expressive equipment of a standard kind that is intentionally, or unwittingly, employed by the individual during the performance. Goffman's perspective on performance and social reality is rooted in the belief of actors in the performance. The performance is believed to

---

[41] The festival becomes a front stage, because of the nature of its making. Only choreographed presentations are done in the spectacle of the audience.

be real by those who are engaged in it and requires no further legitimation as it is situated in what Bourdieu 1998 has referred to as habitus. In addressing this theoretical challenge I will draw on the local notion of performance which is premised in the act of doing culture or playing culture while what is being done is referred to as a performance. In the context of this discussion the performances as conceived by the two groups, namely Unongo and Kapata Cultural Groups, are the particular dances and story dramas they perform. This interaction is seen as part of the 'broader doing' act; and it is what gives and brings life to the performance.

I argue that *kulinyanyukisa* and *maliyombiliso* are aspects of the perceived social reality I deal with in the back and front categories of the festival. Backstage and front stage activities in the festival context will not make sense if dealt with separately. Due to what happens in the festival category of *kulinyanyukisa* in relation to the former *maliyombiliso*, it will be of importance to refer to that festival not only as social practice, but a reality all the actors concerned believe in.

In festival encounters, before the competition commences, certain groups (especially those that are not competing) are always invited to 'open the curtain' for performance; the section is locally referred to as *kulinyanyukisa*[42]. People always look forward to this section of the festival as it allows anybody to go on stage and display their dance skills. One can also present tokens of appreciation to an individual dancer who is thought to have expressed good dancing abilities and other performance prowess. That part shows how fluid the fully mediated front stage can be, especially when what transpires on stage has a significant impact on the audience and its response is an adverse one.

Although the circuit festivals are not viewed by some officials at the Maria Mwengere Culture Centre to be as important as the regional festival, they attract large audiences in the areas where they are held. This was interesting, especially in the context of this discussion where I am trying to show the role of local people in the making of the state-sponsored cultural festival. I will describe and discuss the circuit and regional festival I attended at Mpungu and Rundu respectively to showcase how presentations by various groups initiate an interaction among and between those who come to witness the event as audience, invited guest, festival organizer and/or performers in the *kulinyanyukisa* section. I begin with the circuit festival at Mpungu, which was the last event held during the zonal rounds before the regional festival took place in Rundu during 2008.

In the following paragraphs I describe the performance of the Unongo Cultural Group in the Mpungu circuit event and that of the Kapata Cultural Group in the Kavango regional

---

[42] Lit. to make ourselves happy or to entertain ourselves.

culture festival respectively. My special focus is on gatherings and certain performance presentations that initiate interactions between performers and attendees of the event.

The event was to be held in Mpungu in western Kavango. School learners, teachers, and people from the community came to witness the event. Performers from various schools and youth groups from the area could be recognized by the 'traditional' attire they wore. There was the sound of a drum in the environment. In the midst of this were the circuit Inspector of Education, Peace Corps volunteer teachers, the headmaster of the school hosting the event, the hospital matron and officials from Maria Mwengere Culture Centre. The judges were all from Maria Mwengere Culture Centre.

After the national anthem was sung another a prayer was made asking for guidance, fairness for judges and a good mood of enjoyment, "as we enjoy culture".

After the prayer, it was time for welcoming remarks and speeches. The headmaster rose to make a few remarks that dealt with the importance of hosting the event in the circuit. Representing the government, his speech was very short and was made in the local Rukwangali vernacular. It was followed by the circuit inspector. He started his speech in English with a quote from article 19 of the constitution of the republic which states:

> Every person shall be entitled to enjoy, practice, profess, maintain and promote any culture, language, tradition or religion subject to the terms of this constitution and further subject to the condition that the rights protected by this article do not impinge upon the rights of others or the national interest.

Although he was a local he made his speech in English[43]. His speech was to be translated into the local vernacular by the director of ceremonies, but he could not oblige in the local vernacular and instead asked the headmaster to assist, to the laughter of the audience. The inspector continued his speech with a question of what culture is: he continued to answer, with a fairly anthropological interpretation, as follows: "Culture is a shared way of living, not a fossil from the past, but a vibrant dynamic constantly changing complex of ideas and interactions."

He went on to speak about how culture was used to divide people in the colonial past, because people were seen as unequal and thus some of them were perceived to be superior. He also spoke about how the new government started a programme to make use of culture as a force for creating unity. He did not end his speech before listing the various elements such as "customs, "customs of marriage, and inheritance, tradition and how history is told," which he believed constituted Namibian culture. His take and understanding of culture was

---

[43] The speaker may have chosen to communicate in English, because it is the official language in Namibia.

not significantly different from that presented by the Minister of Youth, National Service, Sport and Culture (MYNSC) during the ANCF later in the same year:

> Culture is a shared behaviour, ideas and artifacts. A way of life passed from one generation to another. It is a shared pattern for behaviours and interactions, social constructions and understandings that are learned through the process of socialization. These shared concerns identify the members of a culture group, while also distinguishing one group from another. However culture will never remain static. As a society, times changes, and so will culture develop. Changes in domestic and regional environment and the fast pace of living will continue to shape our mind set and way of thinking. Cultural development must therefore keep abreast of the new environments that we face. However, economic development and social cohesion will remain our two pillars for prosperity and stability[44].

The Minister's definition of culture was elaborate and captured aspects of the changing environments and economic factors and as an important determinant of how people see themselves in relation to others. There was an emphasis on embracing and being abreast of new global developments. However, a Deputy Director in his ministry presented a different perspective in the same context with regard to the outside influences and its impact on local culture in his short speech below:

> The flavour of the music should be Namibian, it must be Namibian, it must touch the heartstrings. If it attains universality appealing cross-culturally it can reveal magical dimensions. It is not that we are discouraging any other music, we have many occasions that we come together with international culture and even some of the best groups from here will become our culture ambassadors. But for our festival, these ones here it is now where we come up with the best Namibian music. The next criterion is the dance, another ten marks. The dance must be inspiring, you know if you come on stage and you are asleep with your dance those of us watching will also sleep with your dance. So the dance must be inspiring. The dance must speak from body and soul: that is the African idiom. We are not somewhere in New York doing some funny things, let us do with body and soul[45].

It appears that the Deputy Director accepted the need to learn from "other cultures" internationally, but the need to brew national music in the festival occasion was of particular importance. The above utterances advocate genuine and original performances and stress that performers must struggle very hard to prevent international influences with which they are in constant contact. It is a clear attempt by the Deputy Director (in this case the representative of the State) to encourage participants to preserve or salvage an essentialized

---

[44] Excerpt from the speech of Willem Konjore of the MYNSC during the ANCF in Kavango during 2008.
[45] Excerpt from the speech of Andre Strauss a deputy director of the NHCP in the MYNSC.

"traditional culture" in Namibia, especially at the festival space. He seemed to construct and imagine the festival as a space, a "neutral grid on which cultural difference, historical memory and societal organization are inscribed." (Gupta & Ferguson, 1992:7) This construction poses a challenge to many participants who incorporate western traits in their performances; a situation that came with postcoloniality. Postcoloniality in this case – as further argued by Gupta and Ferguson (1992) problematizes the relationship between space and culture. I argue that new ways of life[46] (hybrid culture) that have outside influences, came about at independence. If international influences are to be set aside at the festival moment as the Deputy Director advocates, signs of contestation will manifest in another space.

Then it was time for the senior cultural officer to say something about the gathering. He gave the background to the festival and spoke about the new projects in the office, which were about a collection of oral accounts of traditional rituals and histories of the people of Kavango before turning his attention to the event of the day:

> The dance aspect is confusing a lot of people, for them when they see a group that dances excellently they do not consider other criteria then they go to Mudukuli and say "vana fukire[47]". We look at all the above criteria, but it is true dance is important. We don't want to see you dancing kuduru[48] when it is suppose to be Epera[49]. If it is Epera let it be Epera. ... So out of these criteria we will give you marks so that we can determine the winner, but most importantly you are all winners, he concluded.

The above instances show the unevenness of the state discourse of culture at its various levels of administration. When the senior cultural officer finished his remarks, he returned the microphone to the director of ceremonies who then went on to call the first group to entertain the audience and visitors. It is traditional to have a section of *kulinyanyukisa* in every festival competition in which the audience is shown what is believed to be the best in that category. The group that was invited to entertain was the Unongo Cultural Group. Unongo

---

[46] In 1989 just before independence, the people who came from exile under the SWAPO movement had a musical or cultural group known as Ndilimani. Ndilimani was used as a culture vehicle during the days of liberation. It played music which consisted of a fusion of native songs from all corners of Namibia, however the melody and dance was influenced by West African music. It has since undergone massive change in terms of style, but most of its dance remains rooted in Congolese musical rhythms.
[47] They call in to the radio program and complain that "they have been cheated".
[48] Kuduru is a sort of dance that was introduced during the late 90s from Angola. It is a back and forth round movement of the waist area, the dance itself is not well received by the older folk of the region as it is seen to be explicit and contaminating the traditional dances.
[49] Epera is a traditional dance commonly done in western Kavango. See preceded section "note on Kavango traditional dances."

is a youth category group that had won the youth category during the circuit festival held at Nkurenkuru some time ago. The group was composed of eight female and six male dancers, including three drummers. Both the female and male dancers were dressed in costumes made of maroon cotton fabrics. The females wore short skirts and tops, which covered their breasts. They complemented their look with white beads around their arms, ankles, neck and below the knees. The fabric skirt symbolized the traditional skin dress worn by women before the arrival of missionaries and colonial officials. They sported a head gear locally known as *vihiho*[50]. The males wore the *marudeve*[51] around their waists emitting a rattle sound whenever they moved. Most of the male dancers were bare breasted except for two who wore white beads around their necks. The décor they created for their play consisted of a clay pot, a calabash, three baskets each filled with maize, mahangu and sorghum seeds and three different types of fish hooks.

The drummer started and led the songs while drumming simultaneously. As they entered, there was no excitement from the audience despite successive urging from the director of ceremonies to cheer for the group. It was only after their second and third *Ukambe* dance that there was significant interaction between the group and the audience. The second song started after the play, which focused on the types of traditional foods that the group displayed in its décor. The song *daya ngoma* (lit. hit the drum) is believed to have urged the drummer to beat the drum efficiently and very hard. When the song began, we all watched with wonder the skills of the drummer who did many things at the same time. He led the song, beat the drum and danced, and ended the dance. Two dancers, a female and male danced moving towards the judges in a horse-gallop style, and returned moving in the direction of the lead and backing drummers. When they approached the lead drummer, the female dancer joined the rest in the half moon circle while the male dancer repeated the routine. On his way back as he danced towards the lead drummer he faced him and danced vigorously. The drummer moved an inch towards him and beat the drum intensely! The audience was excited and clapped hands wildly as they ululated. Notable was the middle-aged man who ran on the stage in the direction of the drummer with a two hundred dollar bill (N$200[52]) raised in his hand for everyone to see and inserted it in the waist of the drummer who paused for a little while to acknowledge his gift. The other dancers still danced to the tunes of the backing drums. When the man returned to the audience, the drummer

---

[50] Vihiho (sing: sihiho) is a form of headgear. It is a long snarl that hangs down to the female's shoulders and is made of tree inner bark.
[51] Marudeve (sing: rudeve) is clothing made of reeds which grow along the Kavango River. The reeds are cut into pieces and joined together with a string and tied around the waist like a skirt. When a person clad in a rudeve and dances it emits rattle sound.
[52] N$1=R1

intensified his drum act. Before we knew it the drummer was on his back and the sound of his drum overpowered any other sound as it pitched on high note. One young male student from a local high school ran onto the stage towards the drummer who was still on his back as he beat the drum. In his hand he had a 10 dollar note, which he put in the waist of the drummer who had gone into a trance. The crowd chanted "*Ana tumuka!*[53]" while they shouted and clapped hands. His eyes were closed, the drum was tightly gripped between his legs and he beat it without stopping for over twenty minutes. The only male dancer had also gone into a trance as he danced the horse-style gallop. Spectators also danced to the drum's tune. The rest of the dancers in the group clapped their hands and responded to the song announcement of the lead drummer. The invited guests and the judges clapped their hands. The drum sound was contagious. I imagined that I also danced although, I know very well that I cannot dance; I am not good at *kumhyaka* despite repeated attempts. The dancers could not signal the end of dance to the lead drummer until he was also on the ground and felt by the drummer, and only then did he close the performance. The crowd continued to chant "*daya ngoma!*". It took a long while before the director of ceremonies managed to calm the audience.

Due to the relationship between the two events in the front stage I will analyze the circuit and regional festivals simultaneously. First I give a snapshot description of the performance by the Kapata Cultural Group at the region's central festival, which took place in Rundu. Their performance in the section of *kulinyanyukisa* further illustrates the dynamics and interactions that transpire at that level of the festival.

The regional festival at Rundu attracted many spectators, including important people in the regional government. At the regional festivals, the winning groups from the circuit compete in the different categories for the prize of being the region's best cultural group. Compared to the circuit festival, the regional fair is a large event with a lot of preparations at official level and many groups that would like to participate in the competition. The officials and institutional staff go to great lengths to make a success of the regional festival, held in this case in the recently renovated amphitheatre. The officials appeared to be very involved. During the circuit festivals, officials from the centre judged performances during the competition, whereas for the regional festival the centre invited judges from the head office in Windhoek and local teachers who they believe to have knowledge about Kavango tradition.

The regional festival took place over two days. On both days the 2008 regional festival was well attended. Every seat in the amphitheatre was taken; more spectators, mostly chil-

---

[53] Lit. He is in trance!

dren, sat on the ground a few inches from the stage. Invited guests included the mayor of Rundu, the regional governor, councillors, senior education officials, local business people and religious leaders. The Kapata Culture Group from the Gciriku area in eastern Kavango was scheduled to perform in the *kulinyanyukisa* session. The group consists mostly of elderly male and female dancers who usually compete in the festival's premier category. However, this time the group did not make it through during the circuit festival competition, and was to entertain the waiting audience.

The director of ceremonies, Gelasia Shikerete, announced that Kapata would perform next. People cheered when they heard the name of the group. The group came on stage to set their décor theme. The group performed an entrance song followed by a drama about two women who worked in their fields. The two women always went together to the fields to cultivate and tend to their crops. However, one of them did not really work hard and would usually go home early, in fact soon after she had arrived. The other one worked very hard and always left last. They later returned to the fields to harvest. On their way to the fields they conversed on how they were looking forward to reaping the fruits of their labour. The spectators listened carefully to the unfolding story and occasionally laughed at the comments of the two women. The crux of the story was when the two got to the fields: one was happy and thanked the gods for the good harvest. The other woman was in shock when she found only weeds in her field, and one yellow watermelon. Her reaction attracted laughter and comments from the spectators as she exclaimed: "Nane! Owu mushoni, mo nalimine mu? Evi vya kunkuwa vi! Vyakundohita vhino." (Oh my goodness! And this grass? Is this the place that I cultivated? This cannot be! I must have been bewitched!)

The spectators inside the VIP tent sarcastically retorted to the questions the women asked, to further laughter from the audience and performers: "Kwato vyaurodi." (There is nothing like witchcraft!)

The other women ended the play with a statement about the importance of hard work: "Ukoli wanaumwande! Ira mu va tanta vakhughona shi, ukoli kulya ukoli woye, nange udwa kulya udwa woye!" (This is my hard work! Elders have said if you work hard you eat from your hard work; if you were lazy, you will eat laziness!)

She then started the Shiperu dance, led by the drum. In a short time the stage was filled with people from the audience who joined the Shiperu dance at its high point, at that particular moment. The master of ceremonies then attempted to stop the dance so that she could move on to the next item on the agenda, but the dancers just kept going.

"Daya Ngoma![54]", a Drumming Performance that Had Us Electrified: An Analysis of Front Stage Interactions at the Festival

In order to tease out the social interaction in the festival space, I deliberately selected from the *kulinyanyukisa* category, because it was more neutral and not subjected to intense scrutiny like the adjudicated presentations. I thought this category might have a different impact on audience and participants alike since it was not linked to a festival result. People from all sections of the festival, whether they were spectators, invited VIPs or organizers could join the stage activities unlike in the competition itself where only the performers are allowed on stage.

Performances in this category are meant for entertainment, although they follow the same presentation format as those in the competition. The *kulinyanyukisa* is much anticipated in the festival, because it is the space in which festival-goers freely enjoy, entertain and celebrate the actual event. This category creates an open interactive space between the various sections of people represented at the festival.

Most importantly this is a front stage, a space highly mediated by each master of ceremonies. We expect the front stage to be systematic and fixed in the way Goffman (1959) suggested in his outline of stages. This front stage is mediated by the master of ceremonies even though his powers are at times overruled by persistent performers. However, he or she also has the ability to initiate interaction between the audience and performers through urging the spectators to cheer for the participants. The audience is less likely to respond to those urgings if they do not foresee excitement, although in many cases they do comply. The interaction in this front stage removes the rigid system of the performance.

Firstly, I focus on the circuit festival at Mpungu where the Unongo Cultural Group performed in the category of entertainment. Mpungu is in a rural area and all the modern buildings in it belong to the State. These are either schools or hospitals, which provide employment to local people. The circuit cultural festival is a welcome social activity that attracts the majority of the village people. To the locals it was an important occasion, as one of the two young people I met the evening before at the local cuca-shop said: "At least there is something going on this weekend, it is not going to be boring here[55]."

The Inspector of Education and the matron of the hospital were regarded by the festival organizers as VIPs representing the state. Most importantly, the national anthem and the African Union anthem were sung in order to convey stately significance on the event. Some years into independence, Namibia ruled that the AU anthem be sung along with the

---

[54] Lit. Beat the drum.
[55] My field notes

national anthem. This was said to be in line with the spirit of pan-Africanism and creating a sense of belonging.

The Inspector of Education officiated during the event in order to give the festival its national dimension. He reiterated the message of unity and the rights of citizens to enjoy and practice their cultures as long as this did not infringe on the rights of other citizens. As with many state officials who officiated at festivals that I attended during my fieldwork, he used the term culture in an anthropological sense. However, when he explained and listed the aspects of culture that need to be preserved and celebrated for unity and diversity, the explanation presented culture as an object. In an anthropological sense, we understand it as dynamic and use it synonymously with tradition.

The senior cultural officer, Thomas Shapi, who on this occasion was dressed casually, presented a completely different persona compared to his demeanour at the regional and national festivals. It had been his duty to speak about the background of the festival and the new projects in his office during the circuit competitions. In the process he called on people to participate in projects and cultural activities in order to enhance unity and the independence of the people of Kavango as well as the Namibian nation at large. He also set out an official expectation of the type of local dances to be presented later during the day. His sentiments about local dances were to discourage improvisation and modification of dances and foreign influences, including what he referred to as the *kuduru* dances. However, he also acknowledged the right and freedom of the citizens to complain and protest the festival outcomes in the various media available, especially the local radio phone-in show *Mudukuli,* which means to expose.

These presentations contain stories that are told in drama and song as part of the social discourse. The dances are all modelled on the various traditional Kavango. The dances and ideas in the plays presented in this category are also compared with the models in order to show whether they are symbolic and presented in the utmost original form, or not. Similar sentiments about the importance of observing the originality of dances were expressed by one of my informants. But he blamed the state as follows when I asked him about the state of contemporary dances in Kavango:[56]

> If it is to say people should showcase their culture (tradition) and how it developed, it is good. Now, here and there, you hear people who complain, because of the manner in which culture is performed nowadays. It is not the way our elders did it. If you compare how the youth of today present their culture, there is a big difference.

---

[56] Interview with Karel Shiyaka Mberema at Maria Mwengere Culture Centre, Rundu, 23 September 2008. Mberema is a local historian and linguist and has published on traditions of the vaGciriku. He also recently published a Rumanyo and English dictionary with Mohlig. He also serves as a judge during the culture festivals in Kavango.

> The youth performers especially children try very hard to modify in an apparent [attempt] to draw attention and gain more marks at the national festival, but it is not right. And that is why people are complaining. Recently in the meeting we had about the festival, that issue came up again and it was concluded that what people perform at the festival is not original culture. In that meeting, the senior cultural officer Shapi said that the festival was not necessarily meant for people to perform their indigenous culture, but anybody could perform any culture. He was questioned as to what the purpose of having festivals was, if people were not doing it the way their elders did. How does one protect the tradition? Is it not just proper if anybody sticks to their traditional dances and imitate the way our elders did it?

Mberema thus presents a discourse that essentializes local culture. It speaks of the modification of dances in the front stage of the festival and how they have lost their original sense as expressed in the section on the note of Kavango traditional dances. This discussion points out the type of interactions between the state and the festival-goers. In this interaction the state outlines its expectation to the audience and festival participants of what culture should be. There are local people who contribute to the festival content during rehearsal; those who perform the dances also present the dances in a way that according to them is culture. Both actors in the festival contribute to the festival dances and dramas according to their own conception. While the state views and presents culture as dynamic and yet static at the same time, local people see it as an object that needs protection in the process of transference to the public or the new generation.

However, this does not mean that local people do not acknowledge that the culture they represent in the festival is dynamic, they also present 'their' culture as they imagine it. The conception of culture between the two sides overlaps and as a result becomes complex to analyze, especially when one attempts to locate it within the anthropological conception. However, to echo what Losambe and Sarinjeive 2001 wrote in the introduction of their publication on pre-colonial and post-colonial drama and theatre, it seems as if culture is semioticised in order to demarcate as signifier (vehicle) and signified (communicated meaning of social life).

There is an implicit aim in the festival making, which is to communicate the state's message of "unity in diversity". Clearly this message emphasizes tolerance of difference and belonging. The culture discourse has become prevalent during this specific historical juncture. However, it is interpreted differently by the various levels of the state and local people. The state through its representatives as actors in the making of the festival conveys its message of unity in diversity. In other words, the festival brings people together for the State to deliver its messages to them, before they are allowed to express themselves and their needs through performances that are presented in the various categories such as in the *kulinyanyukisa* moment of the festival.

Now I turn to the actual performance of Unongo and Kapata in the two festival contexts of the kulinyanyukisa category. Both performances have a story to tell. The cultivation of traditional foods and the reasons why people should work hard so that they can gain more from whatever they do was the subject of one of the plays. Learning as an aspect of culture is implicit in all the performances I have observed, as are the statements of the various speeches made during the festivals. The importance of being able to "learn culture" is emphasized so that citizens can know their origins and this will (presumably) help them face the future.

The performance of Unongo and specifically its drummer was particularly interesting. What started as a low-energy performance culminated in a frenetic, energy-charged activity, because of the acknowledgement and appreciation shown by the actors at all levels of the festival. The group knew that the song excited the drummer. The song "Daya Ngoma" and the urging of his partners encouraged the drummer to immerse himself in what he was doing. The spectators also acknowledged his ability to drum by inserting bills of money in his waist as he beat the drum. He in turn appreciated their acknowledgement by increasing the tempo of his drumming to the astonishment of the spectators. Such extraordinary drumming is known to happen only during certain social activities such as healing. Healing (*Mahamba*) or death rituals require elaborate drum beating and it is when the drummer and some of his dancers could enter a trance[57].

Having discussed the above events I argue that the reaction of spectators in the festival was not only excited by the dances, but by the story lines of the dramatic action. The story lines dealt with issues that were in the public discourse. The lazy woman presented in the play by Kapata claimed that she had been bewitched because she did not have a good harvest. A spectator retorted to the claims of the woman in the play. That interaction demonstrated the communication and negotiation of prominent public issues between spectators and performers. Interaction is not only limited to the communication of issues between performers on behalf of the audience to the State representatives in the tent canopy, it goes right across all the festival attendance.

I have discussed the transition of the process from the rehearsal to the actual festival, with special focus on the interactions that take place between the various actors in the event. In the discussion I have highlighted the role of local people in the making of the festival through a discussion of the pre-festival rehearsals of two groups, namely Mayana Primary School and Ukumwe Culture Dance Group in Kavango. I described and analyzed

---

[57] Interview with Jonas Mbambo at Mupapama on 26 May 2008.

rehearsals that took place at two different levels of festival making, the junior category and the highly rated premier category. The ethnography shows how local people participate in and contribute to the making of the festival through teaching and demonstrating traditional dances to participants, who in turn perform them during the festival. Although they are not directly involved in the making of the festival, their contribution makes them active players in the processes of nation building as mediated and prescribed by the state. The cultural material used in the festival in Kavango is local but it has a national dimension (to borrow a term from Lentz, 2001) as presented in a space that is mediated and controlled by the state. It is when local cultural material is presented in that controlled space that it generates interaction at various levels of the festival among the performers, audience, organizers and invited guests. The interaction is between those who are present and compose what is deemed 'proper' dances and the expected conduct and performances of the Kavango 'tradition'. The performances by Kapata and Unongo were viewed as proper by some locals, including officials from the culture office, because of the kind of social interaction they ignited. The interaction was measured (I use the term loosely) by the audience's response to the drummer, the sound he created and the rush of people onto the stage after the master of ceremonies opened the stage to all, to join in and dance along.

Finally I argue that every stakeholder at the festival has a functional role and contribution to make. The state needs the festival in order to communicate its message of unity and tolerance. Local people or festival-goers need the festival to communicate with the State about their grievances, to give praise, and make acknowledgements.

The following chapter is an ethnographic presentation drawing on events at the Annual National Culture Festival of 2008 in Rundu, the capital of the Kavango region in Namibia. The ethnographic description and analysis focus on the culture performances of two groups namely the *Ntunguru Culture Group* and the groups from the *Noordgrens Secondary School.*

8 Deconstructing Postcolonial Ethnic Diversity

Annual National Culture Festival: Discourses of *Difference* and *Belonging* in Postcolonial Namibia

Social scientists writing about the dynamics of festival rituals have analyzed such practices as celebrations of commonality, as the enhancement of social cohesion or as an expression of nostalgia. Festivals have been studied as spaces where information is disseminated to the public. The waves of independence that swept across Africa from the 1950s had left a desire to recapture African culture and history in their wake. As has been shown in a substantial body of literature following the publication of Hobsbawm and Ranger's (1984) influential *Invention of tradition,* culture and history were mutilated and reinvented by colonial interests. Postcolonial states, especially during the 1990s, found themselves faced with enormous diversity and few unifying elements. African leaders developed different approaches to the problem of internal unification and almost all placed much emphasis on the production of national culture. State-sponsored cultural festivals in Africa, and on other continents, became avenues in which cultural representations are produced by Africans in a postcolonial context of nation building and national reconciliation by bringing visions of cosmopolitanism and modernity into critical dialogue with their colonial past. A growing body of literature on the politics of contemporary festival adds to the understanding of the making of postcolonial identity (see for example, Van Binsbergen 1994, Lentz 2001, Askew 2002, Apter 2005 and Flint 2006).

In postcolonial Namibia cultural festivals have become avenues where discourses of difference and belonging are emphasized and contested by local people, festival participants and state officials through a range of ethnic-cultural presentations. The work of anthropologists such as Van Binsbergen 1994 and Flint 2006 informs the subject of this chapter. Van Binsbergen's (1994) investigation of the Kazanga festival in Central Western Zambia shows how festivals have become contexts in which cultural reconstructions are demonstrated. His argument centers on the connections between culture festival performances and the reproduction of ethnicity. Flint's (2006) study of Western Zambia presents interesting intra-ethnic contradictions of the Lozi as regards the representations of their history and heritage. Both Van Binsbergen and Flint show how the festivals they studied created perspectives of difference and, most importantly, how they address the problem of cultural and ethnic demarcation. They demonstrate that cultural and ethnic demarcation is indeed the key question facing festival organizers in terms of the local cultural heritage they choose to stage and celebrate.

I am primarily concerned with the making of Kavango identity as distinctively different from that of other ethnic groups in postcolonial Namibia. This process takes place in a particular political space, that of the culture festivals, which the state has organized and mediated since the mid-1990s. Every year during the Annual National Culture Festivals representatives of Namibia's various ethnic groups gather to showcase and express their diversity where state representatives[1] emphasize the importance of bringing together the country's previously segregated population groups.

This chapter draws on the events of the 2008 Annual National Culture Festival, which took place in Rundu. The festival lasted eight days. My central argument is that while performers act out diversity through dance and other forms of cultural exhibition during these festivals, the importance of belonging to the nation and a larger constituency is significantly highlighted.

My ethnographic description and analysis focus on the culture representation of two groups, namely the Ntunguru Cultural Group and Noordgrens Secondary School. I pay special attention to these specific groups, because of their significance in the local festival space. Both groups have on various occasions been selected by the Rundu regional culture office to represent the Kavango region in festivals, including those that have been organized by the state and other institutions. In the analysis I show how the regional organizers perceive the groups' roles, and present their demographic composition and character to highlight differences and emphasize the significance of the Kavango as a unique ethnic existence in the national festival context. This representation forms part of the political ritual enacted by the postcolonial state in Namibia for its projects of decolonising the mind and nation- building.

The growing body of literature on festivals in Africa has pointed out the different dimensions that these public representations of culture have assumed in different contexts. At the present time cultural festivals have become significant avenues where discourses of difference and belonging are emphasized and contested by local people, festival participants and state officials through a range of ethnic-cultural presentations.

The Annual National Culture Festival

Each year the Namibian government organizes culture festivals nationwide. The Directorate of Heritage and Culture Programmes in the Ministry of Youth, National Service, Sport and

---

[1] See New Era news paper dated 9 August 2006 'Mutorwa Argue for Culture'.

Culture, has offices in all thirteen regions. Culture festivals begin at the circuit level, using the demarcation of school districts, where performing groups that have exhibited their culture to meet the expectation of judges[2] are selected to participate in the culture festival of their respective regions. Eventually, the regions' top performing groups compete in the Annual National Culture Festival.

Circuit festivals attract large audiences even though these are held during the week. The national festival draws many spectators including the local elite and numerous officials from the national government who attend the occasion on behalf of their respective ministries. The national event is held with pomp and ceremony to demonstrate its importance.

Members of the participating groups rehearse intensively. Rehearsals involve the choreography of dances, drama and learning lyrics. The majority of participants in the festival are students and pupils from schools in the region. The event is held as a competition which, as the organizers never fail to point out, is used not as an end in itself, but as a means to an end. On one occasion, in response to a question on how cultures could compete, the Kavango region's senior culture officer explained on the local radio show *Mudukuli* ('saying it'):

What we do is not gathering to compete, but to 'showcase' our culture. However, we need a guideline that guides how we award marks so that we have one group that wins in its effort of showcasing culture. We cannot compete at culture level, because of the diverse cultures we have.

The March Through Town

The first item on the event's itinerary was the march from the centre of town to the Rundu stadium. As instructed by the director of ceremonies, the members of cultural groups from all over Namibia had donned their traditional costumes. Several culture groups displayed banners advertising the names of their regions of origin. They lined up in the following order: Kavango, Oshikoto, Otjozondjupa, Oshana, Ohangwena, Omusati, Caprivi, Karas, Hardap, Erongo, Omaheke, Khomas and Kunene. However, it was clear that the public exhibition of cultures during the march was about specific ethnic groups resident in the various regions since the participants were all clad in traditional costume. Each group sang a different song, groups seemed to compete about who could sing the loudest. One listen hard to make sense of what was being sung. The police were present to coordinate the march, together with culture officers from various regions.

---

[2] The judges are drawn from among the circles of local government officials and other local luminaries.

I believe that the march not only signified the symbolic representation of Namibia's different ethnic groups but was also a display of power mediated by the state through the presence of its staff and security personnel that led the march. The spectacle can best be understood as an attempt to institutionalize the festival and its world of meanings among the citizens. Residents stood on the roadside to witness a large number of people moving through the town centre; a very rare sight unless there is a funeral or wedding procession, particularly one involving the local elite. As the march entered the stadium, the participants kept singing and dancing, all the while exhibiting the banners and costumes.

Inside the Stadium

Inside the stadium seating arrangements were demarcated according to the participants' region of origin. Each cultural group had been allocated a different marquee, which specified the name of its region. Only a small section was not demarcated, presumably to accommodate local festival goers. There was also a sunshade under which the officially invited guests and other dignitaries were seated. The first to arrive and be seated under this canopy was the Deputy Minister of Youth, National Service, Sport and Culture, Pohamba Shifeta. He was followed by the Ministry's Permanent Secretary, Peingondjabi Shipoh. The Acting Governor of the Kavango region arrived shortly before Rundu's town Mayor. Next was the Vambunza chief, Alfons Kaundu. The Roman Catholic Bishop arrived a few minutes after him.

However, for a long time the Festival could not go ahead since the Minister of Youth, National Service, Sport and Culture, Willem Konjore, who was to officiate at the opening, arrived more than two hours later. People became agitated because of this prolonged wait; some lost patience and started demanding that proceedings go ahead as planned[3].

Finally the vehicle carrying the Minister appeared at the gate, from where it was driven straight onto the lawn and came to a stop a few meters from the VIP marquee. The Director of National Heritage and Culture Programmes (NHCP), his Deputy, followed by the Mayor and other government representative approached the Minister's vehicle to receive him in line with the elaborate protocol customary at such occasions. The Minister then took his seat between the Deputy Minister and the Acting Governor.

The Permanent Secretary started by greeting the crowd in various languages that are commonly spoken in Namibia. Judging by their enthusiastic response, the audience appreciated his manner of greeting. I understood it to be an enactment of the state principle of

---

[3] It appears that Konjore is notorious for keeping people waiting. In another incident, about which I read in the media, he kept people waiting for a very long time in another Namibian region where he was expected to officiate at an event.

unity and diversity, where all ethnic groups present at the gathering were acknowledged. Following the singing of the anthems, the director of ceremonies sternly reprimanded some men for not removing their hats while the anthems were sung. He said: "In other countries, you will be shot dead if men have their hats on, when people are singing the national anthem, please remember that." Following the singing of the anthems, the Roman Catholic Bishop said a prayer. The Acting Governor was next to express words of welcome. As he made his way to the podium, the audience applauded. Clad in a black suit, he started with a prolonged greeting that acknowledged all dignitaries present. His prepared speech touched on wide ranging aspects of culture and tradition. He emphasized the importance of showing the "true color of our origin and embrace culture as a diverse and unique exercise of different ethnic groups on this universe." He went on to share his expectation that he was looking forward "to see how happy Herero, Damara, Tswana, Caprivians and other tribes are dancing around at the podium."

I could not fail to notice how the (ethnic) difference between the various population groups that make up the Namibian nation state was emphasized by the senior regional government officer. The crowd cheered loudly when he read such sections of his presentation. He closed his speech by welcoming people to the "mighty Kavango". His presentation of Kavango as a mighty region can be read in various ways, depending on one's reading of the region's current political context. Although Namibia is generally seen as politically and economically stable, some residents of Kavango that I interviewed during my fieldwork felt that an unfair distribution of the national wealth prevailed due to the uneven recognition of the contributions to the liberation struggle made by residents of different regions. As I discussed earlier in chapter six sentiments of neglect, ethnic recognition and unfair distribution of wealth are not only expressed in public discourse, but also in songs. For some time now there has been a sense of neglect and discontent with the state of national affairs among local people in Kavango, especially those belonging to the tiny local elite[4].

Minister Willem Konjore, the main speaker of the day, greeted the audience in the various languages spoken in Namibia, followed by the official protocol of addressing state gatherings. Clad in a navy suit and black hat, the minister approached the podium carrying his speech in one hand, and holding onto a carved cane with the other, thereby embodying

---

[4] One prominent member of the regional government remarked during the closure of a conference in the region two years ago: "Ose kumoneka asi vakwatesiko tupu" (Lit: 'We are regarded as hand lenders.). He was referring to the role played by people of Kavango during the liberation struggle, which is considered secondary. At the time of the 2008 ANCF a new political party had just been launched in the region. It has been labelled as an ethnic political party in speeches by the ruling party, SWAPO during recent election campaigns and the increasing number of presidential visits to the region.

symbolized seniority[5]. Before he read his prepared speech, he conveyed greetings from the Head of State who had been invited to officiate at the event, but who had failed to attend.

The Minister's prepared speech started with what sounded like a (dated) anthropological definition of the culture concept. He presented culture as a "thing" in Handler's (1988) sense, a thing that can be shared and used as a tool to identify differences in identities. Konjore presented culture as something that should embrace global developments in order to enhance economic development and social cohesion. From the Namibian government's perspective therefore, culture is presented as a commodity that can change the economic aspects of people's way of life[6].

Halfway through his speech the Minister warned that people should not regard their particular culture as superior to others. Encouraging the audience to acknowledge diversity, he emphasized that the event should be celebrated with the "sure knowledge that we are different." Konjore presented the festival as an arena where a greater understanding of cultural diversity could be achieved because different people came together not only to celebrate, but to showcase their cultures and origins.

When he finished his short speech, Konjore declared the festival officially open. The crowd clapped hands and ululated in appreciation. The other VIP guests gave him a standing ovation, each of them shaking the Minister's hand. Konjore's speech demonstrated a skillful political articulation. He concentrated on nationalistic sentiments about culture, and presented himself as a representative of the nation as a whole rather than of a particular interest group within the society.

'Performances' of Culture

For my discussion of performance at the festival, I deliberately chose to focus on the stage presentations of two groups, namely the culture group of the Noordgrens Secondary School and the Ntunguru Cultural Group. Officials at the Maria Mwengere Culture Centre attached special sentiment and significance to these two groups. When the national festival programme was being prepared, the senior culture officer, Thomas Shapi, motivated for Noordgrens Secondary to be included although during the competitions it had not made it beyond the circuit stage. For Shapi and his colleagues, Noordgrens presented and signi-

---

[5] In several communities in Namibia people move around with a cane in their hands once they have reached an elevated status in the community, or seniority in age.
[6] The commodification of culture is not the topic of this chapter, but it was evidently a significant part of the event. I observed that throughout the week of the festival some people recorded dances and took pictures that were developed and sold on site. Many times when I attended festivals during my fieldwork, people asked me whether I was in the business of selling 'culture products'.

fied something special because of its demographic composition. Noordgrens Secondary was comprised of both white and black youth. Like any other school in the region that participated in the festivals, however, it presented what is believed and imagined to be Kavango culture. Although its performance was not considered particularly successful, the officials considered its inclusion in the National Festival as crucial because of the group's demographics and the way in which it locates the region within the national principle of unity and diversity.

The Ntunguru Culture Group, on the other hand, was perceived to represent Kavango-ness in an exemplary way. It is an adult group from the eastern Kavango and has participated in the finals on many occasions. Ntunguru is regarded as a group of performers in the premier category that has represented the region in many local, Africa-wide and international contexts. The group has been officially endorsed by the regional culture office as the representative of Kavango and its people. It has also been accorded national status, which has not delighted everyone. As discussed above, officials from culture offices in several of the country's regions complained publicly that groups from Kavango were given opportunities to travel abroad far more frequently than other groups (Informante, February 11, 2010).

The Noordgrens group was the first to enter the stage, but not before the Director of National Heritage and Culture Programmes had read the guidelines and rules of the festival to everyone present. The Director stipulated the criteria that judges would use during the adjudication process. He emphasized that the audience and performers should not view the adjudication process as being aimed at ranking or demeaning any act being presented on stage, nor should the process be seen as favoring any cultural presentation over others. He stressed that the process should simply be viewed as a guideline to identifying the most original performance. He maintained that in the fourteen-year history of the national festival, judges had always demonstrated and upheld high levels of integrity in order to promote and enhance fair play.

Noordgrens's act was in the category of kulinyanyukisa[7], which I discussed at length in the previous chapter. The category of kulinyanyukisa is for entertainment purposes only. When the group from the Noordgrens Secondary School appeared at the entrance to set the stage for their performance, many spectators seemed shocked by the composition of the group and its costumes. Several people exclaimed in disbelief amidst applause: "tatu tarere neina" (lit: We shall see today what they will show us.) The girls wore brown skirts and tops with strings of blue and white beads over their skirts and around their ankles and

---

[7] See discussion in chapter 7.

arms. The white girls in the group sported blonde vihiho.[8] The boys wore marudeve[9] around their waists. These items of clothing supposedly signified Kavango culture. One of the black boys wore a blazer and a white hat for his part in the group's drama presentation. First, the youngsters came on stage and arranged the props of their performance: a reed mat, a tape recorder, three cloths, a small chair, a big basket made of palm leaves and two plastic plates. Items such as plastic plates, blazers and fabric hats are regarded as foreign to the traditionalist notion of Kavango culture. Their use in the context of the Festival represented the ability of local people to appreciate and incorporate objects from other cultures in their own lives; a matter that had been loudly emphasized during the Minister's opening speech.

After laying out the props, most of the group members left the stage. Three male drummers remained behind to welcome the other members of the group as they began the performance from the entrance. On stage, they danced to the tunes of the drums amidst loud cheers and ululation. Some sections of the audience egged them on, shouting "Forward, forward", while others exclaimed, "Wee, culture, wee!" The director of ceremonies drummed up even more applause and ululation from the audience. As the group prepared to present their last item the senior culture officer for the Kavango region unceremoniously took to the podium for a little impromptu speech:

> Noordgrens has been a good example in the whole Namibia. We chose Noordgrens because it is a group that displays all kind of population groups in Namibia. And that is what we mean when we say unity in diversity. Noordgrens! Give them a big applause. Last year when we went to Ohangwena region people were left speechless to see our composition and they could not stop but praise Kavango region for promoting unity and diversity. Thank you, thank you!

To end their performance the group sang a song about "Kavango the good land" in Rukwangali, praising the region's abundance of food, animals, people and culture. The song urged people to take care of what they have. Then the two last dancers moved towards the drummers to stop the song. The audience clapped wildly as the group left the stage.

After this symbolically charged performance the director of ceremonies announced that the first competitive performance in the adult category would be by the local stars from the Ntunguru group. The male dancers had their marudeve wrapped tightly around their waists and wore mutjeketje[10] around their ankles. Some of the male performers wore headgear

---

[8] *Vihiho* (sing: *sihiho*) is a form of female headgear. It is a long snarl that hangs down to the female's shoulders and is made of tree inner bark.

[9] Marudeve (sing.: rudeve) is clothing made of reeds which grow along the Kavango River. The reeds are cut into pieces and joined together with a string and tied around the waist like a skirt. When a person clad in a rudeve dances it emits sound.

[10] Mutjeketje are seeds of the camel-thorn tree. They are attached to a string and tied around the

made from animal skin. They wore necklaces made out of green beads with an engraved symbol of a star. The men's upper bodies were not uncovered. Both men and women were barefoot the latter, however, wore tops to cover their breasts. They wore headgear known as vihiho; their brown petticoats were decorated with white and orange beads. Around their ankles, arms and wrists they sported bands made of white beads. In addition, the women showed off green star necklaces. The group members carried a big canoe and fresh river reeds onto the stage to present a river scene. Other props included small axes and small baskets containing millet, sorghum and nongongo.[11] They arranged two black pots and storage baskets. Through their costumes and material items such as the nongongo fruit, the group presented the locally essentialized image of the typical traditional Kavango[12] way of life. As became evident from the presentations of other groups from the region, so-called traditional Kavango dress and life have evolved and incorporated new influences.

When the Ntunguru group entered the stage to lay out the props for their performance, the director of ceremonies called on the - already cheering - crowd to clap their hands. After they prepared the stage, 13 of the performers walked toward the entrance of the arena, where they waited for the three drummers left behind on stage to invite them with the beat of the drum. As the drumming began and the group re-entered the stage already dancing, the audience cheered and ululated loudly. The dancers entered in two parallel lines which later fused to become one as they formed a half circle. Each dancer carried a small basket containing maize or millet seeds; she or he announced the contents of the basket and explained what it was used for, for instance, "Mumahangu ghakulima twe Vakavango kuwana mo vitima" (lit: This is mahangu. It is used to make porridge by the Kavango people).

The group moved to the front of the stage holding baskets high before they placed them on the ground and returned to their original half circle position. As the song progressed, three female dancers separated from the rest and danced towards the drummers who danced as they beat the drum to end the first song. As the three women got close to the drummers, the drum stopped to signal the end of the song.

When the group began to sing their exit song at the end of their performance, the director of ceremonies encouraged the audience to give a round of applause as the group was leaving the stage: "Thank you, thank you Ntunguru! We have learned Kavango culture from you, and I hope everybody will take it forward", he concluded as their drum beat faded. Over

---

ankles, producing a sound when the performers stamp their feet on the ground.
[11] Nongongo are dried nutty plums which are stored for the extraction of their nutritious oil.
[12] My usage of terms such as culture and tradition follows local usage and is not meant to suggest that I see earlier forms of Kavango social history as timeless and preserved in their entire integrity which has been disrupted. All evidence shows that life has changed significantly and continues to do so.

the next few days, all the other groups that had entered the national competition carried out their performances.

At the end of the festival, every participating group received a certificate of attendance and prize money, which had been raised by the Ministry. The director of ceremonies stepped forward, carrying three large envelopes containing cash and certificates. He announced the winners and runners-up of the different categories and briefly reported on how the results had been arrived at. He called the Deputy Minister to assist him with the prize-giving (the Minister had already left). While the Deputy Minister was making his way to the stage, the director of ceremonies announced business-like:

> Everybody who participated today is a winner. Each group will receive a certificate of participation and prize money of N$300[13]. The runner up gets N$650, second winner receives N$900 and first winner will take away a whopping N$1200 and a certificate. I request the group leaders to collect their certificates and prize money when I call the group names and kindly sign for receiving the money.

All the groups received their certificates amidst cheers from the spectators. The director of ceremonies read the names of the groups and the points they had been awarded in the runner-up category. In the adult category, Ntunguru came second behind the Ondjondjo Culture Group from the Oshana region (in Owambo).

Analysis of the Festival Representations in Kavango

To make sense of these events, I shall take a closer look at the roles of the various actors. The state-organized National Culture Festival is an annual event that constitutes social capital in associational life. The performances can best be read as embodying postcolonial Namibia's official narrative of 'unity in diversity'. The Festival is performative in that it encompasses bodily practices that produce meaning and highlight interactions between social actors and their environment. It is a social process which is sanctioned by the state, but which constitutes practices that are strongly influenced by citizens. During the national festival people from all of Namibia's 13 political regions are represented. The state, through its Ministry of Youth, National Service, Sport and Culture, organizes the event that rotates among venues in the regions.

It appears that, although it is ostensibly an event of national significance, the Festival becomes centered around themes that are important to the host region. The theme for the festival was "Keeping our diverse cultures amidst globalization". Since it was held in Ka-

---

[13] 1 N$ = 1 Rand

vango in 2008, Thomas Shapi, the region's senior culture officer and a teacher by profession, made sure that all the local dignitaries were personally invited. Together with Shapi, the then Director of National Heritage and Culture Programmes coordinated the event. He, some believed, had a personal interest in this particular festival since he too hails from the Kavango region, although since his appointment to the central government he has settled in the national capital. Herbert Ndango Diaz[14] holds a PhD from the department of religious studies at the University of Cape Town and has written novels and poems in the Kavango dialects.

The immense importance that was placed on the possible presence of President Hifkepunye Pohamba at the event deserves greater consideration. The fact that it was never quite known whether or not the Head of State would arrive makes for some very interesting reflection. The enduring uncertainty and the anxiety that this produced in the regional culture office in Rundu, seems to suggest that the arrival of the Head of State had perhaps become a power tool. The Head of State had to be kept in mind during all the preparations because of this uncertainty.

Except for the senior culture officer who played a major logistical role in the preparation of the festival, most of those seated in the VIP marquee were dignitaries representing foreign embassies, national leaders, and the local state administrative elite. The presence of national leaders, together with the local leadership and the wider local audience, as well as the participating performers, gave the Festival gathering a particular significance. All parties, especially the local officials involved in the planning and organization of the Festival, were fully aware that this event would not "make any sense" without the presence of national dignitaries. As Pye 1963: 27 pointed out half a century ago, there is always a human dimension in the celebration of nationhood and the presence of the national leadership since it has to "appeal for an undifferentiated public" which presents itself as different through performance.

The ordinary audiences of the festival, mostly Rundu residents, were seated to one side of the stadium. Some members of the public obviously saw the economic potential from selling snacks and pictures and DVDs of culture groups, which reminded me of the Comaroffs' suppositions of the commodification of culture. (Comaroff and Comaroff 2009) The selling of culture products was in line with what the state emphasized in its culture policy i.e. stipulating the event as an economic possibility for its citizens.

The Ntunguru Cultural Group ('the star') from the eastern part of the central Kavango area of Shambyu is composed of 16 younger and older adults; some of the older members

---

[14] Before he retired from the civil service in 2009, he was accused by several ministry staff members of favouring the Kavango region in many aspects of culture programmes.

have retired from civil service positions in Rundu and moved back to the village. Six members of the group are male, ten are female. Ntunguru boasts several trophies and certificates. The Noordgrens Secondary School's group includes 16 young white, coloured and black performers[15]. During South African colonial rule this school accommodated the children of white civil servants only. Since independence it has become a mixed race school and is the school of choice for the children of (black) civil servants from other Namibian regions who settled in Rundu after independence. Before and shortly after independence in 1990 the school did not participate in culture activities. One of the previous local culture officers told me that he had unsuccessfully attempted to have the school participate in festivals shortly after independence. The school only started participating in the regional culture festivals in the late 1990s after the festivals had been officially proclaimed by the new Namibian state.

The interactions of these social actors in the environment of the Annual National Culture Festival demonstrated how the official principle of unity and diversity serves as the basis on which difference among the people of Namibia is constructed.

Debates on local radio shows around the start of the annual festival season give a good illustration of these complex issues. Radio debates on the festivals included topics such as how the region could participate in the national unity projects implemented by the central government. Presenters and callers also debate, however, how ethnic groups in Kavango contribute to regional unity. For instance, the senior culture officer, Thomas Shapi, called in to the early morning radio programme, Pinduka ('wake up') to announce an upcoming festival. He urged people to attend the festival, for it would be "a perfect opportunity to come together as Kavango people and nation[16]". Shapi's statement triggered a debate on the radio chat show, Mudukuli, later in the morning, which carried on for several days. A few days after the regional culture festival, for instance, an anonymous caller asked the presenter, "Nani wolye Vakavango?" (Who are the Kavango people?')

The discussion on the radio pointed to the origin of the five groups namely the Kwangali, Mbunza, Shambyu, Gciriku and Mbukushu who, according to royal oral histories, can rightfully claim to be Kavango people as I discussed in chapter four in this study. This postcolonial construction of Kavango-ness does not include the people collectively known as Vanyemba, who have been resident in Kavango since time immemorial, as some local history narratives have it. There was a palpable sense of exclusion in the radio discussion. Although the senior culture officer did not mention who makes up the Kavango on this, as on other occasions, the discussion routinely led to the point of who is a (legitimate)

---

[15] Strictly-speaking, secondary school students are in their teens but, as is common Namibian parlance, as school going youth they are locally referred to as 'children'.
[16] My field notes.

part of Kavango? His statement apparently created a situation that Handler 1986 would refer to as an anxiety of being which befalls people when their being and belonging are questioned.

During the ongoing radio show discussions of the purpose and merits of the festival, notions of the allegiance and true commitment to Kavango ethnicity emerged as issues of regional unity and diversity. The radio programme allows for an open discussion, which at times reaches a crisis point especially when touching on local ideas of inclusion and exclusion. In this context, the debates about the belonging of the residents referred to as Vanyemba are particularly significant.

The Vanyemba are believed to have migrated from areas in Southern Angola to Kavango at different times, and for different reasons. A smaller group is said to have lived along the Kavango River at the time when it became the border between Namibia and Angola. They claim that they migrated to the Namibian side, because of who lived there. These smaller groups of Vanyemba are locally accepted as *vandambo,* which means "familiar". The tentative inclusion of these earlier migrants from present day Angola is in contrast with the exclusion of those who arrived with the more recent and much larger influx of Vanyemba and Vimbundu[17] during the war of liberation in Angola[18]. This group is often seen locally as *vatywayuki*[19] or refugees, who supposedly have influenced the local culture with their 'alien' ideas, practices and processes of meaning making.

The colonial state's construction of the five Kavango legitimate peoples (or 'tribes') still seems to be commonly accepted. When I asked the leader of the Ntunguru group what the star in their name and ornament symbolizes, he answered that it represents the people of Kavango, namely the five groups of Hambukushu, Vashambyu, Vagciriku, Vambunza and Vakwangali. This is despite the fact that the Vanyemba are the largest of the groups. However, as I discussed earlier dissenting views insist that the Vanyemba have been around in Kavango for a long time and that many, if not most, of the region's traditional songs and dances are actually of Nyemba origin, in contrast with those who claim to be the 'real' locals. This viewpoint maintains that since the Vanyemba have been living among the so-called local people for a long time, trading and intermarrying with them, their songs and ways of life have been appropriated into Kavango cultural practices. As one very knowledgeable informant pointed out:[20]

---

[17] Vimbundu is an ethnic group mostly found in southern Angola. It is generally believed that they supported Unita rebels during the civil war against the MPLA government in Angola.
[18] Brinkmann (1991) deals in detail with issues of Vanyemba identity in postcolonial Kavango.
[19] I have critiqued Brinkman usage of this phrase in reference to the Vanyemba. See chapters four and five.
[20] Interview with Immanuel Shikukumwa; Safari, January 2009

Many traditional songs, dances and tales in Kavango are not of Kavango origin; they were told and sung in Nyemba languages. That is how it has been even long time ago. Well, there are also songs and dances that were sung in, say, Mbukushu, Shambyu, Gciriku and Kwangali, but the majority of the songs and dances belonged to the Nyemba, and they dance them. When some people are saying that it is Vanyemba who are spoiling everything, that I do not believe.

Surprisingly, the belonging of Vanyemba to Kavango-ness remains fiercely contested despite the state's recognition of the Vanyemba as part of the region's people and culture by including them in an official publication about the identity of the Kavango people (MYNSC 2006:13). This concise publication on the history and dances of the Kavango people, designed by the Kavango culture office, has become known as the culture booklet. The booklet, as I discussed in chapter six, is based on interviews that the culture office conducted in the region in order to reconstruct the history and traditional activities of the Kavango and is presented to the judges during the Annual National Culture Festival. While all participating groups at the festivals independently produce their own culture booklets to explain their background and performances purportedly to convey a sense of their culture and dances to the judges,[21] the regional culture office prepares what I will call a master cover narrative. The individual booklets of all participating groups are then bound according to the official account and presented to the judges.

In the culture booklets produced by the individual groups there is a clear assertion of the group's origin. All the booklets boldly state whether the group originated from Mbukushu, Gciriku, Shambyu or Mbunza and Kwangali, that is, one of the officially recognized legal Kavango 'tribes' of the colonial time. Even today the Vanyemba are presented as those without an ancestral land in the region, although a large number of culture booklets show that most of the songs in the booklets were written in and performed in Runyemba. This may explain why many Kavango dances continue to be hotly contested.

Reflections on Kavango Identity

The culture booklet emerged as a tool to signify and confirm Kavango-ness, encompassing the different ethnic groups represented in the festival space. The booklet's ostensible role is to guide the judges during the festival presentation, yet I conclude that it should also be seen as a tool of differentiation. In what started as a colonial project to present an

---

[21] The judges then use the culture booklet and an adjudication form to judge the act. Groups are judged according to criteria such as how they enter the stage, their décor, costume, song, originality, and the booklet.

objectified Kavango, the culture booklet has become a vital tool in the present administration's nation building project. In particular, it has become a mode through which the state imagines and emphasizes regional identities, which are presented in a homogenized form, although they encompass a complex diversity. Furthermore, we need to locate this complex matter within the wider discourse of ethnicity and differentiation as an aspect of identity. I use identity in this context as a category of practice as suggested by Brubaker and Cooper 2000. Here we need to return to the two groups whose representations I discussed earlier in the chapter.

For the organizers of the Festival, the Ntunguru Cultural Group signified Kavango-ness. As adults they were ascribed a position of experience in a cultural hierarchy from which the young are supposed to learn. This passing down of culture to a younger generation is a common moral narrative in postcolonial Namibia. Arguably, the confirmation of material culture and cultural performance is aligned with hierarchies of authority.

The group from Noordgrens Secondary is seen as a product of the local nationhood factory. Because of its multiracial composition, the group's participation in the "performance of sovereignty" (Hansen and Stepputat 2005: 26) is particularly important to the Kavango region. Moreover, Noordgrens Secondary, at one time an all-white school, makes it a good example of the imagined unity in diversity propagated by the state. (Anderson, 1983; Brinkel, 2006) In this way, past impositions of difference become reconciled with postcolonial notions of national belonging. The notion of unity in diversity is based on what Brown 2001 refers to as the shared problematic regarding South Africa, which acknowledges a mutual history of difference as well as local and global affiliations. Another important aspect of the participation of Noordgrens is the demonstrated ability of the group's white members to speak native Kavango languages and to perform local traditional dances. Therefore, the group is regarded by culture officials and spectators alike as the embodied willingness and ability of those born-free[22] to learn local culture thus providing an example for others to emulate.

Finally, it is tempting to ask why it is apparently deemed proper for whites to perform the perceived Kavango culture, while the performance of Nyemba dances remains disputed? This is quite a complex question. Another one follows: should we view these intra-Kavango tensions and contestations as an attempt to establish ties of community or tools for empowerment? One can conclude, perhaps, that these tensions are about "modern senses

---

[22] 'Born-free' is a local term used to refer to those who were born around the time of Namibian independence and thereafter. It is used to indicate that they have only experienced peace and not the wrath of colonial oppression.

of belonging", which are expressed through ethnic allegiance and emphasis as suggested by Guss 2000:63 in the Venezuelan context in South America.

When groups join the march with banners that display their regions of origin, they signify and assert their differences. However, the motive of the gathering is of utmost importance. The Annual National Culture Festival is held to bring people together for the common good, namely that of unity. I have shown that the culture festival is a state mediated space which is strongly influenced by the participation of the local community. In conclusion, the National Culture Festival is a space of cultural representation that allows and enables Namibia's different regions to present themselves as a "cultural community" within a wider "political community" (Kymlicka, 1989:135), thus constituting the nation despite all local contestations of belonging.

9 The Postcolonial Nation as Curated by the State Through Dance

Conclusion

> All of us as Namibians have the right to take pride in our diverse culture and heritage. While exercising and practicing our cultural heritage and beliefs we urge every one of us to celebrate the colorful diversity of our nation and accept the culture of others instead of pointing the differences and encouraging tribal division. The onus is on each and every one of us to build a unified and dignified culture because failure to do that will result in to disintegration and hopelessness. It is my hope that an event like the annual national culture festival will serve as an event that will foster understanding amongst the different cultural communities in the region and the country as a whole and ensure that respect and genuine understanding of culture, which other traditional communities have to offer[1].

The above statement by Minister Konjore identifies diversity as an important feature in the process of making the Namibian nation. While diversity is fully embraced as a distinguishing aspect, it is to be tolerated and treated cautiously for it could lead to hopelessness and disintegration. Disintegration implies that there is a possibility that this diversity can lead to either unity or destruction in terms of social cohesion. However, harmonious co-existence can only be emphasized in a festive state in which the diversity can be presented through cultural performance in a celebratory mood in order to showcase unity. The assertions of the minister and many other national leaders in Namibia in the festival space provoked my aspiration to undertake a study towards understanding the purported "diversity in unity" which I have come to understand as an emphasis of "difference" and "belonging" of Namibian citizens. It is important to understand this awareness of diversity within the global context in which people have become more open to other ideas and influences. Habermas 1996:849 poses the question, "Should citizens' identities as members of ethnic, cultural or religious groups publicly matter and, if so, how can collective identities make a difference within the frame of a constitutional democracy?"

Habermas's question on the issue of multiculturalism is of particular importance in the context of my study where relations between the Nyemba and other cultural groups are contested in order to illuminate the philosophical aspects of inter minority group conflict and the relationship of minority cultures and political identities to the majority culture within

---

[1] Excerpt from the speech of Willem Konjore, the Minister of Youth, National Service, Sport & Culture at the official opening of the Annual National Culture Festival in Kavango in 2008.

a constitutional democracy. His argument is that various aspects of communitarian and libertarian theories can be combined to produce a universally shared civic culture, one which recognizes and accommodates cultural difference while providing a neutral public sphere in which groups can communicate, compete and carry out a democratic project. With the same question in mind I approached the making of the postcolonial culture festival as a 'neutral' space in which the project of democracy is carried out through representation of difference in a cultural sense and emphasis of a united imagery belonging to the Namibian nation. The festival space is where the nation-state and citizens meet in order to interact on key social issues. This interaction is not between the state and citizens only, it also takes place among citizens.

In the study I documented activities at Maria Mwengere Culture Centre in Kavango. I argue that such a centre and its activities serve as a 'strategic factory' of the perceived national culture which the postcolonial nation-state imagines. This seems to indicate similarities to what Askew found in Tanzania, namely the increasingly dominant concern for state strategists of how to even out or navigate the inconsistencies of cultural expressions and present a unified national front that blankets dissent and masks diversity. (Askew, 2002) At Maria Mwengere I focused on the museum, the making of culture booklets and culture festivals as activities through which local cultures and heritage can be preserved according to the state's perception. I showed how local culture officials deal and attribute importance to the activities such as festival dances and the museum at Maria Mwengere Culture Centre. I have seen how these activities are indeed ways through which the state constructs its citizens according to its imagination. I realized too that citizens could participate actively in these endeavours. Through their culture festival performances and the preparation of their culture booklets participants become active agents in making and imagining postcolonial Namibian citizenship. In the process local people create an image of themselves within the state platform which, in turn, has the authority to amend and modify what it desires to showcase.

This study has addressed the issue of nationalism and nationhood as expressed in the state sponsored culture festivals in Namibia. There are various festivals taking place in the Namibian social space organized by agents outside the realm of the state such as the Witbooi, Omagongo, Lusata, Damara festivals which take place in different regions of Namibia. (Kossler, 2003)

Two perspectives are addressed in this study. The first one is that of the state as administrator and custodian of the state-sponsored culture festivals. My interest lay in the state's turnabout from its initial rejection of the colonial festival to reclaiming it as the Annual Culture Festival. Secondly, I was interested in the perspectives of people who attend or participate in the event.

The main question of how the practice of state-sponsored cultural festivals, which was considered to be a colonial representation of the "other", has been reinvented and appropriated with new meanings in postcolonial Namibia is addressed. The colonial culture festivals were discontinued at independence as they were perceived to be contravening the interest of nation building and reconciliation. However, five years later the new Namibian state reintroduced state-sponsored cultural festivals. My ethnographic study of the state sponsored culture festival in Namibia, with its specific focus on the Kavango region, as a case study in order to gain insight into the professed notion of "unity in diversity" shows that the 'new' festival is significantly different in principle from its predecessor, even though the model appears to be similar.

Two points emerge in this respect. Both the new festival and the colonial sangfees contain elements of a competitive nature, incorporate regional participation according to geographic ethnic presence and, most importantly, are produced by the state. Postcolonial regional boundaries frequently coincide with the old Bantustans divisions, especially in north-eastern Namibia. Despite the apparent similarities to the colonial festival, the current festival is different in conception. It has acquired a new meaning. This is crucial if we are to clearly understand the making of the postcolonial Namibian nation state. The new festival making emphasizes difference, which is informed by Article 19 of the constitution. This clause guarantees people's right of association, practice to enjoy any culture, tradition or religion. This guaranteed right was non-existent during colonial times. These guaranteed and tolerated differences do not suggest disregard for the state ideology of belonging to the nation. People who attend these festival gatherings, politicians included, emphasized the importance of national belonging. Politicians and state representatives would, however, urge citizens to use these differences to enhance their social being towards social cohesion through representations of their imagined culture. This suggests that such difference should be used for the economic betterment of citizens. The state through its directorates of arts and culture has created support programmes to assist people in all regions to create cultural villages and identify heritage sites, which could generate income through cultural tourism.

Central to the question of meaning are the issues of difference, exclusion and belonging. This difference and exclusion discussed in my study does not refer to racial distinction, which would have been central in pre-Independence Nambia, but to cultural or ethnic diversity. The issue of difference, exclusion and belonging has become topical in social and cultural scholarship of late both locally as well as in a global context. Currently it seems more important to express oneself ethnically or culturally rather than in terms of race, a practice supported by many leaders in Namibia and local people.

For instance the first head of state in Namibia expressed and emphasized the constitutional right of each individual to practice their own culture during our interview. Nujoma's view about people and their culture suggests that people would feel 'Namibian' if they were legally allowed to practice their own culture. As I discussed in the preceding chapters, this ideology of difference was not welcome during the early stages of independence and the national discourse was that of "one Namibia, one nation". Geingob 2004 demonstrates how the state formation at the time promoted the national discourse which discouraged difference. As we witness and as I have shown in the study, five years into independence the state began to promote and enhance diversity.

Beyond the politics of difference and nationalism, my research shows that ideas which are transformed through cultural representations produce meanings about being and belonging to a particular culture, which are relevant at the regional level. In both national and regional contexts ethnicity is emphasized as a signifier of difference. In the case of Kavango people could display difference and yet belong, or be excluded from the mainstream regional identity. As Ngondo has suggested in our wide-ranging interview, difference seems to have been inherent in the history of Kavango. Many of those interviewed in Kavango do not recognize the notion of Kavango-ness as a product of colonial times. Although it is evident that Kavango identity as a category is a colonial construction, it seems to have been appropriated locally to signify and emphasize belonging and association in the postcolonial moment. As Ngondo inferred, appropriation of Kavango-ness is situational, especially in the postcolonial context where for instance the Vanyemba and others such as Vaherero from outside the region can claim Kavango-ness. However, that does not mean that they are Vakavango. In the festive space the state reminds and assures its citizens of their belonging to the nation. This type of difference defines some sense of implicit commonality at the national level. Festival representations show Kavango-ness as rooted in history, legends and myths, which have been emphasized and affirmed by the earlier colonial administrations.

Finally, the study shows that interaction in the festival space is not only about ideas of difference and belonging, there also exists advocacy through song. The citizens interact with the state about its needs and vision by outlining social issues in the culture booklet and in the lyrics of songs. I argue that the cultural festival event conceived during the colonial administration and reinvented in the postcolonial period is a social space of interaction. The postcolonial festival is a space in which society and the state produce and practice ideas of association. While the idea of the festival is conceived differently by its participants, audiences and producers, findings in this study show that the event is deemed important by the state and by the people for the conservation of heritage. I emphasize that it should not be viewed in isolation of the state's ambition of economic prosperity.

What the state is striving for is the creation of national culture and a space of association, which can be placed in the global gaze as the tourism and heritage industry is one of the notable contributors to the national wealth. Culture is the most important aspect in the festival context, now seen and regarded as a commodity to be purchased and consumed in many ways. Although the scope of the study does not cover the issue of culture on sale[2], it remains the goal of the state to make it a wealth creating resource.

Theoretically, the study contributes to literature on performance as an act and analytical concept of social life and nationalism. (Goffman, 1959; Turner, 1979; Askew, 2002 and Ebron 2002)

Two perspectives on performance emerge. Firstly, the postcolonial Namibian state views performances as a system of representation consisting of intensively rehearsed acts of creativity. This perspective is contested by participants in the festival. The second one is that of participants and spectators who believe that they are involved in a performance through 'doing culture' which is not rehearsed, but 'real'. For instance, the cultural representations at the festival are about daily occurrences. Representation of birth rituals, witchcraft discourses, and types of food displayed and materials are not merely brought out during performance as process, they are integrated into the daily social life of both participants and spectators. In order to analyze the festival in question as a performance we must contextualize it as a process which is sanctioned for a particular purpose. A festival is an elaborate process constituting practice in a Bourdieian sense. Overall, the above discussions give us an insight about the state-sponsored culture festival as the social capital of associational life as a practice with meaning, a space, which is treated as an object of value.

Culture festivals are presented as important dramatizations that enable participants to understand, criticize and even change the worlds in which they live, a conclusion similar to that made by studies done in Canada (Handler 1988), Venzuela (Guss 2000) and Nigeria (Apter 2005). Without doubt such reflexive quality is what is appreciated as the most important aspect of cultural representations as my study has shown. Specifically it speaks to the work of Guss 2000, Corr 2003, Van Binsbergen 1993 and Flint 2006 who have dealt with festivals in the context of ethnicity as an imagined construct and resource. With particular reference to the current contestations around Nyemba-ness, my study shows how sentiments of ethnicity have been used for the articulation and mobilization of recognition.

---

[2] There is evidence in my fieldwork data that there were people who recorded the dances, took pictures of the various culture groups at the festivals and processed them into DVDs and photos and sold them to the public who attended the event. I have also been asked on various occasions whether I was making DVDs for sale as I was always seen with the video camera at the festival. For more discussion on commoditization of culture see the recent publication Ethnicity Inc. by Jean and John Comaroff (2009).

Below I briefly outline the significant concluding insights and themes in order to show the importance of studying nation building through festivals.

Festivals and 'Nation Building'

Throughout the African continent the 1990s brought a "turn to new rituals of belonging, which differed substantially from the older ones that had been developed during the earlier postcolonial periods." (Geschiere, 2009:213) Yet the specific practices of nation building continued to influence the "crystallization of alternative forms of belonging in every part of the continent, albeit along quite different trajectories." (Geschiere, 2009:213) Geschiere 2009 historical approach to belonging and nation building demonstrates that there are always competing forms of authority, each one imbued with different myths of legitimacy and principle of allegiance. (cf Lonsdale 1981) I have used history and festival analysis to better understand the politics of difference and belonging to Kavango specifically and to Namibia in general. In Kavango there is an ongoing discourse of difference and belonging in the local perspective, which is transmitted to the national level in a festival context. These differences are based on the historical legends of origin. They imply that Kavango as a space supposedly belonged to five ethnic groups, whereas other groups such as the Vanyemba and the San are mostly regarded as outsiders. This is particularly the case for the Nyemba. The Vanyemba are regarded as outsiders who had recently come to the territory and are therefore not included in the collective of what became known as the Vakavango especially after colonial time. The San are regarded as those who have lived in the bush very far from Kavango.

The study shows that the politics of difference and exclusion and belonging in the context of Kavango has its roots in historical legends, which present people as distinct.

Shortly before beginning my research, a debate within the Shambyu traditional authority about recognition of Runyemba as a language to be used in schools and on local radio took place. It coincided with the call for recognition and demand for space, which can be referred to as an ancestral land for the Vanyemba. Even though there was certain support for these calls (the former was supported by certain officials[3] and the latter by Nyemba headmen in Shambyu), they led to serious consequences; all Nyemba headmen who had previously been under the Shambyu traditional authority were removed by Hompa Matumbo Ribebe. Since then, there have been no Nyemba headmen in the Shambyu area. A campaign by local teachers and certain prominent officials called for the removal of Nyemba teachers and education officials who supported the official recognition of the Nyemba language.

---

[3] I may not mention their names for reasons of confidentiality.

These observations suggest that previously unrecognized ethnic groups are now able to claim recognition under the new dispensation. I view it as such because the current political situation through the constitution guarantees people the right to express themselves according to their imaginations. There is no legal instrument which suppresses such manifestations[4] as was the case during colonial time.

The most interesting aspect in this discussion is the usage and celebration of history, which differentiates and determines belonging in the festival context. Although there is not much written about the San and Vanyemba in the postcolonial culture booklet, the Vanyemba dances and art displays especially are said to be making an impression.

While there are serious contestations of post colonial Kavango identity[5], the region presents a different image at the national festival context, emphasizing ethnic and racial harmony. The regional office used the Noordgrens Secondary School ensemble of black and white students showcasing the Kavango culture to present an example of the imagined unity and diversity which the state propagates in its body politic. (Anderson, 1983; Brinkel, 2006) As I have shown, these past impositions of difference have become reconciled with postcolonial notions of national belonging. The state sponsored culture festival presents a space in which nation building takes place, while acting as an important element nation building. It will be safe to conclude that the postcolonial festival is not only a state affair but indeed a social process which involves both the state and its citizens.

The Kavango region remains on the fringes of academic discourse. The current contestations around belonging and exclusion and particularly the claims for the recognition of Nyemba-ness in itself offers a relevant area for further investigation both academically and politically. Another important research potential in Kavango especially in the field of Humanities and Social Sciences is the study of the San. Further historical research about their origin and contemporary discourses of marginality will contribute to the rather complex foundation myth of Kavango and its people.

---

[4] I am aware of the similar cultural politics of new claims for recognition in Southern African. See Robins (2001)
[5] I use identity as a category of practice as suggested by Brubaker and Cooper (2000)

Picture 1: Dances at Ekongoro during the 1970s. Source: Ministry of Information and Communication Technology

Picture 2: Variety of activities at Ekongoro during the 1970s. Source: Ministry of Information and Communication Technology

Picture 3: First senior youth officer Elrich Pretorius during the local festival at Ekongoro. Source: Karel Mberema Shiyaka

Picture 4: People in this image are believed to be Ezuva recruits during one of the field gatherings. Source: Ministry of Information and Communication Technology

Picture 5: Gathering during the Annual National Culture Festival in Kavango during 2008. Source: Michael Akuupa

Picture 6: The group from Kavango Region readies for the street march in Rundu town during the Annual National Culture Festival. Source: Michael Akuupa

Picture 7: Minister of Youth, National Service Sport and Culture Willem Konjore delivers a keynote address during the Annual National Culture Festival in Kavango. Source: Michael Akuupa

Picture 8: Kapata Cultural Group at the Kavango Regional Festival. Source: Michael Akuupa

Picture 9: Noordgrens Secondary School Cultural Group readies to enter the stage during the Kavango Regional Festival. Source: Michael Akuupa

Picture 10: Sam Shafiishuna Nujoma and author. Source: Office of the Founding President

List of Abbreviations

ANCF	Annual National Culture Festival
AU	African Union
APP	All People's Party
COD	Congress of Democrats
DRC	Democratic Republic of Congo
FESTAC	Second World Black and African Festival of Arts and Culture
GRN	Government of the Republic of Namibia
MAN	Museum Association of Namibia
MDC	Movement for Democratic Change
MPLA	The People's Movement for the Liberation of Angola
MYNSSC	Ministry of Youth, National Service, Sport and Culture
NANSO	Namibia National Students Organisation
NB	Namibia Broadcasting Corporation
NHCP	National Heritage and Culture Programmes
SADC	Southern African Development Community
SWAPO	South West Africa People's Organisation
SWANU	South West Africa National Union
SWA	South West Africa
SWAUK	Suidwes- Afrikaanse Uitsaai Korporasie
S&T	Subsistence and Travel Allowance
OPO	Ovambo People's Party
UN	United Nations
UNITA	The National Union for Total Independence of Angola
TRC	Truth and Reconciliation Commission
PWA	Portuguese West Africa
RDP	Rally for Democracy and Progress

Bibliography

Abu-Lughod, Lila (1991) Writing Against Culture. Recapturing Anthropology. Working in the Present. Eds. Richard G. Fox. Pp. (137-162). Santa Fe, New Mexico: School of American Research Press.

Agar, M. H. (1980) The Professional Stranger: An informal introduction to ethnography. London, Academic Press, INC.

Akuupa, M. U. (2007) "Checking the Kulcha:" Local Discourses of Culture in Kavango Region of Namibia. Bellville. University of the Western Cape. (unpublished MA thesis)

Akuupa, M. U. (2010) "We can be united, but we are different": discourses of difference in postcolonial Namibia. Anthropology Southern Africa. Vol.33. No.3&4. Pp. (103-114).

Anderson, B. (1991) Imagined Communities: Reflections on the Origins and Spread of Nationalism. London. Verso.

Appadurai, Arjun (1996) Modernity at Large. Cultural Dimensions of Globalization. Minneapolis & London: University of Minnesota Press.

Apter, A. (2005) The Pan African Nation: Oil and the Spectacle of Culture in Nigeria. Chicago and London, University of Chicago Press.

Arnoldi, M. J. (2006) Youth Festivals and Museums: The Cultural Politics of Public Memory in Postcolonial Mali. Africa Today. Vol. 52. No.4. Pp. (55-76).

Askew, K. M. (2002) Performing the Nation: Swahili Music and Cultural Politics in Tanzania. Chicago and London, The University of Chicago Press.

Barber, K. (2001) Cultural Reconstruction in the New South Africa. African Studies Review, Vol. 44, No. 2 Pp. (177-185).

Bauman, R. (1971) Differential Identity and the Social Base of Folklore. The Journal of American Folklore. Vol. 84, No. 331. Pp. (31-41)

Bauman, R. (1986) Performance and Honor in 13th-Century Iceland. Journal of American Folklore. Vol.99 No.392. Pp. (131-150).

Bayart, J. (2005) The Illusion of Cultural Identity. Chicago, University of Chicago Press.

Becker, H. (1995) Namibian Women's Movement 1980 to 1992: From Anti-colonial Resistance to Reconstruction. Bremen. Verlag für Interkulturelle Kommunikation.

Becker, H. (2003) Sites of Violence & Memory. Mapping the Namibian Liberation War. Paper presented at the 5th Northeast Workshop on Southern African Studies, Burlington, Vermont. 5-7 September 2003.

Becker, H. (2004) Efundula- Women's initiation, gender and sexual identities in colonial and post-colonial Northern Namibia. Re-thinking Sexualities in Africa: Ed. S. Arnfred. Pp. (35-54) Uppsala: The Nordic Africa Institute

Becker, H. (2007) Making Tradition: A Historical Perspective on Gender in Namibia. Unraveling Taboos: Gender and Sexuality in Namibia Eds. S. LaFont & D. Hubbard Pp. (22-38) Windhoek. Legal Assistance Centre.

Becker, H. (2008) "We remember Cassinga": Political Ritual, Memory, and Citizenship in Northern Namibia. Paper presented at the biennial conference of the VAD, Basel.

Becker, H. (2011) Commemorating Heroes in Windhoek and Eenhana:Memory, Culture and nationalism in Namibia, 1990-2010. Journal of the International African Institute, Vol.81 No.4 Pp. (519-543).

Beeman, W. (1993) The Anthropology of Theatre and Spectacle. Annual Review of Anthropology. Vol.22. Pp. (369-393).

Berman, B. J. (1998) Ethnicity, Patronage and the African State: The Politics of Uncivil nationalism. African Affairs, Vol.22, Pp. (305-341).

Boonzaier, E. A.& Sharp, J. (1994) Ethnic Identity a Performance: Lessons from Namaqualand. Journal of Southern African Studies. Vol. 20. No 3 Pp. (405-415).

Bosch, J. L. (1964) Die Shambiu van die Okavango: 'n volkekundige studie. Stellenbosch. University of Stellenbosch. (unpublished PhD thesis)

Bourdieu, P. (1998) Practical Reason: On the Theory of Action. Stanford, California. Stanford University Press.

Bourdieu, P. (2003) Participant Objectivation. Journal of the Royal Anthropological Institute. Vol. 9, No.2 Pp. (281-294)

Brinkel, T. (2006) Nation Building and Pluralism: Experiences and Perspectives in State and Society in South Africa. Den Haag, Sdu Uitgevers.

Brinkman, I (2005) A War for People: Civilians, Mobility, and Legitimacy in South-East Angola during the MPLA's War for Independence. Cologne. Rüdiger Köppe Verlag.

Brinkman, I. (1999) Violence, exile and ethnicity: Nyemba refugees in Kaisosi and Kehemu (Rundu, Namibia). Journal of Southern African Studies Vol. 25, No. 3 Pp. (417-437).

Brown, D. (2001) National Belonging and Cultural Difference; South Africa and the Global Imaginary. Journal of Southern African Studies, Vol. 27, (No. 4) Pp. (757-769).

Brubaker, R. & Cooper, F. (2000) Beyond "Identity". Theory and Society. Vol. 29, No.1. Pp. (1-29)

Brumann, C. (1999) Writing for Culture. Why a Successful Concept Should Not be Discarded. Current Anthropology Vol. 40, Supplement: S1-S27.

Buckner, M. (2004) Book Review: Kelly Askew, Performing the Nation: Swahili Music and Cultural Politics in Tanzania. Anthropological Quarterly. Vol. 77 No.2 Pp. (395-401).

Carstens, J. (2000) Cultures of Relatedness: New approaches to the study of Kinship. UK, Cambridge University Press.

Chanock, M. (2000) '"Culture" and Human Rights: Orientalising, Occidentalising and Authenticity'. Beyond Rights Talk and Culture Talk: Comparative Essays on the Politics of Rights and Culture, Ed. M. Mamdani. Claremont; David Philip Publishers.

Cohen, A. (1993) Masquerade politics: exploration in the structure of urban cultural movements. Berkley and Los Angeles. University of California Press.

Cohen, A. (2007) Self-Conscious Anthropology. In: Ethnographic fieldwork: an anthropological reader, Eds. A C G M Robben & J A Sluka. UK and USA; Blackwell Publishing.

Cole, C. M. (2010) Performing South Africa's Truth Commission: Stages of Transition. Bloomington and Indianapolis. Indiana University Press.

Comaroff, J. & Comaroff, J. (2009) Ethnicity, Inc. Scottsville. University of Kwazulu – Natal Press.

Comaroff, J. L., Comaroff, J. (1997) Postcolonial Politics and Discourses of Democracy in Southern Africa: An Anthropological Reflection on African Political Modernities. Journal of Anthropological Research, Vol. 53, (No. 2) Pp. (123-146)

Comaroff, J.L., Comaroff, J. (2001) Nurturing the Nation: Aliens, Apocalypse and the Postcolonial State. Journal of Southern African Studies, Vol. 27, (No. 3) (Special Issue for Shula Marks) Pp. (627-651)

Cornell, S. & Hartmann, D (1998) Ethnicity and Race: Making identities in the changing world, California, Pine Forge Press.

Corr, R. (2003) Ritual, Knowledge, and the Politics of Identity in the Andean Festivities. Ethnology, Vol. 42, No. 1. Pp. (39-54)

Diescho, J. B. (2006) Potential Economic Development in Kavango. A paper presented during a public lecture at Kavango Regional Council in Rundu. A report prepared by K M Likuwa.

Diescho, J.B. (1983) 'A Critical Evaluation of the Odendaal Commission of Enquiry into South West Africa Affairs 1962-1963', with Specific reference to its Findings, Recommendations and Implementation in respect of Kavango, a Juridico-Socio-Political Analysis (unpublished M A thesis, University of Fort Hare).

Du Pisani, A. (1987) Namibia: The Historical Legacy. Namibia in Perspective. Eds. Totemeyer, G. & Kandetu, V. and Werner, W. Windhoek, Angelus Printing.

Du Pisani, A. (2000) State and Society under South African Rule. In State, Society and Democracy: A Reader in Namibian Politics. (Ed.) Keulder, C. Windhoek: Gamsberg Macmillan.

Ebron, P. (2002) Performing Africa. New Jersey. Princeton University Press.

Eckl, A. (2007) Reports from 'beyond the line':The accumulation of knowledge of Kavango and its peoples by the German colonial administration 1891-191. Journal of Namibian Studies, Vol.1, Pp. (7-37).

Eyoh, D (1998) Social Realist Cinema and Representations of Power in African nationalist Discourse. Research in African Literature, Vol. 29, No. 2 Pp. (112-127).

Fairweather, I. S. (2001) Identity Politics and the Heritage in Post-Apartheid Northern Namibia (unpublished PhD thesis University of Manchester).

Fairweather, I. S. (2003) 'Showing off': Nostalgia and Heritage in North Central Namibia. Journal of Southern African Studies. Vol. 29. No.1 Pp. (279-296).

Fairweather, I. S. (2006) Heritage, Identity and Youth in Postcolonial Namibia. Journal of Southern African Studies, Vol. 32, No. 4 Pp. (719-736)

Fisch, M. (2005); History of Roman Catholic Mission Shambyu: 1930-2005, Windhoek: Solitaire Press.

Fisch, Maria (2008) The World of the Traditional Hunters along the Kavango River. Windhoek. Macmillan Education of Namibia Publishers Ltd.

Fleisch, A. & Mohlig, W. J. G. (2002) The Kavango Peoples in the Past: Local Historiographies from Northern Namibia, Cologne: Rudiger Koppe Verlag.

Flint, L. (2006) Contradictions and challenges in representing the past: The Kuomboka Festival of Western Zambia. Journal of Southern African Studies 32 (4): Pp. (701-717).

Fumanti, M. (2003) "Youth, Elites and Distinction in a Northern Namibia Town. (unpublished PhD thesis, University of Manchester).

Fumanti, M. (2004) The making of a fieldwork-er: debating agency in elites research. Anthropology Matters Journal. Vol. 6, No 2. Pp. (1-9)

Geertz, C. (1973) Thick Description: Toward an Interpretive Theory of Culture. Interpretation of Cultures. New York. Basic Books.

Geingob, H. G. (2004) State Formation in Namibia: Promoting Democracy and Governance. (unpublished PhD thesis, University of Leeds).

Geschiere, P. (2009) The Perils of Belonging: Autochtony, Citizenship, and Exclusion in Africa & Europe. Chicago and London. University of Chicago Press.

Gibson, D.G.; Larson, T.J.; McGurk, C. R. (1981) The Kavango Peoples. Wiesbaden, Steiner Verlag GMBH.

Goffman, E (1959 reprinted in 1990) The Representation of self in everyday life. USA Anchor Books.

Gordon, R. (2005) The making of modern Namibia: A Tale of Anthropological Ineptitude? Kleio. Vol.37, No. 1. Pp. (26-49).

Gottschalk, K. (1987) Restructuring the Colonial State: Pretoria Strategy in Namibia. Namibia in Perspective. Eds. Totemeyer, G. & Kandetu, V. and Werner, W. Windhoek, Angelus Printing.

Gupta, A. (1995) Blurred Boundaries: The discourse of Corruption, the Culture of Politics, and the Imagined State. American Ethnologist, Vol.22, No. 2 Pp. (375-402).

Gupta, A; Ferguson, J. (1992) Beyond "Culture": Space, Identity, and the Politics of Difference. Cultural Anthropology, Vol. 7, No. 1 Pp. (.6-23).

Guss, D.M (2000) *The Festive State: Race Ethnicity, and Nationalism as Cultural Performance.* Berkeley, Los Angeles London. University of California Press.

Habermas, J. (1995) Multiculturalism and the liberal state. *Stanford Law Review.* Vol. 47, No. 5. Pp. (849-853).

Hall, S. (1996) Introduction. *Questions of Cultural Identity.* Eds. Hall, S. and du Gay, P. London. SAGE Publ.

Hall, S. (1996) The Meaning of New Times. *Critical dialogues in cultural studies.* Eds. Morley, D. & Chen, K. (pp. 222-236), London. Routledge.

Handler, R. (1986) Authenticity, in: *Anthropology Today,* Vol. 2, and No.1. Pp. (2-4)

Handler, R. (1988) *Nationalism and the Politics of Culture in Quebec.* London, The University of Wisconsin Press.

Hannerz, U. (1992) *Cultural Complexity: Studies in the Social Organisation of Meaning.* New York. Columbia University Press.

Hansen, B.; Stepputat, F. (2005) Introduction. *Sovereign Bodies: citizens, migrants, and state in the postcolonial world.* Eds. B. Hansen and F. Stepputat. New York. Princetown University Press.

Hayes P, Silvester J, Hartmann W. (1998) *The Colonising Camera: Photographs in the making of Namibian History.* Windhoek. Out of Africa.

Hayes P, Silvester J, Wallace M, Hartmann W. (1998) *Namibia under South African Rule: Mobility & Containment 1915-46.* Windhoek. Out of Africa.

Hobsbawm, Eric & Ranger, Terence Eds. 1984. *The invention of tradition.* Cambridge: Cambridge University Press.

Hughes-Freeland, F. (1998) Introduction. *Ritual, Performance, Media.* Eds F. Hughes-Freeland & M.M. Crain. London. Routledge.

Hummel, H. C., Craig, A. (1994 for 1992) *Johan August Wahlberg: Travel Journals (and some letters) South Africa and Namibia/Botswana, 1835-1856*. Second Series No.23, Cape Town, Van Riebeeck Society.

Hunke, H. (1996) *Church and State: The political context of 100 years of Catholic Mission in Namibia*. Windhoek. John Meinert Printers.

July, R. (1983) Toward Cultural Independence in Africa: Some Illustrations from Nigeria and Ghana. *African Review*, Vol. 26, No. 3 / 4 Pp. (119-131).

Kampungu, R. (1966) *Okavango marriage customs: investigated in the light of Ecclesiastical Legislation*. (unpublished PhD thesis Pontificia Universitas Urbaniana De Propaganda Fide, Rome).

Karapo, H. K. (2008) *Living memory in a forgotten war zone: the Ukwangali district of Kavango and the Namibian Liberation struggle, 1966-1989*. (unpublished MA thesis, University of the Western Cape).

KjÆret, K. & Stokke, K. (2003) Rehoboth Baster, Namibian or Namibian Baster? An analysis of national discourses in Rehoboth, Namibia. *Nations and Nationalism*. Vol.9, No. 4. Pp. (579-600).

Kössler, R. (2003) Rebuilding Societies from Below: Reflections on Heroes Day, Gibeon, Namibia. In Discussion Paper 21: *Development from Below- A Namibian Case Study*. Nordiska Afrikainstitutet, Uppsala.

Kössler, R. (2007) Entangled History and Politics: Negotiating the Past between Namibia and Germany. *Journal of Contemporary African studies*, Vol. 26. No.3 Pp. (313-340).

Kymlicka, W. (1989) *Liberalism, Community and Culture*. Oxford. Oxford University Press.

Lentz, C. (2000) Colonial Constructions and African Initiatives: The History of Ethnicity in North Western Ghana. *Ethnos*, Vol.65. No. 1 Pp. (107-136).

Lentz, C. (2001) Local Culture in the National Arena: The Politics of Cultural Festivals in Ghana. *African Studies Review*, Vol. 44. (No.3) Pp. (47-720)

Likuwa, K. M. (2005) *Rundu, Kavango: A case study of forced relocation in Namibia, 1954 to 1972*. Bellville: (unpublished MA thesis, University of the Western Cape).

Likuwa, K. M. (2007) A critique on "Reports from beyond the line": The Accumulation of knowledge of Kavango and its peoples by the German colonial administration 1891-1911. Paper presented at the "Recording and Restoring our Past in the Past" conference on 23-24 August at Kavango Regional Council in Rundu.

Lindholm, C. (2008) *Culture and Authenticity*. Malden and Oxford, Blackwell Publ.

Lonsdale, J. (1981) States and Social Processes in Africa: A Historiographical Survey. *African Studies Review*. Vol. 24. No 2/3. Pp. (139-225)

Losambe, L. and Sarinjeive, D. (2001) *Pre-colonial and Post-colonial Drama and Theatre in Africa*. Claremont. New Africa Books.

Mafeje, A. (1971) The Ideology of Tribalism. *Journal of Modern African Studies*. Vol. 9. No. 2 Pp. (253-261)

Magubane, B.M. (1969) "Pluralism and Conflict Situations in Africa": A New Look. *African Social Research*. Vol.3. Pp. (529-554).

Mamdani, M. (1996) *Citizen and Subject: Contemporary Africa and the Legacy of Late Colonialism*. Princeton, New Jersey, Princeton University Press.

Mans, M. (2002); Constructing Cultural Identities in Contemporary Musical Traditions-Strategies of Survival and Change. *Namibia Sociology Society*. Eds. Winterfeldt, V.; Fox, T.; Mufune, P. Windhoek, University of Namibia Press.

Mascarenhas-Keyes, S. (1987) The native anthropologist: constraints and strategies in research. *Anthropology at home*. Eds. Jackson, A. Tavistock Publications Ltd. London.

Mbambo, S. K. (2002) *'Heal with God': Indigenous Healing and Religion among the Vagciriku of the Kavango Region, Namibia*. Utrecht, Unitwin.

Mbumba, N. & Noisser, N. H. (1988) *Namibia in History: Junior Secondary History Book*. London and New Jersey, Centre for African Studies, University of Bremen.

McKittrick, M. (2008) Landscapes of Power: Ownership and Identity on the Kavango River, Namibia. *Journal of SouthernAfrican Studies*, Vol. 34:No.4. Pp. (785-802)

Meredith McKittrick (2002) *To Dwell Secure: Generation, Christianity and Colonialism in Ovamboland*. Portsmouth, New Hampshire: Heinemann; Oxford: James Currey, Cape Town, David Philip.

Meyer, B. (1999) Popular Ghanaian Cinema and "African Heritage". *Africa Today*, Vol. 46, No. 2. Pp. 93-114.

Mfecane, S. (2010) *Exploring Masculinities in the Context of ARV use: A study of men living with HIV in a South African Village*. Johannesburg. University of Witwatersrand (unpublished PhD thesis).

Mufune, P. (2002) Youth in Namibia-Social Exclusion and Poverty. *Namibia Society Sociology*. Eds. V. Winterfeldt, T. Fox, P. Mufune. Namibia: University of Namibia Press.

Museum Association of Namibia (2009) *MAN's Three Year Development Plan 2010-2013*.

Mutorwa, J. (1994) *The Establishment of the Nyangana Roman Catholic Mission Station During the Reign of Hompa Nyangana*. Windhoek, Gamsberg Macmillan.

Nambadi, A. H. (2007) *The Kavango Legislative Council 1970-1979: a critical analysis*. Bellville: (unpublished MA thesis, University of the Western Cape).

Narayan, K. (1993) How Native is a "Native" Anthropologists? *American Anthropologists, New Series.* Vol. 95. 3. Pp. (671-686).

Ndhlovu-Gatsheni, S. J. and W. Willems (2009) Making Sense of Cultural Nationalism and the Politics of Commemoration under the Third Chimurenga in Zimbabwe. *Journal of Southern African Studies.* Vol. 35, No. 4. Pp. (945-965)

Olivier, M. J. (1961) *Inboorlingbeleid en Administrasie in die Mandaatgebied van Suidwes-Afrika.* (unpublished PhD thesis, Universiteit van Stellenbosch)

Oomen, B. (2005) *Chiefs in South Africa: Law, Power & Culture in the Post- Apartheid Era.* Oxford, Pietermaritzburg, New York. University of Kwazulu- Natal Press.

Opoku, K. A. (1970) Independence of the Mind. *Journal of Black Studies.* Vol.1. No.2 Pp. (179-186).

Owusu-Frempong, Y. (2005) Afrocentricity, the Adae Festival of the Akan, African American Festivals, and Intergenerational Communication. *Journal of Black Studies*, Vol. 35, No 6. Pp. (730-750).

Pierre, J. (2009) Beyond Heritage Tourism:Race and Politics of African Diasporic Interactions. *Social Text.* Vol. 27.No.1 Pp. (51-81).

Preller, G. S. (1941) *Voortrekkers van Suidwes: Geskiedenis van die land en sy volke met hul oorloë; van die Dorsland-trek; die Smit-trek uit Piketbrg en die Duitse en Britse veroweringe.* Kaapstad, Bloemfontein en Port Elizabeth. Nasionale Pers Beperk.

Pye, L.W. (1962) *Politics, Personality, and Nation Building: Burma's Search for Identity.* New Haven and London, Yale University Press.

Report of the Presidential Commission on Education, Culture and Training Vol.1 published 1999.

Republic of Namibia 2001. *Policy on arts and culture, unity identity and creativity for prosperity.* Windhoek.

Ross, F. (2005) Special Issue on Ethics. *Anthropology of Southern Africa.* Vol. 28 (No 4-5) Pp. (57-61).

Sahlins, M. (1993) 'Goodbye to Tristes Tropes: Ethnography in the Context of Modern World History' In: *Journal of Modern History*, Vol. 65, No.1. Pp. (1-25).

Schechner, R. (1990) reprinted (1993); *Magnitudes of performance.* By Means of Performance: Intercultural Studies of Theatre and Ritual. (pp.19-49) Eds. Schechner, R. & Appel,W. Great Britain. Cambridge University Press.

Schieffelin, E. L. (1998) Problematizing performance. *Recasting Ritual: Performance, Media, Identity.* Eds. F. Hughes-Freeland & M.M Crain pp. 198-208.London. Routledge.

Schildkrout, E. (1995) Museums and Nationalism in Namibia. *Museum Anthropology.* Vol. 19, No. 2 Pp. (65-77)

Shiremo, S. (2005) The role of Kavango kings in the anti colonial resistance: 1903 a year of unity and resistance. A paper presented at conference the Rundu College of Education.

Shiremo, S. (2010) *The reign of Hompa Nyangana over the Vagciriku.* (unpublished MA thesis, University of Namibia)

Sichone, O. (2001) Review: Pure Anthropology in a highly indebted Poor Country. *Journal of Southern African Studies.* Vol. 27. No. 2. Pp. (369-379) Special Issue on Fertility in Southern Africa.

Skalik, P. (1988) Tribe as colonial category. *South African Keywords: the uses and abuses of political concepts.* Eds. Boonzaier, E. & Sharp, J. Pp. Cape town: David Phillip.

Sluka, J. A. (2007) Introduction. *Ethnographic fieldwork: an anthropological reader.* Eds. A C G M Robben & J A Sluka. UK and USA; Blackwell Publishing.

Sonyika, W. (1990) Twice Bitten: The Fate of Africa's Culture Producers. In: *PMLA*, Vol. 105, No. 1 Special Topic: African and African American Literature Pp. (110-120)

Spiegel, A. & Boonzaier, E. (1988) Promoting Tradition: Images of the South African Past. *South African Keywords: The Uses and Abuses of Political Concepts.* Eds. Boonzaier, E. & Sharp, J. Cape town: David Phillip.

St John, G. (2008) Introduction. *Victor Turner and contemporary cultural performance.* USA. Bergmann Books.

Stone, Linda (1997) *Kinship and Gender.* Boulder: Westview Press.

Strathern, M. (1987) The limits of auto anthropology. Anthropology at home. Eds. Jackson, A. Tavistock Publications Ltd. London.

The Constitution of the Republic of Namibia (1990) adopted in Windhoek.

Thornton R. J. (1988) Culture: A Contemporary Definition. South African Keywords: The Uses and Abuses of Political Concepts. Eds. Boonzaier, E. & Sharp, J. Cape town: David Phillip.

Tsuda, T. (1998) Ethnicity and the Anthropologist: Negotiating Identities in the Field. Anthropology Quarterly. Vol. 71, No.3. Pp. (107-124).

Turner, V. & Turner, E. (1986) Performing Ethnography. The Drama Review, Vol. 26, No 2. Pp. (33-50).

Turner, V. (1979) Dramatic Ritual/Ritual Drama: Performative and Reflexive Anthropology. The Kenyon Review, New Series. Vol. 1, No.3. Pp. (80-93)

Turner, V. (1980) Social Dramas and Stories about Them. Critical Inquiry, Vol.7, No.1. Pp. (141-168).

Turner, V. (1990) reprinted (1993) Are there universals of performance in myth, ritual, and drama? By Means of Performance: Intercultural Studies of Theatre and Ritual. Eds. Schechner, R. & Appel,W. Great Britain. Cambridge University Press.

Vale de Almeida, M. (2002) Citizenship and Anthropology: Perplexities of a Hybrid Social Agent. Paper presented at Plenary session- 'The challenges of Engagement', 7th EASA Conference, Copenhagen.

Van Binsbergen, W. M. J. (1994) The Kazanga Festival: ethnicity as cultural mediation and transformation in central Western Zambia, in: African studies: a quarterly journal devoted to the study of African Administration cultures and languages. Vol. 53, No.2. Pp. (99-125).

Van Heerden, E (2009) Liminality, transformation and communitas Afrikaans identities as viewed through the lens of South African arts festival: 1995-2006. (unpublished PhD thesis, University of Stellenbosch).

Van Tonder, L. L. (1966) The Hambukushu of Okavangoland: An Anthropological study of a South Western Bantu People in Africa. (unpublished PhD thesis, University of Port Elizabeth).

W. A. Haugh (2009) A Luta Continua: Coping with Threats to Prosperity and Health in Post-Independence Namibia. Journal of Southern African Studies. Vol. 35. No. 1. Pp. (99-113).

Wa Thiongo, N. (1986) Decolonizing the mind: The politics of language in African literature. London. James Curry.

Westphal. E. (1970) Review: The language of the Dciriku. Phonology, Prosodology and Morphology by W. Mohlig. Journal of the International African Institute. Vol.40 No. 3 Pp. (291-293)

William Beeman (1993) The Anthropology of Theater and Spectacle. Annual Review of Anthropology. Vol. 22. Pp. (369-393).

Wilson, R. A. (2001) Politics of Truth and Reconciliation in South Africa: Legitimizing the Post-apartheid State. Cambridge; New York: Cambridge University Press.

Witz, L (2003) Apartheid's Festival: Contesting South Africa's National Pasts. Indianapolis & Bloomington, Indiana University Press.

Wright, S. (1998) The Politicization of "Culture". Anthropology Today, Vol. 14 No.1. Pp. (7-15).

Newspapers

'Andrew Matjila and Traditional Festivals in the Caprivi: The Other Side of the Coin' New Era 06 October 2006

'One Namibia, One Nation? The Case Of The Caprivi Revisited' New Era 31 July 2009

'Farmers to protest Kavango issues as tensions run high' The Namibian, 23 November 2005

'Kavango grazing standoff continues' The Namibian, 23 June 2008

'Rundu road not delayed' The Namibian, 18 July 2007

'Kavango leaders complain of being left out by government' The Namibian, 13 February 2003

'Tribalism allegations rock Ministry of Youth and Culture' Informante 11 February 2010

'Better Late than never' The Namibian 05 May 2011

'In culture we are one' Polynews 05 August 2011

'Former Youth director denies tribalism allegations' Informante 15 February 2010

'Work on cultural villages, centers awaits UN fund' New Era, 19 January 2009

'Rehoboth Journal; Fearful Namibian Tribe Raises Flag of Freedom' NewYork Times 04 April 1990

Archives

NAT1/1/54 File 25 Official Communication dated 1937/2/21 Tribal Trust Fund: Okavango Native Territory

NAT/1/1/54/S/U-20/File 25

NAT1/1/54 File 25 Official Communication dated 1937/2/21

NAR/11/55, File 9 and Vol.3

NAR/11/55, File 20 "unregistered confidential correspondence, 1962-1967"

NAR1/1/55 File N1/12/7/2 Letter dated 1968/05/11

NAR/1/155

NAR/155 File N1/12/6 dated 1967/10/25 Official Communication from Afrikaanse Universiteit van Die Witwatersrand

NAR/1/155 File BB/0276 SWA- A Five Year Plan- for the development of the Native Areas

NAR/1/155 File F002-JX10006- KAVANGUDI (1973 April) homeland official newspaper published by the Department of Information.

NAR/1/155 File F002-JX10006- KAVANGUDI (1974 April)

NAR/1/555/ File F002-JX10006 KAVANGUDI (May 1974)

NAR1/1/55 File JX/0256 KAVANGO ONDERWYSNUUS (1983 December)

NAR/1/1/55 File JX-0257 MURULI NUUSBLAD VIR KAVANGO (December 1984)

NAR/1/1/55 File JX-0257 MURULI NUUSBLAD VIR KAVANGO (January 1986)

NAR/1/55 Letter dated 1964/03/28 to the Chief Bantu Affairs Commissioner from Bantu Affairs Commisioner of Kavango motivating her return to the territory to complete her research

NAR/1/55 Letter dated 1967/10/29 to the Bantu Affairs Commissioner in Kavango from Dr. W Mohlig in Germany

NAR/1/55 Letter dated 1967/11/09 to Dr. Mohlig in Germany from the Bantu Affairs Commissioner of Kavango

NAR1/1/55 File N1/12/7/2 Letter dated 1968/05/11 to the Chief Bantu Affairs Commissioner detailing the demands of the Vagciriku King Shashipapo for recognition and teaching of Rugciriku in schools.

NAR/1/55 File AP/7/1/1 Jaarverslag (Annual Report) 1978 Departement Van Onderwys-Kavango Regering

Interviews

Interview with Samuel Hausiku headman of Sauyemwa village on 11 April 2007

Interview with Sam Nujoma, Office of the Founding President, Windhoek 25 November 2008

Interview with Linyando Manfred Mukoroli, joined by Kletus Muhena Likuwa at Safari, Rundu, 16 January 2009

Interview with Karel Mberema Shiyaka, Maria Mwengere Culture Centre, Rundu, 23 September 2008

Interview with Irma Jericho, Tutungeni, Rundu, 18 December 2008

Personal communication with Elrich Pretorius at Maria Mwengere Culture Centre during 2008

Personal communication with Kandali Nangolo at the Annual National Culture Festival held in Kavango during 2008 December

Interview with Magdaleena Pessa Kasera, Theresia Sikongo, Anastasia Mufenda and Helena Nasini, they are teachers responsible for culture at Sauyemwa Junior Primary School, 20 January 2009

Interview with Queen Maria Kandambo at her homestead in Gciriku, January 20, 2007

Interview was held with *Hompa* Alfons Kaundu Mattias on 14 April 2007 at Sigone

Interview was held with *Hompa* Maria Kandambo on 24 December 2006 at Gciriku

Interview with Shidonankuru at Ndiyona 24 December 2006

Interview with Djani Kashera on 20 January 2007 at Kambowo village

Interview with Mbambangandu waShihako; Kambowo, January 20, 2007

Interview with Simon Kandere on 28 January 2007 at Safari

Interview with Jan Bradley, Tutungeni, Rundu, 20 September 2008

Interview with Selma Negumbo at City of Windhoek 29 October 2008

Interview with Immanuel Shikukumwa; Safari, January 2009

Interview with Lukas Dikuwa on 09 July 2009 in Mbukushu.

Interview held with Rudolf Ngondo, 15 January 2010 at Katjinakatji

Index

202 Battalion 98, 101

A
Aakwaluudhi 44
Aakwanambwa 44
African Second World Black and Festival of Arts and Culture (FESTAC 77) 35
African Union (AU) 149, 164
African Union Summit 149
Afrikaans 33, 75, 96, 100, 108
Afrikaanse Universiteit van die Witwatersrand 78
Agar, Michael 47
Akan 32
Akuupa, Dorkas 38
Akuupa, Lukas 38, 71
Akuupa, Maria 7–9, 12, 46, 49, 59, 64 f., 67, 72, 84, 87, 92, 94 f., 97–101, 109–112, 115, 117, 119, 120 f., 123, 125 f., 132, 137, 145 f., 157 f., 165, 174, 186
Akuupa, Michael 7, 15, 33, 36, 38, 42, 44, 108, 114 f., 119, 127, 142
All People's Party (APP) 133
America 16, 36, 44, 184
Andara 70 f., 99 f.
Anderson, John 59, 183, 191
Angola 53–55, 65 f., 69, 75, 91, 108 f., 133, 145, 160, 181
Annual National Culture Festival (ANCF) 2, 5, 11, 38, 105, 159, 173
Anti-Colonial Resistance and the Liberation Struggle (AACRLS) 83
Appadurai, Arjun 104
Apter, Andrew 35, 169, 189
Arnoldi, Mary Jo 34
Askew, Kelly 6, 14 f., 22, 112 f., 140, 169, 186, 189

B
Bantu Affairs Commissioner 79
Barber, Karin 2
Basterland 88
Bauman, Richard 17, 19, 132, 139
Becker, Heike 4, 25, 31, 73, 88, 103, 140
Beeman, William 19
Bennett Kangumu 98
Boer Administration 102
Boma Namibia 113

Boonzaier, Emile 7, 21 f., 36
Bosch, Johannes 76
Botswana 27, 53, 61, 69, 91, 133, 149
Bourdieu, Pierre 22 f., 26, 29, 36, 52, 139, 157
Bradley, Jan 97, 101 f., 123–125
Brinkel, T 183, 191
Brinkman, Inge 55, 108, 181
Britain 112
British 77, 85
Brother Georg Russ 70
Brother Johannes Rau 70
Brother Konrad Heckmann 70
Brown, Duncan 25, 27, 183
Brubaker, Roger and Cooper, Frederick 29, 183, 191
Bruwer, Johannes 57, 75
Budack 79
Bunya 70
Burger, Louis 89, 94

C

Cameroon 27
Canada 16, 28, 111, 189
Canikwe 60, 63
Caprivi 54, 74, 85, 88, 98, 106, 132, 171
Caprivians 173
Carstens, Janet 40, 44
Cassinga 91, 93
Catholic 69, 70–72, 76, 85, 148, 172 f.
Central Western Zambia 112, 169
Chanock, Martin 30
City of Windhoek 106
Cocky Hahn 73, 124
Cohen, Anthony 42
Cole, Catherine 15 f., 20
Comaroff, John and Comaroff, Jean 25, 27, 33, 89, 135, 179
Congress of Democrats (CoD) 133
Cuando Cubango 55
Cuca 8, 43
Cuito 65
Cuni 69

D

Damara 58, 80, 106, 132, 173, 186
Damara Annual Cultural Festival 106
Damaraland 58

Dciriku Tribal Authority 79
de Almeida, Vale 46
Democratic Republic of Congo (DRC) 133
Department of Education 12, 87, 89, 93, 96 f., 99
De Wet, Jannie 81
Diaz, Herbert 38, 132, 179
Diergaardt, Hans 88
Diescho, Josef 55
Dikumbwata 144
Dimbare, Frans 94
Diyeve 68
Donaveltha 116
Dr. Alpo Mbamba Junior Secondary School 153
Du Pisani, Andre 4, 74, 80

E

Ebron, Polla 6, 14–16, 23, 140, 189
Eckl, Andreas 57, 68, 70–72, 83 f.
Eedes, Harold 61, 72, 114
Efundula 104
Ejuva 81
Ekongoro 7–9, 12, 49, 87, 92, 94–102, 110 f., 115, 119, 120 f., 123–126, 132, 137, 157, 158, 165, 174, 186
Ekoro, Liro 8, 11, 38, 40, 42
Ekuliko 37, 134
Epera 141, 144, 160
Erongo 106, 171
Etango 81
Ethiopia 75
Europe 9, 44, 120
Ewi lya Manguluka 103
Eyoh, Dickson 27

F

Fairweather, Ian 2, 21 f., 31, 36, 89, 103 f., 128
Father August Bierfert 70
Father Frohlich 72 f.
Father Joseph Gotthardt 70
Father Krist 70
Fergusson, James 21
Finnish 69–71, 74
Fisch, Maria 59, 72, 84
Flint, Lawrence 33, 112, 169, 189
Fumanti, Mattia 48, 78

G

Geertz, Clifford 17, 144
Geingob, Hage 25, 188
German 31, 53 f., 57, 67–70, 72, 78, 83 f., 106 f.
Germany 72, 79, 83, 112, 149
Geschiere, Peter 27
Ghana 16 f., 32 f., 104, 138
Gluckman, Max 144
Goffman, Erving 17 f., 22, 51, 129, 138 f., 150, 156, 164, 189
Gordon, Robert 57
Gottschalk, Keith 80 f.
Guma 60
Gupta, Akhil 160
Guss, David 35

H

Habermas, Jurgen 185
Haididira, Fau 41
Haididira, Nanguroni 39, 41
Haikombo 69
Hakusembe, Leevi 94
Hall, Stuart 107
Hamutenya, Hidipo 133
Handa 65
Handler, Richard 16, 23, 28, 37, 111, 174, 181, 189
Hardap 106, 171
Haugh, Wendi 31
Hausiku, David 60
Hendrik Witbooi 31, 102, 106 f.
Herero 58 f., 80, 106, 132, 173
History Club 108
Hobsbawm, Eric 169
Homeland Department of Information 9, 100
Hompa 64–70, 72, 85, 88, 94, 108 f., 130, 190
Huhges Freeland, Felicia 21, 140

I

Iipumbu yaTshilongo 58, 102
International Court of Justice 75

J

Jao 59, 60, 63
Jericho, Irma 91 f.
Johan August Wahlberg 69
July, Robert 5, 41, 59 f., 71, 84, 120, 133

K

Kabanana 104
Kaisosi 56, 108
Kakube 16 f., 138
Kalanami 113
Kalenga of Nduva 134
Kalikenuke 64
Kambamba 67, 141, 144
Kambembe 141–116, 146
Kambundu Culture Dance Group 148, 155
Kampungu, Romanus 40 f., 58, 62, 69 f., 72, 76 f., 80
Kandambo, Maria 64 f., 67
Kandere, Simon 68
Kandjimi Hawanga 68
Kangumbe 59
Kapako 108
Kapata Cultural Group 138, 145, 157, 162
Karambuka 69
Karas 171
Kashandura 144
Kashera, Djani 59, 63, 69
Katengona 41–43, 47
Kativa kaMutuva 66
Kaundu, Alfons 64 f.
Kavango 8, 41–43, 46 f., 55, 59, 63–65, 67 f., 70–72, 76, 79, 88, 94, 97, 108 f., 114, 125–127, 132–134, 145, 148, 163, 179 f., 182, 190
Kavango Anthem Ovamboland 50, 90, 94, 121
Kavango Elders 59, 83, 85
Kavangoland 58
Kavango Legislative Council 61, 81 f., 101
Kavango Museum 111, 115, 118
Kavango Regional Council 1 f.
Kavango River 12, 53, 59 f., 63–65, 75, 77, 82, 87 f., 90, 109, 116, 161, 176, 181
Kavango Volk 81 f., 90, 92
Kavango Volkslied 90
Kazanga Festival 17, 112 f.
Kazanga, Valesca 16 f., 33, 112 f., 116, 169
Khomas 171
Khowesen 106
Klein Karoo Nasionale Kunstefees en Aardklop (KKNK) 33
Kobine 16 f., 138
Konjore, Willem 159, 172 f., 185
Kossler, Reinhart 31
Kulinyanyukisa 12, 137–139, 145, 157, 160, 162–164, 167, 175
Kunene 171

Kuomboka Festival 112
Kymlicka, Will 132, 184

L

League of Nations 70, 75
Lentz, Carola 16, 17, 33, 75, 138, 168 f.
Libebe 70
Liberia 75
Libya 149
Likuwa, Kletus 47, 55, 59 f., 114, 118
Limbaranda 66, 109
Lindholm, Charles 37
Losambe, Lokangaka 166
Lozi 112, 169
Lukas Dikuwa 71
Lusata 106, 186
Lutheran 22, 69 f., 73, 120

M

Mafeje, Archie 77
Mafwe 88, 98
Mahamba 141, 144, 146, 167
Maharero 102, 106
Maharero, Samuel 106
Majavero, Alfons 81
Makuyombilito 137, 139
Makuzu 55, 58, 65 f.
Makuzu ga Muntenda 65
Maliyombiliso 12, 137 f., 157
Mamili, Boniface 88
Mandela, Nelson 25, 35
Mankoto 60, 62 f.
Mans, Minette 2
Maria Mwengere 7–9, 12, 49, 87, 92, 94 f., 97–101, 109–112, 115, 117, 119, 120 f., 123, 125 f., 132, 137, 157 f., 165, 174, 186
Maria Mwengere Camp 87, 95
Maria Mwengere Culture Camp 101, 111
Maria Mwengere Culture Centre 7–9, 12, 49, 92, 94 f., 98–100, 110 f., 115, 119–121, 123, 125 f., 132, 137, 157 f., 165, 174, 186
Maria Mwengere wa Mukosho 7,–9, 12, 46, 49, 87, 92, 94 f., 97–100, 101, 109, 110–112, 115, 117, 119–121, 123, 125 f., 132, 137, 157 f., 165, 174, 186
Marudeve 116, 161, 176
Mascarenhas-Keyes, Stella 45
Mashi 54, 60, 63–65, 67
Masimo 151

Matjaube 62 f.
Mayana Combined School 138
Mbambo, Josef 49, 149 f., 155
Mbambo, Samuel 49, 78, 147, 149 f., 155, 167
Mberema, Shiyaka 80, 99, 165
Mbwalala, Helvi 120
McKittrick, Meredith 67
Meyer, Birgit 32
Mfecane, Sakhumzi 10
Ministry of Information 2, 101
Ministry of Youth, National Service, Sport and Culture (MYNSSC) 38, 114, 171, 178
Mohlig, Wilhelm 62, 78–80, 165
Monyemba 66
Morris 68
Mpungu 70, 130, 138, 156–158, 164
Mpupa 142
Mudukuli 103, 160, 165, 171, 180
Mukavango 49, 61
Mukoroli, Robert 91
Mulyata 134, 142
Mupiri, Robert 94 f.
Muruli Nuusblad 100
Museum Association of Namibia (MAN) 114, 117 f.
Mutjokotjo 67, 141, 144
Mutorwa, John 70 f., 84, 124 f., 170
Muvambo 44
Muyongo, Mishake 88

N

Nakare, Damian 66
Nambadi, Aaron 118
Namibia 7–10, 35, 38, 41, 79, 95, 102, 106, 132, 149, 162
Namibia Broadcasting Corporation (NBC) 114
Nangolo, Kandali 113
Narayan, Kirin 43, 45, 52
National Archive of Namibia 9
National Arts and Language Competition 113
National Heritage and Culture Programs (NHCP) 38, 115
National Union for the Total Liberation of Angola (UNITA) 55, 181
Native Commissioner 61, 68, 72 f., 79
Natural Administration Act 76
Ncaute 63
Ncushe 60, 63
Ncwa 61
Ndjelenga of Mulyata 134
Ndongalinena 63

Ndumba yaTjimpulu 66
Netherland 27, 95
New Era 2 f., 88, 98, 103, 108, 170
Ngara 142
Ngombo 147, 150, 156
Ngondo, Rudolf 58, 66, 93, 141
Ngoro 69
Nigeria 35, 189
Nkondo 61
Nkunki 61
Nkurenkuru 68, 70, 132, 161
nongongo 177
Noordgrens Secondary School 13, 140, 168, 170, 174 f., 180, 191
Ntunguru 13, 66, 168, 170, 174–179, 181, 183
Ntunguru Cultural Group 13, 170, 174, 179, 183
Nujoma, Sam 34 f., 50–52, 102, 133, 155, 188
Nyambi 141, 144
Nyangana 66, 68, 70, 72, 85, 143
Nyembaland 66
Nyumba 142

O

Odendaal Plan 35, 55, 61, 67, 74 f., 77, 79, 81, 93, 98, 124
Ohangwena 54, 129, 133, 171, 176
Okahandja 106
Okavango Delta 53
Olivier, M J 76
Olukonda 22, 70, 120, 128
Omagongo 186
Omaheke 171
Ondjondjo Culture Group 178
Ondonga 70, 129
One Namibia One Nation 24
Oomen, Barbara 30
Opoku, Kofi 34
Oshana 171, 178
Oshikoto 54, 120, 129, 171
Otjiserandu 106
Otjozondjupa 54, 171
Oukwanyama 129
Ovambo 24, 31, 44, 54, 57, 71, 73 f., 76, 113
OvamboKavango 74
Ovamboland 38, 44, 57 f., 70, 73 f., 81, 98, 104, 121, 124, 129
Ovambo People Orgnisation (OPO) 24
Owusu-Frempong, Yaw 32

P

Peace Corps 158
Pinduka 180
Portuguese 8, 43, 55, 62, 68 f., 75, 109
Portuguese West Africa (PWA) 55, 75
Pretorius, Elrich 94 f., 97, 99, 125
Pye, Lucian 179

Q

Quebec 16, 111

R

Rally for Democracy and Progress (RDP) 133
Rand Afrikaanse Universiteit (RAU) 78
Rehoboth 88, 95
Rengo 141, 144
Ribebe, Matumbo 108, 190
Roman Catholic Church 71 f., 76, 148
Rucara 134 f.
Rumanyo 38
Rundu 42
Rundu Secondary School 93
Runtu 73
Runyemba 108, 127, 134, 149 f., 182, 190

S

Sahlins, Marshall 7
San 36, 5 f., 60, 62–64, 67, 75, 82, 85, 96, 104, 107, 121, 127, 145, 190 f.
Sangbundel 12
Sangfees 12, 87, 97
Sankofaism 32
Sarinjeive, Devi 166
Sauyemwa Junior Primary School 128, 132–134, 154
Schechner, Robert 17 f.
Schieffelin, Edward 6, 14, 20, 22, 24, 28, 140
Schildkrout, Enid 95, 119, 120
Schmidlin 70
School and Museum Exhibition (SCAM-X) 114
Senegal 35
Seraphina 50 f.
Shapi, Thomas 39, 47, 49, 115, 132, 165, 174, 179 f.
Sharp, John 21 f., 36, 123
Shashipapo, Linus 94
Shidonankuru 109, 142 f.

Shifeta, Pohamba 172
Shihwameni, Ignatius 133
Shikavedi 141, 143
Shikerete, Gelasia 163
Shimwemwe 142
Shiperu 138, 146, 163
Shipoh, Peingondjabi 172
Shiremo, Shampapi 59, 83
Sichone, Owen 45
Sitentu, Mpasi 65 f., 130
Sluka, Jeffrey 43
South Africa 2, 4, 15 f., 25, 27, 30, 35, 50, 53–58, 61, 66 f., 70, 74–76, 80, 85, 88, 93, 96, 98, 100 f., 110, 112, 129, 180, 183
South African Army 88
South Africans 85
Southern African Development Community (SADC) 132
South West Africa National Union (SWANU) 24
South West Africa People Organisation (SWAPO) 4, 24 f., 76, 81, 88, 90 f., 93, 99, 102, 105, 114, 133, 148–150, 155, 160, 173
South West Africa (SWA) 4, 12, 24, 54, 57, 62, 69, 72, 74–78, 80, 83, 86 f., 90 f., 93, 98, 100, 109 f., 121
Soyinka, Wole 126
Spiegel, Andrew 7
St John, Graham 21
Stone, Linda 44
Strathern, Marilyn 45, 52
Suidwes Afrika Uitsending Korporasie (SWAUK) 94
Swapo Women's Council 148, 155

T

Tanzania 6, 15, 22, 113, 186
Terence 169
The Namibian 2, 8, 88, 105, 130, 133, 135
Thindongo 144
Thiperu 141
Tondoro 70
Truth and Reconciliation (TRC) 15 f., 30
Tsuda, Takeyuki 46
Tsumeb 95, 120
Tswana 173
Tukulikeni 116, 122
Turner, Victor 17 f., 20, 22, 36, 139, 189
Tutaleni 113
Tutu, Desmond 25, 35

U

Ugeni 109
Ukambe 141, 144, 161
Ukwangali Traditional Authority 66, 89, 129
Ulenga, Ben 133
United Democratic Party (UDP) 88
United Nations (UN) 24, 74
United States of America 120
University of Cape Town 48, 179
University of the Western Cape 47, 120
Univesity of Cape Town 48, 179
Unongo Cultural Group 138, 157, 160, 164
Uukwambi 58, 70
Uyambi 141

V

Vachokwe 56, 75, 96
Vaduni 56, 63 f., 145
Vagcu 56, 145
Vakafumwa 64
Vakandjadi 59 f., 62 f., 65, 69
Vakankora 44, 59, 64, 67
Vakavango 41, 46, 54–61, 64–68, 70, 74, 76 f., 80–82, 94, 96, 108 f., 121, 127, 131, 134, 141, 144 f., 147 f., 155, 172, 180–182, 188, 190 f.
Vakwasipika 64 f.
Valutyazi 56
Vanantjoka 135
Van Binsbergen, Wim 16 f., 33, 112 f., 169, 189
Vandambo 108 f., 181
Vangangela 56, 108
Van Heerden, Esther 33, 36
Van Tonder, L. L. 77 f., 80, 121, 124
Vanyemba Vangangela 108
Vatywayuki 108 f., 181
vihiho 116, 146, 161, 176 f.
Vimbundu 109, 181
Volk 81 f., 89, 92 f., 100
Volkekunde 75, 78, 94, 121

W

Wandjongoka 152
Warmelo, Nicolaas 76
waShivako, Mbambangandu 61
Wa Thiongo, Ngugi 34, 37
Western Caprivi Zipfel 74

Willems, Wendy 30, 34
Wilson, Richard 29 f.
Witbooi Festival 106
Witz, Leslie 36

Y
Youth Division 93, 96

Z
Zambia 16 f., 21, 33, 54, 60, 91, 104, 112 f., 132, 149, 169
zaMukuve, Kapango 65
zaMukuve, Mate 65
Zawada 68
Zimbabwe 30 f., 133

EKONGORO

Ekongoro Wet.

1. 'n Lid van Ekongoro is 'n gelowige.
2. Hy ondersteun Wet en orde.
3. Hy is altyd eerlik en opreg.
4. Hy is vriendelik en behulpsaam.
5. Hy is hardwerkend en spaarsaam.
6. Hy is 'n liefhebber van die natuur.
7. Hy respekteer die oues.
8. Hy eer sy volk se kultuur.
9. Hy het erns met sy studies.
10. Hy is vriendelik.

KAVANGO VOLKSLIED

Statig vloei die Okavango
deur 'n land van groen en grys
ongeskonde maar gebonde
vind ons volkie hier 'n tuis
maar die skemering skeur die
donker
deur die chaos breek die lig
soos pêrels lêes deur jou modder
vlam van hoop beskawingsplig
ons was gedoem geen hoop in sig
o diep rivier o donkerstroom
ons het ontwaak ons vind die lig
o diep rivier o wonderstroom

www.ingramcontent.com/pod-product-compliance
Lightning Source LLC
Chambersburg PA
CBHW082227010526
44111CB00040BA/2907